NEW DIRECTIONS IN INTERNATIONAL STUDIES

PATRICE PETRO, SERIES EDITOR

New Directions in International Studies expands cross-disciplinary dialogue about the nature of internationalism and globalization. The series highlights innovative new approaches to the study of the local and global as well as multiple forms of identity and difference. It focuses on transculturalism, technology, media, and representation and features the work of scholars who explore various components and consequences of globalization, such as the increasing flow of peoples, ideas, images, information, and capital across borders.

Under the direction of Patrice Petro, the series is sponsored by the Center for International Education at the University of Wisconsin–Milwaukee. The Center seeks to foster interdisciplinary and collaborative approaches to international education by transcending traditional professional and geographic boundaries and by bringing together international and Milwaukee-based scholars, artists, practitioners and educators. The Center's book series originates from annual scholarly conferences that probe the political, economic, artistic, and social processes and practices of our time—especially those defining internationalism, cultural identity, and globalization.

MARK PHILIP BRADLEY AND PATRICE PETRO, eds.
Truth Claims: Representation and Human Rights

ELIZABETH SWANSON GOLDBERG
Beyond Terror: Gender, Narrative, Human Rights

LINDA KRAUSE AND PATRICE PETRO, eds.
Global Cities: Cinema, Architecture, and Urbanism in a Digital Age

ANDREW MARTIN AND PATRICE PETRO, eds.
Rethinking Global Security: Media, Popular Culture, and the "War on Terror"

TASHA G. OREN AND PATRICE PETRO, eds.
Global Currents: Media and Technology Now

BEYOND TERROR

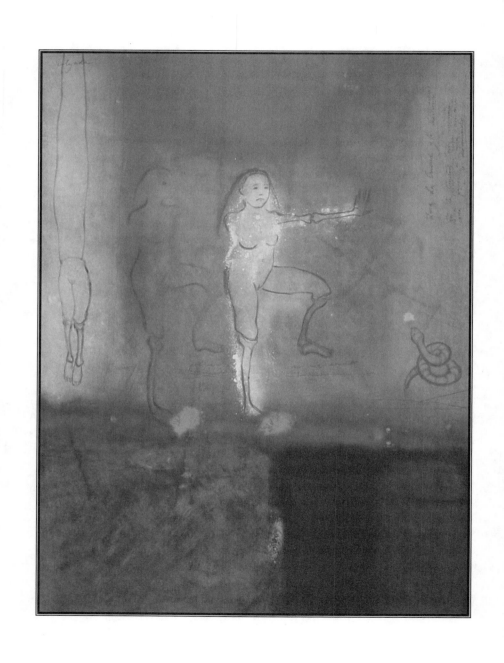

BEYOND TERROR

GENDER, NARRATIVE, HUMAN RIGHTS

ELIZABETH SWANSON GOLDBERG

RUTGERS UNIVERSITY PRESS

New Brunswick, New Jersey, and London

LIBRARY OF CONGRESS CATALOGING-IN-PUBLICATION DATA

Goldberg, Elizabeth Swanson, 1966–
    Beyond terror : gender, narrative, human rights / Elizabeth Swanson Goldberg.
        p.   cm.   –   (New directions in international studies)
    Includes bibliographical references and index.
    ISBN-13: 978-0-8135-4060-3 (hardcover : alk. paper)
    ISBN-13: 978-0-8135-4061-0 (pbk. : alk. paper)
    I. Human rights in motion pictures.   2.   Sex role in motion pictures.   I.   Title.

    PN1995.9.H83G65 2007
    791.43'658—dc22

                                                                    2006031263

A British Cataloging-in-Publication record for this book is available from the British Library.

Portions of this text were previously published as "Living the Legacy: Pain, Desire, and Narrative Time in Gayl Jones's *Corregidora*." *Callaloo* 26.2 (Spring 2003): 446–472. © Charles H. Rowell. Reprinted with permission of The Johns Hopkins University Press.

Portions of chapters I and 2 were previously published as "Splitting Difference: Global Identity Politics and the Representation of Torture in the Counter-Historical Dramatic Film." *Violence and American Cinema.* Ed. J. David Slocum. New York: Routledge, 2000. 245–270. Reprinted with permission.

Frontispiece: Claudia Bernardi, *Zora: The City and the Memory*, 2004, monotype, 30 × 22½ in. Courtesy of Segura Publishing Company, Mesa, Arizona. See page xiii for an author's note.

Visit our Web site: http://rutgerspress.rutgers.edu

For my mother, Geraldine, and my daughter, Marcelle

In memory of Leah Evens

CONTENTS

ACKNOWLEDGMENTS

The support—intellectual and otherwise—that I have received in writing this book is immeasurable, and words are inadequate to describe it; however, I will attempt to express my appreciation here. I gratefully acknowledge Miami University's Sinclair Memorial Dissertation Fellowship, which allowed me to complete the original work that has become *Beyond Terror*. The generous support of the Babson College Board of Research, along with a Babson College Faculty Resource Facility Grant, provided me time and support with which to reconstitute that original work in light of dramatic changes in the human rights landscape since 2001. A grant from the Babson College Faculty Research Fund enabled me to reproduce in full color the cover art by Claudia Bernardi. I have relied upon the research staff at the Horn Library at Babson College, especially Kate Buckley, Christine Drew, and Barbara Kendrick, who are unfailingly professional, resourceful, and—not least—full of good cheer. I am also indebted to my extraordinary research assistant, Laurie Ball, for her intelligence, her thoughtfulness, and the impeccable standards of her work.

I am grateful for the insightful comments of Patrice Petro and an anonymous reader of the manuscript in its early stages. Thanks also to Steve Collins, who discerned and encouraged my intellectual voice; Sheila Croucher, who helped me to navigate the political aspects of the manuscript early in the process; Kathleen Kelly, whose sharp eyes and pen found clarity in the midst of chaos; Lydia Moland, who provided philosophical resources and unstinting writerly solidarity; Greg Mullins, an early and inspirational interlocutor in the quest to read the disciplines of literature, film, and human rights together; Oyekan Owomoyela, for his generous critical reading; J. David Slocum, whom the fates have deemed an intellectual collaborator and mentor, and whose generosity of time, intellectual spirit, and editorial insight have been invaluable; and Jill Swiencicki Martins and Dean Woodring Blase for scholarly support and sisterhood. Mary Jean Corbett, Lori Merish, and Victoria L. Smith remain a formidable troika of intellectual and creative guidance. Their belief in my work and their tireless readings and rereadings of each chapter guided this book from seed to fruition. My deep gratitude also to Maryemma Graham, who has taught me more by her being and presence than I could learn from books in a lifetime—and who so unstintingly continues to share with me her vast knowledge and pragmatic sense of possibility. Infinite respect and appreciation to my teacher, Raghurai Michele Damelio, who uncannily offers me the lessons I need at precisely the moment I most need them. Bobbe Needham's generous and careful reading was a surprise gift; the text is much stronger as a result of her insights. I cannot begin to express my thanks to Marcy Jane Knopf-Newman for picking me up and setting me back on the path more times than I can count, for providing almost instantaneous feedback on my work, and for being a living example of political and intellectual passion in action. Finally, without the vision and support of Leslie Mitchner at Rutgers University Press, this book simply would not be.

It remains to offer deepest gratitude to my father, Ronald W. Swanson, who gave me my first anthology of poems; Sylvia Swanson, whose presence is a gift; Harold L. Goldberg and Elma Simpliciano Goldberg, who make room for me and my laptop in their island paradise every year, and who keep the espresso, orange muffins, and support flowing; and the late Guido and Sally Sasdelli, who never gave up on their "little brat."

And at last, to David and Marcelle, my source and my life: thank you.

A NOTE ON THE FRONTISPIECE

Zora: The City and the Memory, reproduced in full color on the front cover, is part of a series inspired by Italo Calvino's *Invisible Cities*. In the context of diaspora, political displacement, and economic exile, the concept of home, community, and "our place in the world" seems elusive, unobtainable. The work recovers images that constitute the luggage of personal history and the legacy of shared memories.

Born in Buenos Aires, Claudia Bernardi works as both an artist and a human rights activist. She has worked in collaboration with the Argentine Forensic Anthropology Team (AFAT), established in 1984 in Argentina to supply evidence of violations of human rights carried out against civilian populations. The team utilizes the rigorous methods of traditional archeology to examine, document, and publicly expose mass burial graves. AFAT has conducted exhumations of mass graves all over the world and has reported its findings to the United Nations. Bernardi joined AFAT in investigations of human rights violations in El Salvador, Guatemala, Argentina, and Ethiopia. Part of Bernardi's responsibilities included the creation of the archeological maps and transcribing the testimonies of families of the "disappeared ones." From these experiences, Bernardi realized how art could be used to educate, elucidate, and articulate the communal memories of survivors of human rights atrocities.

She calls the artistic process that she has developed "frescoes on paper," a method in which she applies layer after layer of pure pigments to wet paper and runs that paper repeatedly—sometimes hundreds of times—through a printmaker's press. No solvents or binders shape the pigments' flow across the paper. Upon and between the layers of pigmentation, Bernardi uses a porcupine quill to engrave images, sometimes words. She also incorporates shards of bone, fragments of clothing, and other artifacts in the work.

Portions of this statement are from a biography written by Kevin B. Chen for Intersection for the Arts, San Francisco, and from the Web site of Creative Work Fund.

BEYOND TERROR

We are struck by the brutality just beneath the surface of quotidian life. . . . It is the task of contemporary literary theory to move into marginal space and to converse with those authors who cross boundaries between living and dead, silent and vocal.

—Sharon Patricia Holland, *Raising the Dead*

INTRODUCTION

Theoretical discourses of witness, testimony, and representation in the context of grave violations of human rights have emerged over time from the experiences of wounding and therefore occupy the temporal ground of the *post-*, the aftermath of injury. For many who have survived the purposefully inflicted wounding of torture, rape, or genocide, injury itself takes on the outsized proportion of causal root for ideas, speech, and actions that follow. In narrative terms, the wound becomes subtext, motivation, and exposition for the emergent traumatic plot of its aftermath. The *longue durée* of the wound that occurred in an "instant of time," experienced through "that time which flows only slowly" (Braudel, qtd. in Ricoeur 103), influences the maturation of the the-oretical discourses of witness, testimony, and representation, and the unfolding stories that comprise their referents, in incalculable ways.

At the same time, through the sign of the (purposefully inflicted) wound, these discourses occupy the elongated time of the threat that structures an as yet unknown future. This threat imperils not only the corporeal integrity of the person or group of people whose rights may have been (or may yet be) violated, but also the ways of knowing, of being, and of being ethical that have engaged the global community since at least the emergence of ethical narratives in Buddhist, Hindu, and Muslim teachings in Asia and North Africa; of pantheis-tic discourses and rituals of tribal life in sub-Saharan Africa; and of the philo-sophic inquiries of the classical Greco-Roman, and later, Judeo-Christian periods of Eurasian history. Invigorated during the European Enlightenment and by the events of the French and American revolutions, interconnected ideas about being ethical in the context of being human reemerged as central to global intellectual, political, and historical life at the end of World War II.[1] Currently these theories, developed over time by survivor-intellectuals and by intellectuals and activists concerned with human rights more broadly in the wreckage of mid-twentieth-century history, are under new threat from post-9/11 challenges to international human rights norms and conventions. *Beyond Terror* is situated in the intellectual and corporeal environs of this triple threat.

Since the articulation of the United Nations Charter with its explicit acknowledgment of and protest against the "barbaric" nature of man's actions against man, and since the ratification by the UN General Assembly of the Universal Declaration of Human Rights, 10 December 1948, the movement of political, legal, and cultural approaches to human rights may be described as expansive. That is to say that for the most part, and often in surprising ways, members of the international community have built upon the early edifice of the UN Declaration by drafting and ratifying conventions that address particular sets of rights accruing to membership in specific groups in a variety of regional contexts. In spite of setbacks, gaps, and exclusions, the movement has been largely progressive, ethically aligned with other global progressive movements concerned with civil and social rights, freedom, and democracy. Arguably the greatest exclusion remains the address and application of social and economic rights, split from the body of civil and political rights by the drafters of the UN Declaration because of disagreements about Communist or Socialist ideologies in the context of the emergent cold war and, to some extent, of decolonization movements gaining momentum in Africa and Southeast Asia.[2]

Arguably for the first time since 1945, however, the event of 11 September 2001 and responses to it by the United States and a small number of its allies have reversed the expansionist momentum of global human rights and have constricted, scaled back, and deconstructed its discourses, conventions, and practices.[3] This regressive movement—nicely captured by Art Spiegelman's comic image of minions of the post-9/11 Bush administration drawn upside-down, facing backward, and shouting "Backward, March!"—poses specific challenges to standard operating procedures of the human rights community. These challenges, in turn, carry critical implications for the cultural representation of human rights violations.

Imagine for a moment an address in these introductory paragraphs from the perspective of an activist, rather than of a literary critic/academic. Better yet, imagine an address from the very project of human rights activism: the massive struggle to intervene in the perpetration of human rights violations around the globe in order to prevent and, ultimately, to abolish them. Consider the modus operandi of this collective activism: a method that requires looking, enunciating, and, finally, either celebrating or mourning. For example, an activist in Amnesty International's Urgent Action Network (the organization's

"Backward, March!" From *In the Shadow of No Towers* by
Art Spiegelman, copyright © 2004 by Art Spiegelman.
Used by permission of Pantheon Books, a division
of Random House, Inc.

emergency room, dedicated to protesting on behalf of persons known to be in immediate danger of mistreatment, torture, disappearance, or execution) receives in the mail each month descriptions of one or more cases of threats against or harm done to a human or group of humans. The activist then writes a letter and sends copies to various officials: the head of state, the chief of police, a representative of the judicial branch (if such branch exists), the local or international media, representatives of local human rights organizations, and the country's ambassador to the U.S. The goal of these letters—which will, the theory goes, arrive in a flood—is to make government officials in a position to intervene in the course of events aware that people from the international community are watching; that as a result of a well-trained network, citizens from every corner of the globe know as if they had seen with their own eyes what is happening in a torture chamber, on the dirt roads of a tiny pueblo, or in a sports arena doubling as clandestine prison—in spite of government or nongovernmental agents' best efforts to keep such extralegal events (and their victims) quite literally in the dark.

Those with the power to intervene are made to feel the burn behind that multitude of eyes by the enunciation of what has been "seen" in letters that at the same time respectfully request that the violation of rights be halted immediately, that a fair and impartial investigation be made into their perpetration, and that the perpetrators be brought to justice. This act of enunciation constitutes a repetition of brute fact, inscribed in each of the individual letters, telexes, faxes, and emails that comprise the flood. In short, the process purposefully turns into long-distance witness observers thousands of humans removed in time and space (and often also in experience, culture, and history) from the actors and events in question.[4]

The theory is simple: governments and nongovernmental actors will be less likely to persist in barbarous acts such as torture, rape, extrajudicial execution, and genocide if they know that others are watching, that the torture chamber is not a secret, that the mass grave will be unearthed and the evidence catalogued. The emotional analogue is shame, and relevant international human rights documents and covenants are invoked in the letters as shades of disapproving authority. The recipients of such enunciations are, for instance, repeatedly reminded to "refer to Article Five of the UN Universal Declaration of Human Rights, to which your nation is signatory, which prohibits the use of any cruel, inhuman, or degrading treatment." However, such shaming, and the motivating force of potential consequences of overstepping lawful bounds of detention and treatment of citizens and/or prisoners, can be effective only in the context of an international community, led by its putative superpowers, committed to the assumptions upon which existing human rights conventions and laws are based. The method of such human rights work is also embedded in the theoretical and pragmatic function of the witness, as evidenced in the official Amnesty International description of Urgent Action Network efficacy once the Urgent Action network of individuals in more than seventy countries has been mobilized to send letters, telegrams, emails, and telexes: "Over the following hours, days and weeks, . . . officials receive thousands of individually written messages. These are a powerful signal that their actions are being witnessed by an international audience deeply concerned about the fate of those involved" (Amnesty International Urgent Action Network). The international constriction of human rights norms has placed at risk the crucial warrant that governments and their agents may be moved to change their behavior by the response of an international audience to brutality it has "witnessed."

Beyond shaming, deeper pressures may be brought to bear upon offending nations, such as sanctions or other signs of diplomatic ill will or, ultimately, intervention on the part of the international community (read: the West) for unreformed bad behavior. In some cases (Somalia, Bosnia, Kosovo), the United States has undertaken military intervention strictly for purportedly humanitarian reasons.[5] Indeed, the occasion for the revivification of the classical discourse of human rights in mid-twentieth-century Europe was the massive intervention that ended the Nazi Holocaust, motivated at least in part by a response to the mass murder of Jewish, Roma, and other targeted categories of people. After the stunning defeat of Germany for the second time in less than half a century and the excessive spectacle of atomic weaponry used against Japan, which gave rise to the paradigmatic international forums for justice at Nuremburg and Tokyo, the specter of invasion (and the national devastation that would, it seemed certain, accompany it) was thought to haunt the would-be butchers and torturers of brutal regimes. The flood of letters from unknown citizens around the world was meant to raise that specter to preclude its necessary materialization in force.

In spite of its successes, the human rights movement has always been marked by a bit of the sense of whistling in the wind. One can identify righteousness and hope in the Amnesty slogan "Light one candle in the darkness," but a parallel sense of futility lurks in the work, in the endless witnessing and enunciating. Urgent Action activists wait for their monthly newsletters, which include case updates when available. One opens the newsletter with a sense of hope that is rewarded, dashed, or suspended, depending upon the fates reported. One tends to identify more with the cases upon which one has written personally, of course, and so fragile human connections are forged. And yet. The volume of cases, of rights violations around the globe witnessed in person or via radio, television, newspaper, magazine, or Internet accelerates; the movement staggers under their weight. And yet. New developments reinvigorate hope: the convening of the International Criminal Court; the extradition and arrest of former Chilean dictator Augusto Pinochet; the trial of Slobodan Milosevich and the conviction of three Bosnian Serb soldiers for rape as a crime against humanity; the delivery of former Liberian President Charles Taylor to the Hague for prosecution of crimes against humanity; the successful prosecution of Toto Constant, Haitian torturer and rapist, living comfortably in New York since his tenure during the Duvalier regimes. And so a fragile rhythm takes hold: hope, despair, cynicism, optimism . . . where will the whirligig stop?

Abu Ghraib.

The words are a cipher, both magnifying and scrambling decades of theorizing and attempts at comprehension. The inner corpus of the torture chamber, usually veiled in secrecy, brought to light by the written word of human rights reports and action letters, has finally been seen, enunciated, and witnessed globally via photograph and testimony.[6] Consider the figure of the cipher: not in this case the zero of nothingness, void, but rather, says the online *Oxford English Dictionary*, "a symbol or character of no value by itself, but which increases or decreases the value of other figures according to its position." What other figures have been increased or decreased according to their relation to images from Abu Ghraib? With what obscenity must I tangle to assert that these images—and therefore the bodies that comprise their referents—possess no value by themselves?

When one adds zero to the figure 100,000, the zero itself does not gain value but occasions a prodigious leap in value for the number one. Let us select one image from the files of Abu Ghraib—the now iconic image of a hooded and cloaked figure with wires extending from its fingertips and from under its cloak, balanced precariously on a small box—as the cipher that will occasion such a leap (increasing or decreasing value) for the figures to which it has

Abu Ghraib Prison, Iraq, 2003. AP/World Wide Photos

been added or against which it has been juxtaposed.[7] If we define the relative "value" of a photographic image delivered in a journalistic context in terms of intelligibility, of information transmitted to or emotion evoked in its viewers, how might we assert that this image—this body—contains no value by itself?

First, while revealing the utterly debased inner workings of a torture chamber, the image does not depict the pain of the human beneath the cloak; rather, it hints at the threat of pain, or of pain that may already have been experienced, depending upon the success or failure of the body in maintaining its balance over time in the terrifying world of darkness within its hood. In the seeming stillness of the body depicted—not visibly in the process of tipping, falling, or receiving the threatened jolt of electricity—the pain evoked in this photo remains invisible to those who would gaze upon it, in an uncannily more palpable invisibility than that of images depicting blood, bruises, or other tangible signifiers of bodily pain. Even bodies marked by these physical signs cannot truly signify pain, as Elaine Scarry so convincingly taught us in her groundbreaking study *The Body in Pain*, given that pain opens an irretrievable epistemological gap between the person in pain and others who are not experiencing pain, to the extent that "to have great pain is to have certainty; to hear that another person has pain is to have doubt" (7). According to Scarry, it is this epistemological gap that enables torturers to continue their work rather than succumb to a natural empathy or revulsion and rush to the aid of the prisoner, or at least halt the delivery of harm. It is also this verbal and epistemological chasm that renders pain so politically efficacious, so easily removed from the body of the person in pain and translated into "the insignia of power, . . . an emblem of the regime's strength" (56). This translation undergirds the structure of the torture chamber itself.

A second way in which we might explain the lack of organic meaning or value in the Abu Ghraib image is through its metonymic function in reference to the massive whole of torture worldwide, over time.[8] Although the identity of the man under the hood has been tentatively revealed, this image cannot be taken as referent of one individual's experience of pain and terror. (I say "tentatively" because, while a man has claimed that he is the one depicted in the image, pointing to distinguishing marks on his fingers, to the blanket-cum-cloak in the image which he claims to have made for purposes of warmth and modesty, and to this treatment as precisely what he experienced while incarcerated at Abu Ghraib, the practice of hooding and terrorizing prisoners in this way was simply too widespread, and the erasure of distinguishing

human features by the hooding and cloaking too complete, to make a definitive identification.)[9] As Susan Sontag notes, "Photographs echo photographs,"
and in this case, the photographs—arguably the first of their kind so massively disseminated to the global public—echoed images ingrained in the
memories and testimonials of torture survivors outside the bounds of temporality and regional or historical specificity (*Regarding the Pain of Others* 84).
For many torture survivors and witnesses, this image more immediately referenced the terrifying, ungraspable ubiquity of the practice of torture, rather
than depicting an individual experience of purposefully inflicted mental and
physical anguish. As metonym, then, the function of the image is to ground
an uncannily collective experience in the face, name, and identity of the individual under erasure, who has been reduced to sign of the global threat and
practice of torture. While the goal of human rights movements is to restore
the face, the name, and the identity to the individual body in pain, and thereby
to lift it from the nullity of the cipher, some survivors claim that such restoration is impossible and, indeed, unnecessary; for them, testifying to their pain
is a testimony to the phenomenon of torture as it is practiced in secret upon
the bodies of victims who in their sheer abundance become nameless, iden-
tityless. As one survivor claimed: "To assert my name as a survivor is not necessary, for these violations are universal" (Arestivo, "Testimonial").

If the individual and his experience in the iconic Abu Ghraib image have
been effectively evacuated of meaning and identity, then what is the value
that the image adds or takes away from the "figures" to which it is related?
The Abu Ghraib images increase the accuracy—indeed, the prescience—of some
theories of testimony and witness, for instance, the epistemological experience of "doubt" on the part of witnesses with regard to the pain of others and
the efficiency with which the body in pain may be translated into an "insignia"
of the regime's power. In this case, while the Bush administration perhaps
suffered some shame at the revelation that the heart of its liberating mission
in Iraq was housed in a refurbished torture chamber, still the images symbolically referenced the abnegation of the enemy by the forces of good. And
since the war in Iraq had always been emptied of meaning, inasmuch as it
was a displaced projection of military might against the vulnerability invoked
by the attacks against the United States on 11 September 2001, the nebulous-
ness of Arab and Muslim bodies, humiliated and tortured regardless of their
identities or relationship to the desire or intention to commit terrorist acts,
served well as corporeal "insignia" of the U.S. response to "evildoers."

As a mathematical figure, the cipher adds value only when it remains to the right of the decimal point that divides "positive" from "negative" (terms which lose substance in the rhetorical jumble of the war on terror and its effects). One figure that has substantially decreased in value since the release of the Abu Ghraib photos has been the credibility of the discourse of human rights itself. Keep in mind that the online *Oxford English Dictionary* also defines a cipher as "a secret or disguised manner of writing by . . . methods intelligible only to those possessing the key. . . . Also, the key to such a system." Abu Ghraib: at once puzzle and solution, lock and key. The puzzle: U.S. policy since 11 September 2001, increasingly elliptical and obfuscating, based upon denials, half-truths, and significations presented by a handful of advisors without sufficient evidence, acted upon with cataclysmic force, unintelligible to the majority of people living its effects. The images from Abu Ghraib, then, de-cipher the code for a world's worth of witnesses, reassembling the immense violence scrambled into phrases like "shock and awe," "sensory deprivation," or "stress and duress" in the momentary light of the camera flash and its extension in the *longue durée* of the image.

The images unlock yet another truth from the unintelligible code that has come to be policy as usual: that in spite of an initial desire to read the Abu Ghraib photos as symbolic of a regime's accumulation of power, the images, along with a series of electoral and policy decisions that followed their release, provide perhaps deeper insight into the relation of a populace to its founding democratic principles. In other words, the images reveal evidence of the paradoxical gap between the administration's denunciation of the acts they depict and the simultaneous support of political representatives and policies that would ensure that such acts continue. In spite of ongoing dissent against the global war on terror in general and the Iraq War in particular, it is certainly a crushing blow to have discovered, upon viewing the inner corpus of that torture chamber, that its abjection is us. The United States—sign and putative keeper of freedom, democracy, and the rule of law—is unmasked by a series of widely circulated images followed by reams of repetitious testimony to be the torturer himself. As Sontag noted: "What is illustrated by these photographs is as much the culture of shamelessness as the reigning admiration for unapologetic brutality" ("Regarding the Torture of Others" 29). The photos signify the extent to which we are trapped in a cultural moment suspended in time between the increasingly exhausted sentiments that characterize our founding religious and secular ethical groundings, and the increasingly normalized culture of brutality that our modes of entertainment and self-representation reflect. The lived hypocrisy of occupying this cultural moment is breathtaking. As Charlotte Bunch argued in a mock tribunal that heard testimonies to the violation of women's rights globally at the 1995 UN World Conference on Women in Hairou, China: "It is often remarked that the U.S. has 'no culture,' that we have lost touch with rituals, performances, ceremonies, and texts that seem to endow other regions and peoples with what we might call 'culture.' The U.S. absolutely has a culture and a set of cultural traditions: the cultures and traditions of violence" (Goldberg, "Notes").

To be sure, this is not the first time that evidence of U.S. advocacy, practice, and dissemination of torture has surfaced. U.S. militarism over the course of the nineteenth and twentieth centuries consisted not only of overt and covert wars and coups, but also of the training of thousands of torturers who went on to serve in militaries and paramilitaries around the globe. Perhaps the most notable evidence in this regard is the series of torture manuals found to be part of the curriculum at the School of the Americas, Ft. Benning, Georgia, which trained more than sixty thousand Latin American soldiers between 1946 and 2001.[10] Still, evidence of these events was restricted to testimonies, military papers, and legal and governmental documents, and often only those who actively sought the information (often at great personal risk) possessed it. Never before have we seen the dissemination of images from the torture chamber on such as a scale as the Abu Ghraib case.

More crippling, then, is the dull nullity of response after the image, the abject revelation that received no official response beyond the requisite denial, typically elliptical and obscured: "[These acts] were inconsistent with our policies and our values as a Nation" (Bush, "President's Statement"). Obscene in its banal hypocrisy (particularly given that an ABC News poll indicated that 47 percent of U.S. citizens found "some degree of torture to be acceptable if it could help save innocent lives"), the response was also characteristic in its offering of the few low-level perpetrators, the proverbial bad apples, for punishment (Morris and Langer).[11] The unofficial response is the more consequential in its challenge to human rights: the actions and decisions taken in the wake of Abu Ghraib that work precisely to multiply the lingering pain of its images, among them the ripple effect of a purported majority of citizens voting to reelect the government that produced the cipher that is Abu Ghraib; the subsequent confirmation as attorney general of the United States of Alberto Gonzales, legal apologist for the torture at Abu Ghraib; the "unsigning" of the Rome Statute that created the International Criminal Court, originally signed by President Bill Clinton on 31 December 2000; approval by Secretary of State Condoleezza Rice of extradition for suspects to countries that use torture in the process of interrogating suspects.[12] Shortly after the revelation of images from Abu Ghraib, Susan Sontag posed the question: "What makes some actions representative and others not?" For Sontag, "the issue is not whether the torture was done by individuals (i.e., 'not by everybody')—but whether it was systematic. Authorized. Condoned. All acts are done by individuals. The issue is not whether a majority or a minority of Americans performs such acts but whether the nature of the policies prosecuted by this administration and the hierarchies deployed to carry them out makes such acts likely" ("Regarding the Torture of Others" 26). Upon publication of her essay in the 23 May 2004 issue of the *New York Times Magazine*, Sontag could not have anticipated the extent to which these acts would be made likely by the decisions not only of the Bush administration, but also of a large percentage of the U.S. voting public and its representatives in Congress.[13]

A fundamental assumption of the human rights movement—that if one could reveal the workings of a torture session in process, the citizens of the regime engaged in the torture would seek to end that torture, especially if that regime was a democratic nation-state with a free, independent press; free, independent judicial and legislative branches; and a free, independent populace capable of organizing and engaging in dissent and protest—has been seriously compromised, if not outright negated. The contemporary human rights movement was, in a sense, built upon the shame of Nazi collaborators or of those "innocent bystanders" who remained silent and complicit and claimed not to have known about the atrocities being carried out around them. Countering that degraded silence with a vehement "Never again!" the movement vowed that once atrocity had been unearthed, it would be acted against; a case in point would be the images of ethnic cleansing in 1990s Bosnia, which provoked a "humanitarian intervention" on the part of an international force led by the United States. And while, again, this premise was undermined by gaps and exclusions (most egregiously, the Rwandan genocide of 1994 and, currently, the genocide in Darfur, Sudan), still an attempt to realize the underlying link between seeing, speaking, and acting remained as an epistemological and ethical foundation for global humanity.

The premise of looking, enunciating, witnessing, then, is sorely challenged by the hard fact that citizens of the United States (taken as a whole, in a massively expanded notion of the role and function of the witness) looked inside the torture chamber and, rather than being moved to act, seem to have chosen mostly to look away. Perhaps better put, these citizens (taken as a whole) chose to look inward to the self, valorizing protection of that self, linked to its national context, from the ubiquitous threat of the (national, racial, cultural, religious, political) other as reason enough for what they saw in those images. In her treatise on the ethics of producing and viewing images of atrocity, *Regarding the Pain of Others*, Sontag describes several photos of what amounted to torture that acted, by their massive dissemination, as catalysts for the cessation of war—most famously, perhaps, images from the war in Viet Nam such as those depicting the My Lai massacre, the point-blank execution of a young Viet Cong fighter, and a child in flight, burning with napalm. Part of Sontag's critique, also articulated in her article for the *New York Times Magazine* on the impact of the Abu Ghraib images, is that images are limited in their ability to create space for the kind of empathy that might produce change; indeed, rather than describing an event in a way that renders it comprehensible and that therefore enables action in response to it, an image comes to substitute for the event itself. Narrative is arguably the more potent vehicle for comprehension, as Sontag notes, and it is narrative—the fictional sort in both cinematic and literary form—that will be our subject as we return to the realm of the academic.

Unspeakable

Of the decreases in value occasioned by the Abu Ghraib cipher, one of the most drastic has been a shared notion of the unspeakable. Beyond the broad claims of integrity, dignity, and good taste that have informed this notion is a basic premise of scholarship in the areas of trauma, witness, and testimonial studies: that in a formal sense, the pain accompanying gross violations of human rights is by nature impossible to fully articulate. The problem then, both in narrative terms and with regard to theories of pain and trauma, became one of representability: how can one represent that which is fundamentally unable to be spoken, or even conceptualized? Consider some scholarly examples. Elaine Scarry asserts that "whatever pain achieves, it achieves in part through its unsharability, and it ensures this unsharability through its resistance to language" (*Body in Pain* 4). Cathy Caruth notes that "the traumatic reexperiencing of the event thus *carries with it . . .* the impossibility of knowing that first constituted it" (Introduction, 10, emphasis in original). In his essay "Historical Emplotment and the Problem of Truth," Hayden White describes the position of "a number of scholars and writers who view the Holocaust as virtually unrepresentable in language" (43). The title of an essay by Peter Haidu is "The Dialectics of *Unspeakability*" (emphasis added). Judging from this pervasive phrasing, the representability of torture has been, paradoxically, a function of that inarticulability which came uncannily into being as its representational surrogate.

This condition of inarticulability may be broken into two parts. The first has to do with the nature of pain itself, which is marked by both verbal and epistemological resistance to language. According to Scarry, pain "bring[s] about an immediate reversion to a state anterior to language, to the sounds and cries a human being makes before language is learned," precisely because it has no referent, no external sign or object (4). The second manifestation of inarticulability, rather than emerging organically from the physiognomy of the body in pain, is a product of the higher-order human need first to express, and then to narrate, that experience of purposefully inflicted pain. Indeed, the urge to testify, the centrality of testimonial forms and procedures in legal, historical, psychoanalytic, and, more recently, literary and cinematic contexts has been shown to emerge from a basic human need. As Dori Laub notes with regard to the testimonies of Holocaust survivors: "Survivors did not only need to survive so that they could tell their stories; they also needed to tell their stories in order to survive" (63). For these survivor testimonials, the problematic of finding "revealing symbols and codes that could serve as a beginning" to convey how a tortured person feels is linked to pain's capacity to destroy systems of meaning making.[14]

Beyond finding language sufficient to the telling of such experience, the primary question haunting such testimonials has to do with veracity. Is what the survivor relays true in the sense that it happened as the survivor has claimed to the survivor him- or herself? Such prioritization of factual veracity occurs, I should add, within the epistemological tenets of individualist western notions, contexts, and applications of truth-value. Some important recent rights work in legal, psychoanalytic, and even literary testimonial forums challenges such limits to the forms and contexts of legitimated truth-telling. Such work includes, for instance, the efforts of lawyers representing torture survivors seeking asylum in the United States to interpret the survivor's narrative for the court. The attorney's job in this case is to make clear to the court how norms and mores specific to a survivor's language and culture, along with the trauma and shame that often shape the survivor's account of—or her reluctance or inability to describe—certain forms of torture endured, may cause the survivor's testimony to diverge in form from accepted juridical norms of narrated testimony. As these attorneys seek to demonstrate, however, these divergences do not necessarily compromise the testimonial's essential truth value. In the therapeutic context, some psychologists have turned to somatic therapies that use dance, movement, and other nonverbal forms of communication wherein the clinician mirrors the movements of the survivor as she nonverbally describes her experience and its effects in order to validate or affirm that experience. Such approaches acknowledge that torture may remain for the survivor literally unspeakable, or that traditional forms of talk therapy may so closely recall the experience of interrogation as to produce the risk of secondary trauma. Finally, in the literary context, critic Leigh Gilmore has explored the potential of autobiographical literary forms to provide a fuller archive of the testimonial than the one currently linked to the juridical model (101).

The problem of representability extends well beyond the attempts of survivors, those authentic "I's" who have seen, felt, and witnessed the violence themselves, to narrate their experiences. Moving out from the relative truth-value of individual survivor testimonials, the larger problem of representability emerges when artists, writers, and filmmakers who were not present at the historical event, who are not survivors, and who may well be removed by time or distance from the event attempt its representation in historical or artistic terms. The problem here has an ethical cast: how to do justice to the memory of those who suffered, or who were lost to, the event. How not to do further violence to these humans, their loved ones, or their descendants by spectacularizing, eroticizing, or otherwise *getting wrong* the representation of pain inflicted in a grave violation of human rights. How to create cultural images that will not perpetuate cycles of violence and revenge. If they are to reach toward the ethical, cultural representations of torture and terror must achieve a fragile balance between the difficulty of presenting that which is too painful to think of or to speak—and perhaps too painful to be heard—and the imperative of presenting that very material in the service of remembering those events and the people lost to them, and of resisting continued enactment of such violences. We must also attend to the warrant, often left unexamined, that narrativizing atrocity in the form of novel, testimonial, or film is in some way an effective means of creating a deeper consciousness in viewers about the event, and even of encouraging viewers to act in a way that would contribute to efforts to decrease the occurrence of such events in future.

Synthesizing these problems of veracity and narrativization as part of his commitment to a representational ethic for narratives and images of atrocity, Saul Friedlander identifies a "distanced realism" that approximates in artistic terms the unspeakable condition of the Nazi Holocaust: "It is easier to point to literary and artistic works which give a feeling of relative 'adequacy' in bringing the reader and viewer to insights about the Shoah than to define the elements which convey that sense. . . . A common denominator appears: the exclusion of straight, documentary realism, but the use of some sort of *allusive or distanced realism*. Reality is there, in its starkness, but perceived through a filter: that of memory (distance in time), that of spatial displacement, that of some sort of narrative margin which leaves the unsayable unsaid" (17).

The relationship to realism articulated in Friedlander's remarks is complex. In this formulation, the specific goal of representation is to bring the reader/ viewer to insights about the traumatic event, rather than to provide survivors with space to testify about their experience or audiences with the opportunity to experience a cathartic release of terror (although these may be important effects of such representation). Presumably the majority of reader/ viewers have not directly experienced the event in question, so their revelatory insights might include perception of the structural causes of such an event; recognition of the psychological states of perpetrators, victims, and survivors; and awareness of the ongoing legacies of traumatic occurrences. These insights are meaningful inasmuch as they contribute to a collective consciousness about torture, genocide, and other such violations, a consciousness that not only validates victims' and survivors' experience, but also presumably produces a collective desire to ensure that such atrocities not recur. In this case, the relative adequacy of images is measured by their success as both witness and deterrent, their ability to counter totalizing or official narratives with a nuanced, resistant historical awareness. To strive toward such goals, as Friedlander notes, art that takes torture as its subject must reference the thing itself, the historic event, the materiality of bodily experience. Representational extremes of excessive abstraction, on the one hand, or of raw realism, on the other, might dilute the force of representation, with the result that "[viewers'] capacity for comprehending and perceiving [can be] entirely blunted" (17). Similarly, representations of torture in the realist mode may actually do further violence to their material referents, the bodies who have suffered torture or execution, by spectacularizing them according to the requirements of genre or plot device.

The novels and films under study here negotiate this relation to realism using a variety of techniques. Of particular relevance to my analysis of fictionalized literary and cinematic narratives of historical atrocity are narrative and image structure, emplotment, point of view, and temporality. I am aware that the selection of texts and contexts in *Beyond Terror* risks eclecticism; however, these choices have been made with a desire to explore texts about global human rights violations readily available to a range of audiences in the West—indeed, texts that take as an overt goal the education of western readers and viewers about the historical events they chronicle. Both cinematic and literary narrative are common vehicles for disseminating stories and knowledges of historical violations of human rights, and the text offers relevant context for the events represented in the narratives as well as for the conditions of production and dissemination of the narratives themselves. In spite of the rather substantial critique throughout *Beyond Terror* of the linear progress narrative as a strategy for representing the violation of human rights, the trajectory of the book is itself a kind of loose progress narrative, moving from strategies for representation that I find less responsive to the ethical demands of their subjects to texts that represent more effective and more ethical modes of emplotment. The thrust of the book, not surprisingly, is an argument in favor of less conventional, increasingly experimental generic codes. I do not, however, advocate experimentation in the sense of the difficult, the obscure, or the aesthetically acrobatic. Narrative strategies that include variations on traditional chronological time, linear plot structures, and omniscient or totalizing first-person narrative points of view are better suited to sharing the stories of atrocity because, inasmuch as they are undertaken with the intent to pursue an ethic of witness issuing from the nature of the historical referent, they can meaningfully disrupt conventional narrative forms that reproduce fixed—predictable, and thereby often intractable—identity positions of victim and oppressor.

In its address of a broad range of contemporary literary and cinematic fictions available to audiences in the western world, then, *Beyond Terror* builds upon the premise that fictionalizing historical atrocities necessitates attention to the ethical claims originating from the experiences of victims and survivors of historical atrocities, as well as those of their loved ones and descendents. In legal, psychoanalytic, and documentary narrative contexts, such ethical claims are already widely acknowledged; however, the question of such ethics with regard to fictional cinematic and literary narratives remains unsettled, particularly in the wake of postmodernism—in spite of the recent ethical turn in literary studies.[15] Literary theorists such as Martha Nussbaum and Paul Ricoeur have made the case that narrative is inseparable from the ethical contexts of its referents; indeed, Ricoeur argues against the possibility of "a mode of reading that would entirely suspend all evaluation of an ethical character," articulating that "one of the oldest functions of art" is to constitute "an ethical laboratory where the artist pursues through the mode of fiction experimentation with values" (59). An ethic stemming from theories and practices of witnessing may productively be applied to fictional representations of human rights violations, and chapters 1 and 2 articulate possible parameters for such an ethic.

In chapter 1, "Torture I: Safety," we see the representation of torture in a genre of popular films emergent in the 1980s and 1990s that I term the "counterhistorical drama," which is ethically inadequate to its subject. Specifically, films such as Jon Boorman's *Beyond Rangoon* and Richard Attenborough's *Cry Freedom* use documentary conventions to protest grave human rights violations while paradoxically undercutting that very protest by mobilizing images of torture against citizens of other (nonwestern) places to construct a narrative of safety for western viewers. Yet a film that foregrounds and exceeds the generic conventions of the counterhistorical drama—David O. Russell's *Three Kings*—is able to draw viewer attention to the imbalanced distribution of safety in a global context while delivering a metanarrative critique of the standard representational conventions that reinforce that imbalance.

Chapter 2, "Torture II: Citizenship," locates the source of the narrative of safety examined in chapter 1 in an ideal of citizenship in a constitutional democracy, most often the United States as metonym for the West more generally. In counterhistorical dramas such as Oliver Stone's *Salvador* and Jon Avnet's *Red Corner*, citizenship in a constitutional democracy acts as a kind of geopolitical shield for westerners while simultaneously signifying an elusive remedy for people of nonwestern nations suffering from massive human rights violations. The lack of citizenship in a constitutional democracy tautologically explains and ensures the continued suffering of rights violations by nonwestern (and mostly nonwhite) peoples in this representational context. The chapter ends with a discussion of race and gender in terms of the contemporary experience of citizenship, introducing gender in this light as a central analytical category in the study of the perpetration and representation of torture. In *Red Corner* and journalist Gil Courtemanche's novel *A Sunday at the Pool in Kigali*, gender provides a kind of limit case of vulnerability and otherness against which the white western male as prototypical citizen figure, protected a priori from violations of human rights, is constructed in dominant representations.

A consideration of "gender," another major analytical term of this study, shows that while the climate for human rights has dramatically shifted for the worse in the post-9/11 moment, the status of global gender norms remains relatively consistent—a state that does not feel any more optimistic to report than does the decline in human rights. This is not to say that gains for individual women are not everywhere occurring, or to deny the vibrant development of transnational feminist discourses, alliances, and practices. However, in researching gender in terms of the roles and experiences of women in the changing global context of human rights, and in terms of cultural representations therein, I find that the arguments made in feminist texts from twenty or more years ago—particularly about the reduction of historical women to the unrecognizable sign of Woman within a range of culturally diverse patriarchies—are all too relevant today. One of the most trenchant of those semiotic arguments has to do with the place of women and children in the global background to both event and representation in the context of human rights. Unlike the spectacular and iconic status of images issuing from Abu Ghraib, images and narratives that capture the relegation of women to this global background abound, so ubiquitous as to be unremarkable.

One such image, taken quite literally at random from the 3 March 2005 issue of the *Boston Globe*, accompanies a story headlined "UN Troops Kill Up To 60 Militiamen: Peacekeepers' Response Marks Congo Policy Shift." The news reported in the story has to do with a change in the mandate of the UN Security Council, after the murder of nine UN peacekeepers in the region, to allow peacekeepers to do more than protect UN staff (a limitation eerily reminiscent of the tragic mandate under which UN commander General Romeo Dallaire chafed while genocide proceeded unhindered in Rwanda in 1994). The image foregrounds two heavily armed Bangladeshi peacekeepers guarding what looks like a refugee camp in the background. It is in the recesses of that background that the viewer of the image can make out the tiny blurred figures of two women and a child. One woman seems to look toward the camera, while the other carries a load of what looks like firewood and holds the hand of the small child. The women, in traditional African dress, are located behind a wall of barbed wire. The light of the photo has thrown shadows of trees onto a wall in the background of the soldiers; the women, also blurred in the angle of light and through a haze of dust in the camp, are almost as obscured as these shadows. As I study the peacekeepers in the foreground, I wonder how the women in the scene distinguish from behind their barbed-wire confine between these heavily armed peacekeepers and the heavily armed militia from whom they are ostensibly being protected, especially in light of reports of rape, forced prostitution, and forced sexual favors in exchange for food by peacekeeping forces against women classified as refugees or IDPs (Internally Displaced Persons).[16] As a feminist, I find myself peering into the photo in an attempt to perceive something that will help me to understand the experience of these women consigned so absolutely to the background both representationally and in the world of the referent. I understand from the news article, which reports that "tribal fighters have killed dozens of people, looted and burned homes, and forced more than 70,000 people to

Women in camp for Internally Displaced Persons, Democratic Republic of Congo.
Reuters/MONUC/UN

flee to the hills," that the stories of these women are human rights stories, and that I have no access to either through their representation in the image.

In addition to contributing to conversations about the ethics of reading and writing in the contemporary moment, then, *Beyond Terror* reveals that strategies for narrative representation of grave human rights violations share a common problem with the struggle against such violations. This problem—gender—is connected to the definition of what constitutes a violation of rights, and which kinds of violations are recognized in international legal forums. Starting from the premise that both perpetration and representation of human rights violations are predicated upon relationships to existing norms of gender ideology and difference, an argument builds over the course of the book, but especially in chapters 3 and 4, about the necessity of foregrounding gender as an analytical category in the parallel projects of creating ethical narrative strategies for the representation of human rights violations and developing ethical approaches to human rights norms and policies in the field. This project takes on increasing urgency in light of recent events that highlight the instability of gender as both descriptive term and lived identity—the indictment of a woman on charges of rape as a crime against humanity in the International Tribunal for Rwanda, for instance, or the conviction of a female member of the U.S. Army for acts of torture committed while she was pregnant. As Judith Butler reminds us, the instability of gender as a category is easily exploited and put to nefarious purposes, even as representations of women and the roles available to them in the global public sphere remain remarkably stagnant.[17]

Chapter 3, "Torture III: Desire," further explores gender as limit case in the arena of human rights by examining the centrality of patriarchal ideologies to both the perpetration and representation of torture. Common conceptions of protection from torture as linked to membership in first-world democratic nation-states (examined in chapters 1 and 2) build upon the structure of patriarchal gender norms; conversely, scenes of torture—and, often, strategies for their representation—are saturated with such gendered narratives, and their deconstruction can contribute to the struggle against torture. Here there exists a rhetorical parallel between political and gender/sexual subversion, and the chapter explores the reduction of woman to sign of subversion in the public sphere in three contexts. The first concerns Harvard University law professor Alan Dershowitz's negative response at the CUNY Graduate Center in 2003 to the presence of Sister Dianna Ortiz, executive director of the Torture Abolition and Survivor Support Coalition (TASSC) International, at an academic conference addressing the uses of torture in the post-9/11 world; his response reveals Dershowitz's unwillingness to confront the embodied and, in this case, gendered sign of the consequences of his argument in favor of "torture warrants" in the "war on terror." The second context concerns the experimental narrative strategies in Hanif Kureishi's screenplay for *Sammy and Rosie Get Laid* and their efficacy for exploring the implications of a dominant construction of female sexual desire as subversive. The third context—as revealed in the case of Lynndie England in Abu Ghraib Prison—is the problem of the female torturer as a sign of a public sphere unchanged by its limited accommodation of women, a problem that a reinvigorated transnational feminism in the twenty-first century must address. All three cases provide evidence within dominant patriarchal systems of the continued reduction of women to signs of the subversive or abject; in other words, that which patriarchy would disavow. And in each case, the content of that disavowal is, unsurprisingly, revealed to be at the heart of the patriarchal project itself.

Continuing with questions of gender and representation, chapter 4, "Rape: The Division of Spheres," illuminates the connection between narrative temporality and the gendered division of space in representing rape. Beginning with J. M. Coetzee's *Disgrace*, it becomes apparent that linear emplotment—even when part of a narrative of decline, rather than of progress—has limited ability to negotiate the complexities of private and public aspects of rape as a central narrative event. In Gayl Jones's *Corregidora*, the author critically deploys a circular narrative time that shows how its own radical potential for connection and empowerment is defeated by the repetitive temporality of the traumatic legacy of slavery. In Isabel Allende's *The House of the Spirits*, a narrative model exists that, embracing both linear (epic) and circular modes of time, illuminates the limits of gendered divisions of space and forms a gesture out of the cyclical time of vengeance. Finally, each of these representations of rape occurs in a context of related historical and political events that indicates that temporal exorbitance or excess can help create narratives of rape able to account for the complexity of both personal and historical implications of the event in changing global contexts.

Witness

While the events and images of Abu Ghraib may not have changed the unspeakable, incommunicable nature of pain itself, they have changed the idea that the representations of purposefully inflicted pain are unthinkable, unspeakable, perverse; the assumption that viewers would recoil or be moved to act based upon what they have witnessed; and the belief that there is no language or referential system by which to describe what the images hold or to articulate responses to them. The mass circulation of images that were once by definition clandestine, and the conversations that have emerged around them, including interviews with the prisoners themselves, require that we rethink our understanding of the limits of language and representation.

What happens to the role of the witness when the characteristics of secrecy and shame remain intrinsic to the structural practice of torture but are erased from public discourse about it? When pain may remain essentially unshareable but torture is no longer clandestine? With the publication of the Abu Ghraib photos, conversation about the inner workings of the torture chamber is no longer limited to torture survivors, families of survivors or victims of torture, activists, intellectuals, or political and military personnel with a vested interest in such events. Rather, the conversation is magpie chatter heard on street corners, in cafes, and on radio call-in shows and appearing in newspapers. Not only the content of the debate—comprised of questions such as: Should we or shouldn't we torture as part of the war on terror? Do the actions depicted in the images from Abu Ghraib really constitute torture? Can't we understand the stress these soldiers are facing, and their need to just have fun, let off a little steam? Isn't this just what happens in war?—but also its ubiquity are jarring after years of understanding such images/acts to be by definition clandestine because of their violent obscenity, which also determined that they were essentially, morally unspeakable. Notwithstanding the claims of human dignity and morality exerted by the humanity of persons held indefinitely at Guantánamo, Baghram, and Abu Ghraib (not to mention the multitude of other, less publicized torture sites scattered across the globe), the representational ground has been split wide open and is now up for grabs in a high-stakes game of capitalizing on the possibilities for spin. And the stakes *are* high; as Judith Butler asks with regard to the representational struggle around the images of the 11 September attacks on the World Trade Center: "What can be made of grief besides a cry of war?" (*Precarious Life* xii).

This question occupies the center of the relationship between citizens and their elected representatives in the post-9/11 age. One of the results of the massive dissemination of images of horror from 11 September straight through the Abu Ghraib photos, along with its accompanying magpie effect, is the conversion of ordinary people, otherwise removed in time and space, into witness observers. This process was arguably underway in the years leading up to 2001, with the acceleration of image production and dissemination via the ever-increasing range of media outlets and the Internet. Even after the experience of real-time war coverage in the first Gulf War, deeply sanitized in its hazy night vision, which eerily illuminated regional targets but never persons vulnerable to wounding or death, the 9/11 moment pushed the experience of media exposure beyond what seemed to remain of its limits. The number of people who witnessed the planes in real time as they flew into the twin towers was extraordinary and was exceeded by the numbers who, over the succeeding hours, days, weeks, and now years, have witnessed the moment of contact, followed by the fall of the first and second towers, with an unparalleled repetitive force.

The uncut violence of people jumping to their deaths from the burning towers or of body parts on the ground, or even the real-time viewer propulsion from simple shock at the apparently accidental crash of a 747 into the World Trade Center to the traumatic realization that the attack was well planned and executed, and probably meant that the United States was or would soon be at war, all introduced the diagnosis posttraumatic stress disorder into ordinary parlance as applicable to bystanders in New York and quite literally all over the globe. This shift will necessitate scholarly attention from psychoanalytic and political perspectives to unpack its complexities and implications; for the purposes of this cultural study, however, most pertinent is the expansion of the concept of witness from the first-person survivor or observer, which of necessity limits the number of witnesses for any given event, to a virtual explosion of witnesses all over the globe not only to the event of the 9/11 attacks, but also to the global shifts and cataclysms that have attended it.

As with any other event that rises to the level of a moment to which others bear witness, the 9/11 attacks were available for interpretation by their observers—those who did not directly experience but simply watched the event—and the interpretations varied, not surprisingly, based upon the subject position of the witness. Those connected to a loved one in the environs of the World Trade Center or the Pentagon, or on any cross-country flight that morning, witnessed the event as the horrifying, inexplicable destruction of the lives of beloved innocents. Americans who did not know anyone in the vicinity of the attacks may have witnessed the event as a threat to their own security and well-being. The international community in the western world may have witnessed the attacks with a sense of "shock and awe" (to borrow a phrase rendered obscene in its application to the U.S. bombing of Baghdad in the Iraq War) that such an event could materialize in the most powerful nation on earth. Members of regions that have been the beneficiaries of harmful U.S. foreign policy (Latin America, parts of Asia and Africa, etc.) or that are currently under the political and economic dominion of its neocolonial policies may have found their sorrow at the sudden, inexplicable, and immoral loss of life coupled with a kind of recognition of their own experiences and a hope that perhaps the United States would take this opportunity to appreciate and share the experience of vulnerability so common to most of the rest of the world. Finally, adherents of fundamentalist jihadi movements may have witnessed the event as a triumph, a virtuous action and the ultimate sacrifice dedicated to a righteous cause.

The act of bearing witness, originally a concept in juridical or psychoanalytic contexts, has been in literary terms closely associated with the genre of *testimonio*, the body of Latin American testimonial writing that emerged after the political terror caused by authoritarian regimes in the latter half of the twentieth century. René Jara has described this literary form as possessing a unique historic authority, given that "the one who gives the testimony is the narrator" (qtd. in Agosin 74). The act of witnessing is also central to the production of Holocaust narratives (both testimonial and literary/filmic). Presumably, the purpose of testimony is to reveal a lost or repressed truth, and, while persons with different perspectives may contest such narratives, the ethics of the testimonial as a genre suited to chronicling personal experience are not typically challenged.

Recent literary critical work, however, has posed questions about the limits of witness literature to the authentic witness observer. The expanded notion of the witness in the post-9/11 age begs the question: what does it mean to be a member of a global village unable to expel its own death-driven propensity for hideous, unthinkable violence? Alternatively, what possibilities are opened by the potential that the vast expanse of world citizens-cum-witnesses may embrace the idea that Shoshana Felman has posed, that they (we) too are "from here," radically included in the contamination and the connection?[18] Chapter 5, "Genocide: Witness," considers the reach of this theoretical work in the context of the release of commemorative films ten years after the 1994 Rwandan genocide, simultaneous with the perpetration of genocide in Darfur, Sudan. This chapter analyzes several narratives of genocide, drawing conclusions about some shared techniques that suggest an ethics of representation that stems from the practice of witnessing in the context of human rights. For instance, all four texts under consideration (Pat Barker's *Double Vision*, Edwidge Danticat's *Farming of Bones*, Atom Egoyan's *Ararat*, Edoardo Ponti's *Between Strangers*) employ metanarrative to speculate upon the role of the witness—and of the text itself as witness—in the aftermath of genocide. *Ararat* and *Double Vision* go further, reflecting upon the role of art in testifying to historical atrocity and the power of the aesthetic as a response to collective horror. Finally, in view of the expanded role of the witness after 11 September, these texts provide an essential critical reflection upon gender as a link between constructions of first-world violence as individual/criminal and third-world violence as collective/political. Texts such as *Between Strangers* and *Double Vision* model a manner of human connection that transcends global identity difference by exploring the experience of loss and violence specifically through their gendered aspects. Significantly, these and other theories emergent in the millennial moment have taken a welcome turn in the direction of idealism, what Dominic LaCapra calls "the challenge of utopian aspiration" (42). The turn to such idealism on the part of postmodern literary scholars and historians provides heartening evidence of the efficacy of a partnership between these fields of cultural study and the discipline of human rights, for human rights discourse always occupies the realm of the utopic, the idealistic, the optimistic—to its detriment in the postmodern moment, but to its strength in the post-9/11 one.

The epilogue touches on the idea of authenticity related to the (eye)witness and an expanded notion of witness that will help mobilize the energies generated in distanced-observer witnesses by the onslaught of global images of atrocity. The brevity of the epilogue suggests the tentativeness of its claims, the many questions that arise through the idea of an expanded notion of witness in the context of the global polity and of literary and filmic studies. As with the disciplinary pairing of human rights and literary/cinematic studies more generally, the directions for new research implied by the theoretical approach in the epilogue are in a nascent stage, suggestive or evocative rather than concrete. They are to be found, however, in a broad range of developments in both human rights and literary studies, including a broad scholarly call for vigorous inquiry into what constitutes the human(e) in the context of the humanities, and the relationship between the discourse of human rights and the production, reception, and teaching of art, film, and literature. Interestingly, this call is belated when considered in light of similar appeals made from the other side of the equation: the human rights community has for some time argued that the struggle against human rights violations must be conducted in cultural as well as legal, political, and military spheres, so that the "toxins" of human rights violations are not passed from one generation to the next.[19] Indeed, projects of community treatment, healing, and reconciliation in the wake of devastation caused by civil war, genocide, and even AIDS have often been articulated through testimonial and/or community theatre or oral storytelling forums. With this in mind, *Beyond Terror* offers a response to the strain of postmodern cultural theory that has disparaged the role of cultural texts in helping to shape, change, or even effectively represent real historical events. The book argues that, on the contrary, after grave violations of human rights have occurred, the realm of representation is precisely the ground upon which the struggle for justice in legal, emotional, and cultural terms is waged.

There are many ways in which human rights assumptions may bear upon discussions in literary and cinematic studies—and vice versa. There are debates in postcolonial studies, for instance, regarding what some perceive to be the excessive focus of some of its most prominent practitioners upon representation and discourse, which critics claim excludes attention to the often brutal material realities that characterize the postcolonial world. Such debates could be addressed through a partnership between human rights perspectives and literary and film theories able to address material or corporeal experience in the context of postcolonial textual studies. Applying this framework to literary and cinematic texts can also help to mediate between the postcolonial affinity with local claims of marginalized cultures and its well-documented suspicion of postmodernism's origin in the universalist traditions of European thought. Conversely, advances in the fields of narrative and postcolonial cultural studies hold promise in the search for ways to intervene in repetitious cycles of grave violations of human rights in particular communities. Specifically, narrative strategies that include variations on traditional chronological time, linear plot structures, and omniscient or totalizing first-person narrative points of view might help practitioners in the field of human rights to help both survivors and perpetrators of violations share the stories of such abuses (in public testimonial or personal, familial contexts) in ways that perpetuate neither the fixed identity positions of victim and oppressor nor the desire for revenge. In the developing context of international testimonial forums such as the International Criminal Court, the various international tribunals in the Hague and in Arusha, Tanzania, and local Rwandan tribunals known as Gacaca, the postcolonial location of agency in the voice and in control over stories that have historically been marginalized or silenced gestures toward an alternative over time to more brutal methods of asserting identity and control.

These diverse disciplinary partnerships share an urgency around questions of word, image, and representation in relation to the definition of the human, as well as a commitment to the potential contribution of literary, cinematic, and cultural studies to the development of an ethical global human rights discourse. The obvious philosophical grounding for such a discourse is the cosmopolitan, with all the qualifications and revisions that have attempted to wrest it from its imperial foundations. Beginning with an analysis of representational strategies used to fictionalize atrocity, *Beyond Terror* moves by its close to an examination of broader forms of witness literature concerned with conceptions and legacies of human rights, and with narratives of human connection as alternatives to the endless dramatization of the human ability to inflict pain.

1

TORTURE I
SAFETY

Steven Spielberg's 1994 blockbuster *Schindler's List* is a powerful testament to the Shoah, if critical and audience response are reliable indices. Certainly many of its images of the suffering of victims and survivors of Nazi atrocity are deeply moving. Its focus, however, is split in typical classic Hollywood fashion between the background stories of the Jewish men and women Schindler rescued (and those he did not rescue) and the story of Oskar Schindler himself. Janet Maslin's *New York Times* review of *Schindler's List* is instructive in considering the relationship of such a split focus to the film's effect as historical representation: "Documented exhaustively or dramatized in terms by now dangerously familiar, the Holocaust threatens to become unimaginable precisely because it has been imagined so fully. But the film *Schindler's List* . . . presents the subject as if discovering it anew." Reading further, it becomes clear that the newness of Spielberg's presentation of the Holocaust hinges on his negotiation of the relationship between Schindler and Schindler's Jews; put another way, the lens through which we might imagine the Holocaust anew is Schindler himself. Maslin describes Schindler as "unmistakably larger than life, with the panache of an old-time movie star." It is precisely this authority, this bigness, that problematizes such representations: the character of Schindler, privileged culturally, politically, and economically in relation to the Jewish men and women on whose behalf he ultimately struggles, overtakes the narrative, focusing this story of the Holocaust upon his transformation from Nazi power broker to humanitarian hero in an instance of the bildungsroman narrative of emerging awareness central to the category of film I identify as the counterhistorical drama.[1]

Crossing generic boundaries, the counterhistorical dramatic film employs adventure, romance, suspense, courtroom drama, and war narrative conventions to represent instances of historical atrocity. Over and above these generic classifications, however, it refers to a historic event or to a true story, presenting a counternarrative to an official version of history or to a perceived silence surrounding a historical event. Typically, these films employ a bildungsroman form through which audiences identify with the protagonist's growth to the status of enlightened hero figure over the course of the movie. Into this category, with varying degrees of success in fictionalizing historical violations of human rights, fall such films as *The Year of Living Dangerously* (1982), *The Killing Fields* (1984), *Cry Freedom* (1985), *Salvador* (1987), *Beyond Rangoon* (1995), *Schindler's List* (1993), *Red Corner* (1995), *Seven Years in Tibet* (1997), *Three Kings* (1999), and *Beyond Borders* (2003).

Importantly, such films are about western protagonists operating in other places; that is, places other than the site of western (U.S.) freedom and democracy, although on occasion the films critique U.S. complicity in the undemocratic practices of torture/terror in another nation.[2] In spite of their geographic locations elsewhere, counterhistorical dramas invariably provide a white, western protagonist toward whom audience identification is directed throughout the film. The struggle of the people or country in question provides the context within which the protagonist grows and develops, and may offer a source of alternative values or wisdom that nudges the protagonist forward in his/her quest. There is a basic split in terms of plot and characterization that, not surprisingly, falls along the line of racial/cultural identity: the film traces the story of the collective struggle of the nation/people alongside the story of the protagonist/hero in his personal, professional, or romantic growth. I use the male pronoun mindfully, as the protagonist is almost always male, a fact which has a great deal to do with the development and characteristics of the genre.

In *Schindler's List*, the focus on the Holocaust narrows during the film's narrative span to spotlight the perspective of one hero, a Nazi who experiences a change of heart. The focus then expands, as it does at the end of virtually all counterhistorical dramas, to include the collectivity of victims and survivors of the atrocity. In this case, the actual Jews Schindler saved file through the frame of the camera side by side with the actors who portrayed them, leaving stones at the actual Schindler's grave. This momentary broadening of focus and turn to documentary convention reinstates these survivors as actors in the story only at the moment that the story is over.

To be sure, the film does not wholly romanticize its hero. Spielberg is critical of Schindler's character, demonstrating throughout the film his self-
interest and complicity with Nazi practices. Still, the narrative focus on
Schindler's story, rendered in the generic terms of romance and bildungsroman, compromises the representations of historical atrocity against Nazi prisoners by making those representations meaningful as they force a shift in
Schindler's consciousness that transforms him into a prototypical hero figure,
rather than because they provide witness to the material conditions experienced by those prisoners. Maslin articulates this phenomenon in a description
of one of the film's most poignant scenes, highlighting its blend of dramatic
(classic Hollywood) and documentary-film conventions: "As the glossy, volup-
tuous look of Oskar's sequences gives way to a stark, documentary-style
account of the Jews' experience, *Schindler's List* witnesses a pivotal transformation. Oskar and a girlfriend, on horseback, watch from a hilltop as the ghetto is
evacuated, and the image of a little girl in red seems to crystallize Oskar's horror" (*Schindler's List*). The scene, shot from above to replicate Schindler's gaze,
depicts atrocity enacted upon the Jewish people as the Nazis evacuate them
from the Krakow ghetto; however, that atrocity gathers meaning primarily as a
signifier of Schindler's rise to consciousness. The use of color—the little girl's
red coat painfully vivid against the numbing black and white of the rest of the
scene—brings to life the horror experienced by the victims of Nazi aggression,
illuminating Schindler's realization of this horror, his ability to see it in all its
profundity.[3] In keeping with the conventions of counterhistorical drama, the
film's plotlines converge at the scene of torture or atrocity in an epiphanic
moment. This moment is central to the film's dramatic action, producing the
protagonist's heightened awareness, which in turn becomes a catalyst either
for his action or for deeper suspense and concern for his safety on the part of
the audience. The image is not central to the film as a testimony to the historic
torture enacted upon real bodies. In other words, the relative inadequacy of
Schindler's List as a representation of the Nazi Holocaust does not result from a
negative relationship to the truth of the historic event, but rests upon its use of
the spectacle of tortured bodies within a classic Hollywood film structure.

　　Schindler's List provides an appropriate point of entry to my analysis of the
counterhistorical dramatic film, as I am particularly concerned with the competing demands of narrativization—particularly emplotment—and the representation of tortured bodies. Closer examination of generic and narrative
cues in this series of thematically and generically linked texts exposes their

political ambivalences and paradoxes. Also revelatory are the conditions of production and circulation of the films, and the fate of the unspeakable when the narrative or generic conventions used to represent it are employed in large-scale, high-budget, mainstream Hollywood films about a catastrophic historical event or events. Rather than being mobilized (by survivors or others) to bear witness to people and events and to resist the use of torture and terror, these narrative films balance the market demands of audience appeal and box-office revenues upon the points of their own imperatives to tell the truth about events previously misunderstood, offering a counter-history to official versions. If probed, this ambivalence—or, perhaps better, this overdetermination—of purpose reveals a fundamental instability not only in the ethics of representing torture, but also in terms of the cultural work such representations ultimately perform.[4] That is, in the context of mass cultural circulation of images of torture and death, the wounded body is at once a referent testifying to historical atrocity and a signifier of fear, suspense, desire, even humor, depending upon the interpretive signals of its generic formula and the exigencies of the viewing situation and viewer.

After such images have been widely circulated and consumed by western audiences, then, how are these same audiences to negotiate the often heavy-handed messages in historically situated films meant to critique the use of state-sponsored terror in other places? Given that, as self-described "dramatic historian" Oliver Stone asserts, "movies have to make money, you've got to make them so they're exciting, they're gripping, people want to go see them" (qtd. in Kreisler), politically motivated message movies often borrow unabashedly from classic Hollywood techniques of genre, plot, and characterization, a circumstance that complicates—and compromises—the reception of such films. I am interested in the space between historical films engaged in overt critique of (state) violence, and fictional films whose representations of violence are informed by imperatives of plot or genre. Put another way, this chapter trains its gaze upon the gap opened by the radical shift of interpretive cues (genre, plot, context, and characterization) around the fixed specter of rape, torture, and execution/genocide. Before it is begun, the very delicate work of representing torture is in many ways degraded by the larger context of Hollywood filmmaking, which participates in what Dean MacCannell has in another context termed "the routinization of violence" (198).[5]

Indeed, narrative strategies and cinematic techniques employed by mainstream films that depict historic violence to historic bodies often prioritize a

dominant western subject position over the other cultural and national subject positions represented, an identity politic that mirrors the general global
distribution of safety and harm from a human rights perspective.[6] This
process of identity differentiation accompanies the split plotline characteristic of what David Bordwell terms "classical Hollywood cinema," in which the
protagonist as a "psychologically defined individual struggl[ing] to solve a
clear-cut problem or to attain specific goals" is the "target" of narration, and
the plot is split in two along the lines of a heterosexual romance, on the one
hand, and "another sphere—work, war, a mission or quest, other personal
relationships," on the other (157).

The problem with using such classical Hollywood formulae to structure a
film with an overt message about an international political struggle is implicit
in its definition: according to this formula, the protagonist—in this case differentiated culturally, racially, and economically from the people on whose behalf
s/he protests—retains agency not only with regard to the action of the film, but
also in terms of its narration. The reins of the story, which constitute its narrative point of view, are wrenched from the historic actors and handed to a privileged western observer/participant, resulting in the illusion that there is no
story—no historic event—unless it is witnessed, shaped, and experienced by
western agents. Fortunately, recent films have challenged the presumption that
white western protagonists with major star appeal provide points of recognition and identification for white western viewers, thereby refracting these
viewers' identification with the struggle of the nation or people in question.
Among these is Terry George's *Hotel Rwanda* (2004), which represents the
Rwandan genocide of 1994 through the story of Rwandan protagonist/hero Paul
Rusesabagina.[7] Until recently, however, the conventional counterhistorical dramatic film has imposed an uneven narrative burden upon the plotline of the
individual protagonist. In this way, the genre's normative representations of
historical instances of torture raise ethical problems exacerbated by the insis-
tent differentiation of white, western individual protagonists from nonwhite,
nonwestern collectives made up of minor characters and extras.

Specifically, the demand for viewer identification with the struggles of
other people suffering human rights violations produces a stable U.S. identity
based upon the ideals of constitutional democracy as differentiated from the
systems of the other nations/cultures represented. This political differentiation is underscored by displays of cultural difference, one of which, paradoxically, is the enactment of human rights violations. The frame of this idealized

western identity, then, is built upon the spectacle of the tortured body of the national/cultural other, a spectacle that consolidates identity difference via the figures of both victim and torturer/perpetrator. The body of the victim in its racial and cultural difference from the western viewer (presumed to be white) becomes signifier of the relative safety and security of the western body from such acts, while the acts of the torturer mark the space between citizens governed by the rule of law and morality (that is, by Christian democratic constitutionality) and the brutal irrationality of others who are neither subject to nor subjects of a written law, moral or otherwise. Thus, the use of authoritarian force represents a paradoxical combination of excess and absence of law according to the principles of democratic constitutionality.

The coupling of classic Hollywood generic conventions of split plotline and bildungsroman format with imperialistic conventions employed to represent tortured bodies produces core instabilities in the political positioning of counterhistorical dramatic film: that is, the overt statement of resistance to international human rights violations masks the hegemonic assertion of a mythic western identity and difference in global context. Recent examples include John Boorman's *Beyond Rangoon* (1995) and Richard Attenborough's *Cry Freedom* (1985). However, some recent films borrow from the counterhistorical drama's conventions but foreground such generic conventions or their effects using innovative narrative and cinematographic techniques, and have managed both to do well at the box office and to deliver coherent critiques of the violation of human rights and the global conditions that support such violations. Among these is David O. Russell's *Three Kings* (1999).

Beyond Rangoon: The Problem of Narrative Demand

John Boorman's *Beyond Rangoon* (1995) is a classic example of the counterhistorical dramatic film that offers itself as corrective to a repressed history, constructing its audience as student to the film's didactic treatise on the violent events that followed the Burmese government's repressive crackdown on pro-democracy protests and activists in the late 1980s.[8] Boorman inscribes into several key scenes a critique of the international silence that surrounded oppression of and violence against pro-democracy students and supporters of democratic leader Aung San Suu Kyi by the military junta in the 1980s.[9] In one scene, the protagonist's voiced-over interior monologue describes the struggle of a photographer to get his photos out of Burma: "They were the only photos of the massacre. What the Chinese did in Tiananmen Square was televised but Burma wasn't. So for most of the world, it just didn't happen."[10] The film, then, offers itself as a representation of that lost or silenced historical truth. While it is not only true, but also politically meaningful, to assert that something "happened" in Burma, and that those events included massive human rights violations, Boorman's emplotment and cinematography reveal ideological instabilities that affect the production of historical knowledge accompanying the film's circulation. The representation of tortured bodies in the film also dramatizes the problems that result from the use of the historic referents—that is, government repression in late twentieth-century Burma and extrajudicial torture and execution of Burmese people— as signifiers in the film's generic coding, rather than as testimonials to their own occurrence or experience.[11]

The film deviates somewhat from the standard counterhistorical dramatic form in that, to begin, its protagonist is female. Laura Bowman (Patricia Arquette) travels Burma not in an official capacity, but in a personal one: to heal herself from the effects of (first-world) violence.[12] Like many counterhistorical dramatic films, *Beyond Rangoon* presents potentially fruitful models of relationships between western and native peoples even (especially) at a moment of political extremity. Indeed, the split plotline in *Beyond Rangoon* illuminates the transformation of the western protagonist and her native counterpart, Aung Ko (played by Aung Ko), as a result of contact in the context of state-sponsored brutality in 1980s Burma. Far from representing the flow of influence as unidirectional, from (western) center to (colonial) periphery, the film provides ample evidence of the influence of Burmese culture and philosophy upon the western protagonist, and of positive cultural and personal exchange between Bowman and the Burmese people she encounters. However, it undercuts the radical potential for those representations to act as progressive models of cultural contact, and for the film to advance a coherent protest against the historical human rights violations central to its action, by its use of representations of terror against Burmese people as an element of the adventure emplotment to heighten audience suspense for Bowman's safety and well-being, rather than to act as witness to the material conditions they signify. In this way, the film's narrativization ultimately gives way to the ideological construction central to counterhistorical dramatic films—western identity as safe, superior, and separate from the rest of the world—in spite of the film's formal claims to represent a historic moment and to protest against human rights violations.

Beyond Rangoon begins by offering the fertile premise that pain can be a means of connection between disparate peoples. Yet the imperialist consciousness revealed in Bowman's first interior monologue, a voice-over that accompanies the image of white tourists floating through the lush landscape of Burma on a river boat, immediately undermines the potential of this empathic connection: "The trip was my sister's idea; . . . she meant well. A touch of the exotic East would get me away from all the things that had happened. But it didn't; . . . I thought I might find something in the East, some kind of answer. I stared at those stone statues, but nothing stirred in me. I was stone myself." The presence of orientalist discourse in Bowman's rhetoric of escape, and the specific descriptive "exotic" in relation to the generalized geographic marker "the East" (as opposed to the cultural and political specificity of Burma as independent from and interdependent with other nations and cultures in Asia), is common in dominant representations of cultural contact. However, it becomes clear as the film progresses that this potentially healing exoticism is to be found quite specifically in an eastern ontological approach to pain and suffering, especially as manifested in the tenets of Buddhism. As this interior monologue enlightens the audience about Bowman's emotional state, the camera flashes from shots of the river to shots of a large stone Buddha carved into a hillside, reclining "just before he passed into nirvana." To underscore the didactic significance of an eastern approach to pain, the white tour guide informs his clients that "in the Buddhist world, where suffering is the accepted condition of man, the attainment of perfect detachment is the ultimate achievement." Making the connection, we must assume that the answer Bowman searches for in the East is precisely that detachment from the pain she has experienced as a result of an act of violence.

As if to complete this introduction to Bowman's wounded consciousness, the camera shifts to an aerial shot of a western-style living room with a man and a young boy—Bowman's husband and son—lying bloodied, shot. Thus the audience understands that Bowman is wounded in a specific way: by the loss and grief that accompany physical violence. First-world civilian violence and third-world state violence are set up as congruent, at least in the sense that people experiencing the effects of these different kinds of violence might find ground for an empathic connection that would bind over cultural, national, economic, and gender differences. Importantly, this connection has as much to do with strategies for healing as with the shared experience of the violence itself. The wounded body provides that point of connection, remaining fixed in the specter of its woundedness despite the disparate conditions that have produced it. This congruence between first- and third-world violence is gendered as a woman's violent loss of her husband in the first-world individual experience of Laura Bowman, and as the same loss repeatedly experienced by women in the third-world context of collective, state-sponsored violence in Burma.

The film early establishes gender as an organizing narrative principle, when, traveling alone in Burma, Bowman is repeatedly queried about the whereabouts of her husband. As a traveler, then, she is constructed specifically in terms of a lack that is both symbolic—a woman not subject to the requisite patriarchal restrictions on mobility—and material, in that, having lost her husband to violent crime, she is literally without him. To emphasize this parallel, several of the film's most violent scenes specifically depict the death of a husband. One of the many point-blank executions Bowman witnesses is that of a man whose wife is forced to look on, powerless to intervene. Later in that same scene, Bowman encounters a Burmese woman hiding during the military onslaught of the village who warns her, "Be careful. They took my husband away!" Finally, during the border crossing to Thailand at the close of the film, the only one of Bowman's Burmese companions caught in the crossfire is a young man whom audiences have come to know throughout the film in his role as husband and father. His wife watches as he dies, as does Bowman, whose witnessing of these other women's losses and their public expressions of grief is cathartic, filling the void left by her inability to witness and fully mourn the deaths of her own husband and son.

Bowman's gender also informs her experience of violence in the United States as domestic, taking place in the home—although this representation of violence in the home as perpetrated by random criminals from the outside world displaces the routinized violence most often perpetrated against women in the home by family members.[13] Bowman's healing process involves a certain economy of scale that comes to inform her perspective on violence such that the violent loss of her husband and son in their home, initially threatening to overwhelm her, is diminished in proportion to the immensity of the widespread, state-sanctioned, public atrocity she witnesses in Burma. Such violence, constructed as extraordinary, provides a means for Bowman to re-vision her own experience as manageable, allowing a release of her own terror as she witnesses that of others in a process of exaggerated traumatic mirroring. This process is arguably an undesirable aspect of witness via global media coverage by the collective body of the "over-developed world"

(to borrow Vijay Prashad's apt term) in its privileged relation to the politically traumatic condition of the "global south"[14] (The issue of the distanced
observer who witnesses global violations via the media reappears in chapter 5,
in which a series of texts provides other possibilities for such witnesses.)

In *Beyond Rangoon*, an early scene initiates catharsis through a displaced
act of witnessing: National League of Democracy leader Aung San Suu Kyi, a
woman operating in the public sphere on a collective level heretofore
unknown to Bowman, faces the guns trained on her by a phalanx of soldiers.
Serenely approaching the soldiers, Suu Kyi stares one in the eyes until, his
discomfort so great that he begins to tremble, he drops his weapon. At this,
Suu Kyi pushes aside the guns, walking through them to greet her supporters.
The camera reverts at this moment to a shot of Bowman, glowing at this triumph of a woman who faces the guns and wins, presumably in contrast to
her own absence at the moment that her husband and son were killed. An
onlooker asserts that "Burma will be free when every student, every worker,
every *mother* faces the guns" (emphasis mine). In a sense, this last imperative
drives Bowman's movement through Burma, informing her involvement in
the pro-democracy struggle until she herself has faced the guns and survived
them. Facing the body wounded by guns also specifically occasions Bowman's
healing. Trained as a physician, Bowman has been unable to practice medicine since the murder of her family because she can no longer stand the sight
of blood. When Aung Ko receives a bullet wound which threatens to kill him,
Bowman is forced to perform on-the-spot surgery to remove the bullet and
save his life. In the process of healing Aung Ko, she is healed herself. His
wound is redemptive to her inasmuch as she is able to pull the bullet from
him as she could not from her husband and child, his body providing the
ground upon which Bowman is able to work through her trauma.

At the end of the film, after a perilous crossing into Thailand with hundreds of Burmese refugees, Bowman heads immediately for the medical tent
and begins working on the injured, signifying the completion of her healing
process and thus of the main quest plot of the narrative. We are also privy to
a dream sequence in which Bowman's son visits her, saying, "You've got to let
me go, Mama, I have to go," upon which she wakes to a peaceful starlit scene,
suggesting her ultimate achievement of detachment, her absorption of the
cultural wisdom gleaned from contact with the Burmese people (particular-
ized in the figure of Aung Ko). As in *Schindler's List*, when the plotline corresponding to this protagonist achieves closure, the narrative field opens to

foreground the historic referent, in this case using captions over the screen images of Bowman working in the Red Cross tent (images that underscore the indispensable presence of western aid and knowledge of western onlookers in international crises).[15] The captions read in part: "Thousands of Burmese were massacred in the crackdown of the Democracy Movement. More than 700,000 fled their country. Two million more were driven from their homes and subsist in remote jungles. Torture and oppression continue in Burma to this day."[16]

The idealized narrative closure achieved by the resolution of Bowman's healing process provides a stark contrast to this strikingly nonspecific disclosure regarding the thousands of Burmese people massacred and displaced by state terror and especially to the simple declarative that torture and oppression continue in Burma to this day. This ambiguous and overdetermined time referent places audiences in an equivocal relationship to the assertion of ongoing torture and oppression. That is, while "this day" presumably refers to the moment the film was released, it also uncannily refers to the day that one views the film, which, given the circulation of film via home video, may be years after the film's 1995 release. Apart from its referential haziness, this statement of a historical condition (ongoing oppression and brutality) is problematic not because it represents an ambiguous truth claim, but because of its juxtaposition with the false finitude of narrative closure imposed by its classic Hollywood bildungsroman and adventure emplotment. The act of assigning narrative closure to the story of Laura Bowman, especially as that closure is achieved through the vehicle of the historical struggle of Burmese people, privileges Bowman as protagonist and reaffirms her identity as safe, separate from the ongoing, irresolvable struggles of the Burmese. It is especially significant in this context that closure is equated with healing, a healing unavailable to the Burmese, whose history is represented as an open wound, unsutured to this day. The image of Bowman healing the wounded Burmese man, newly restored and empowered in her training as western physician, re-places her at the imperialist—if liberally altruistic—center of the film, and of the indeterminate vortex of native history.[17]

Safety and Harm: The Wounded Body

Beyond Rangoon's final image of Bowman hard at work in the Red Cross aid tent is the culmination of the film's use of the wounded body to construct a western identity defined by its difference from native people in terms of protection against bodily injury in both national and global contexts. The measure of this difference widens over the course of the film. It is especially evident in the spectacle of tortured bodies used as symbolic capital in exchange for rising audience suspense around Bowman's journey through a hazardous Burma to physical safety and emotional healing.

Such use of the tortured or wounded body is related to the formal requirements of the film's classically split Hollywood structure. Late in the film, a gruesomely stylized representation of the massacre of peaceful Burmese protesters disrupts a typical Hollywood chase scene in which Bowman and her compatriots in their jeep narrowly escape the shots of soldiers. The wild action of the chase is abruptly truncated when they stumble upon the horror of a leisurely massacre, shot in close-up. At the moment the soldiers open fire upon the crowd, the camera reverses to a shot of Bowman screaming, "Stop it!" In slow motion, the film captures in tight close-up the specter of men, women, and girls falling as they are shot, their bodies twisting in grisly, aesthetic movements. These shots are combined with reverse shots of Bowman's screaming face throughout the sequence. And then, as abruptly as the action of the film was arrested to accommodate this baroque depiction of massacre as modern dance ensemble, it bluntly snaps back to the accelerated action of the chase scene, which feels the more rapid and suspenseful—juxtaposed with the deliberate and almost suspended slowness of the massacre. This slowing of cinematic time can be an effective method for capturing the ineffable, lingering temporality of pain and trauma (the *longue durée*); however, its efficacy here is lost in the outsized shadow of the camera's point of view. Bowman essentially moderates the representation of massacre of Burmese people; her horror, untamed by the gloss of aesthetic stylization and occupying the narrative and cinematic focal point of the scene, trumps the suffering of the victims. Perhaps even more important, Bowman's terror has the power of voice the masses of Burmese under attack lack, as audiences distinctly hear her screams on the soundtrack over the collective (background) noise of the crowd. Ultimately, then, the interruption of a frantic chase scene by this spectacle of execution heightens audience suspense and fear for Bowman's safety. The function of these images as testimony to the historic massacre of Burmese protesters is secondary to their use in adventure emplotment.

Representations of the torture and execution of Burmese people intensify the adventure and bildungsroman formulae in similar fashion throughout *Beyond Rangoon*. From the moment the film erupts into its representations of violent struggle between protesters and soldiers—the moment, that is, when the bildungsroman formula takes on the formal characteristics of adventure narrative—the pop-pop of shots fired and the spectacle of falling Burmese bodies distinguish Bowman's many escapes from scenes of conflict. These background sights and sounds demarcate the narrow margins of Bowman's escape as her body literally removes itself from the site of danger precisely when soldiers arrive, firing their assault weapons in the despotic capriciousness characteristic of the military in counterhistorical dramatic films.[18] If the quest of the film involves moving through a space demarcated dangerous to a safe, secure space of redemptive healing and closure, then wounded Burmese bodies provide the material(ity) of suspense for Bowman's safety as she navigates that ground.

Like most counterhistorical dramatic films, *Beyond Rangoon* uses the spectacle of the tortured (native) body to cordon off a particularly hostile danger zone within the relative peril of the whole environment. The narrative time the protagonist spends in that space, then, is a time of intensified fear and suspense, and crossing that border generally signifies a shift in the protagonist's consciousness, a movement toward the achievement of courage or heroism that will signal completion of the quest/narrative. In *Beyond Rangoon*, that shift in consciousness occurs when Bowman enters a village desecrated by military onslaught in order to obtain medicine to heal Aung Ko's gunshot wound. We hear screams as she heads toward the village, and the camera pans the area in time to capture the point-blank executions of two Burmese men, witnessed by their wives. Upon reaching the border of the town, Bowman stops at a hanging and bloodied body, revealed to the audience in pieces congruent to Bowman's gaze as it travels the body's surface. The audience sees, as if through Bowman's eyes, the limp body hanging, blood over its chest, eyes bulging, before the camera jumps to a shot of Bowman running forward again, away from the danger represented *by* this body rather than the harm done *to* the body. Bowman's mediating gaze clouds our view of the Burmese body, forcing us to find its outline through the haze of an adventure plot in which suspense hinges upon threats to Bowman's bodily safety. Thus, the terror inspired by the spectacle of torture of a Burmese person is displaced, as audience attention is removed from that person's body and his or her pain, to the potential of such pain enacted upon the white, western body.

Why this need for a mediating western presence in a film that claims to be about human rights abuses in Burma? If one posits that the presence of

western protagonists (often played by major Hollywood stars) in counterhistorical dramatic films provides a point of identification that ensures the popular appeal necessary to reach a mass audience, then, according to this model,
western audiences (a construction that elides its own racial, class, and cultural differences) are capable of imagining the pain of the other only by imagining the suffering of a composite (white) western person. This strategy of
identification has a long history in the United States, as Saidiya V. Hartman
points out, locating its origins in sentimental activist literature of the ante-
bellum period. In a discussion of the abolitionist writings of John Rankin, a
white man who imagines himself and his family undergoing the brutalities
of slavery as a means of evoking reader identification with the enslaved,
Hartman describes the complexity of an empathy which demands that the
body of the other be replaced by a "proxy" resembling the self in order to be
imagined.[19] As Hartman asserts: "In fact, Rankin becomes a proxy and the
other's pain is acknowledged to the degree that it can be imagined, yet by
virtue of this substitution the object of identification threatens to disappear"
(19). This obliteration of the other's suffering constitutes the representational
violence of counterhistorical dramatic film, which, unable to sustain the tension between cultural specificity and universal humanity embedded in its
own protest discourse, gives way to the totalizing impulse of an imperialist
resurrection of white, western subjectivity as symbol for universal experience.

Cross-Cultural Identification in *Cry Freedom*

Richard Attenborough's *Cry Freedom* manages this tension between cultural
specificity and universal humanity in its protest against human rights abuses
in apartheid-era South Africa by providing a more complicated model of
cross-cultural identification than that of *Beyond Rangoon*. The film also distin-
guishes itself by dramatizing only one explicit representation of torture.
Rather then employing images of tortured and mutilated bodies as spectacles
to provide audience suspense, here the tortured body provides evidence of
the truth against the manipulation of history by those in power. This use of
images to reveal a repressed truth is in keeping with an understanding of ethical representations of human rights abuses as those which assert the validity
of one truth claim over another in service of an argument, as opposed to eroticizing the image as spectacle for narrative pleasure.[20] Although its narrative is
split in classical Hollywood style, *Cry Freedom* also uses narrative structure to
radically contest the official version of the fate of Black Consciousness leader

Stephen Biko (Denzel Washington) in police custody—the manner of his death, the condition of his body—by dramatically reconstructing those events, directing the viewer's identification with Biko to shape a sense of indignation and horror at the tactics of the Afrikaner police and, by extension, the apartheid government.[21] It is only indirectly that the film uses what happens to Biko's body to motivate suspense for the fate of white hero/protagonist Donald Woods (Kevin Kline). Significantly, the film was released during the tenure of National Party (apartheid) rule in South Africa; these images, then, countered an official version of history in progress in ways that are central to the film's status and reception.

While the film does not directly depict Biko's torture, audiences receive evidence of it in the scenes directly following his arrest. Shot in a long, dark hallway, the camera, angled low, frames several pairs of shiny black shoes walking with a set of bare feet dragging among them. The soundtrack is empty but for the click of heels and the low gasps of labored breathing. In the next scene, Biko's body is revealed in parts; however, unlike the cinematic technique in *Beyond Rangoon*, the camera's perspective does not mimic the gaze of a western onlooker. The camera, unmediated, pans up Biko's leg and over his naked body to his beaten, bloodied face. We hear sounds of torture— a whip or a stick banging, accompanied by agonized screams—as further evidence of the cause of Biko's injuries. Biko is taken out, still naked, and thrown in the back of a truck. The camera cuts to a shot–reverse shot formation of Biko's head slamming onto the truck's hard floor interspersed with images of the heavy tires bouncing over ruts in the dirt road. The final shot of Biko's body is in the morgue, where Woods has gone with Biko's wife. Biko's face is twisted and swollen. Woods has brought his photographer to document Biko's condition.

Taken together, these scenes supply evidence of a suppressed reality and counter scenes of Minister of Police James Kruger's formal announcement of Biko's death ("Biko's death leaves me cold. He died after a hunger strike.") and of the official inquest, which acknowledges Biko's brain damage but makes the absurd pronouncement that "the cause of death was brain injury which led to renal failure and other complications. . . . On the available evidence they cannot be attributed to any act of omission amounting to a criminal offense on the part of any person." In this case—rare in the counterhistorical dramatic film— the image of the tortured body bears witness to the reality of its condition. Moreover, the image provides a crucial contradiction to the vehement denials of the apartheid authorities, denials which constitute a secondary trauma central to the experience of torture. Elaine Scarry describes such denial, or disclaiming, as an aspect of state-sponsored torture used to "translat[e] . . . all the objectified elements of pain into the insignia of power, [to convert] the enlarged map of human suffering into an emblem of the regime's strength" (56). *Cry Freedom* uses the image of the tortured body—arguably a "map of human suffering"—precisely to undo the regime's strength by reclaiming that image as signifier of the regime's brutality, as well as testimonial to the body's own repressed material reality. Therefore, the scene is useful to the plot only insofar as the plot presents a counterhistory to the official history asserted by South African security forces under the apartheid regime. In other words, during this scene, the film's imagery and action correspond to its proclaimed intent of protest, all the more real given its release at the repressive height of apartheid power.

In spite of *Cry Freedom*'s clearly oppositional position, however, the incoherence in the film's rendering of torture—and thus, the instability of its politics—hinges on Biko's death occurring approximately halfway through the film. The second half of the film asks viewers to identify with the struggle of Donald Woods to get himself, his book on Biko, and his family out of South Africa after being banned in a fashion similar to that of Biko. The generic vehicles of suspense and adventure are now mobilized in telling Woods's story, which is also the story of the making of a hero. Whatever the film's formal position, indicated by its assertion of and protest against the cause of Steve Biko's death, it still asks audiences to identify for more than half its length with a heroic figure who has benefited from the apartheid system as a member of South Africa's ruling class. Viewers still see black men, women, and children being tortured and murdered and white men, women, and children escaping into the beatific sunset and orchestral crescendo of the quintessential Hollywood ending.

This plotline achieves the requisite classic Hollywood closure through the dramatic border crossings that mark Woods's and his family's escape from South Africa. The plotline corresponding to the life of Stephen Biko and the struggle in South Africa remains typically open, marked as such at the end of the film by a conflation of specific historic events into a montage of third-world misery: documentary shots of military violence against Soweto schoolchildren protesting the use of Afrikaans in the schools in 1977, along with a rolling list of names of people South African police killed in custody after their imprisonment without trial. In considering the relative adequacy of *Cry Free-dom*'s representations of atrocity in South Africa, the problem is not one of truth-value; indeed, *Cry Freedom* is perhaps the counterhistorical drama most at pains to reveal the repressed truth of the historical event as opposed to the dominant, official version. At issue here is the destabilization of representations constructed to do this work by the split in plotline that awards the story of the white hero the lion's share of time, resolution, safety, and closure.

Despite these compromises in the integrity of the film's representations of torture and terror, *Cry Freedom* complicates the issue of identity in the film by constructing the bildungsroman process of character growth—specifically the growth of Woods into a heroic protagonist—as one of cross-cultural exchange and integration. Strategically intercutting flashback shots of Biko with African music tracks and scenery, the film equates heroism with Africanness.[22] Woods's process of becoming heroic coincides with his becoming more African—specifically, more black South African, more like Biko himself. Indeed, the making of Woods into a heroic figure is actually the education of a white liberal by a black radical. Biko states early on that his desire to meet with Woods is really a desire to attempt the "education of a true liberal." Biko is clearly successful, as Woods adopts both his politics and his political tactics over the course of the film in an uncanny reversal of Homi Bhabha's theory of mimicry in a colonial context. Bhabha describes the colonial mimicry of imperial authority as a disruption of that authority (88); here, Woods's odd mimicry of Biko's (heroic) resistance constitutes a usurpation of the authority of the marginalized, an authority that translates to a political and even racial authenticity that gained currency throughout the 1990s with the embrace of multicultural and postcolonial politics by the Left.

The political instability of such representations in the film may be traced to its grounding in Donald Woods's book *Biko: The True Story of the Young South African Martyr and His Struggle to Raise Black Consciousness* (1978), which demonstrates the same desire for authenticity, and the same narrative split, as the film, presenting itself as the (true, authentic) story of Biko but interrupting that story with a narrative thread tracing Woods's own consciousness and experience. The ambivalence of Woods's project is discernible in claims made in the prologue to the book's third edition (1991): "Richard Attenborough's film based on this book *and my friendship with Steve Biko* was shot on location in Zimbabwe. . . . The screenplay relies on incidents from Biko's life and my writings and experiences as the 'foreground,' or personal interest material, for the film. Major historic events of the period serve as the documentary 'back-ground' to reveal the nature of apartheid" (10, emphasis mine). This refer-ence to a plotline split into foreground and background material elides the imbalance within *Cry Freedom*'s foreground plot; that is, audiences see rela-tively few incidents from Biko's life, and those are related to the development of his friendship with Woods. This is not to claim that the story of Woods's rise to consciousness, his relationship with Biko and his family, or his experi-ence of banning and flight from South Africa is not important, worthy of being told and heard. Rather, it is to say that to gather all these narrative droplets under an umbrella classified as the narrative of Stephen Biko's life, torture, and death, and the struggle of black South Africans against apartheid, is to compromise the representation of both the torture sustained by Biko and the collective political struggle of black South Africans. It is to participate in the imperialist representation of the struggle of an-other through the lens of the white observer, who is privileged in every way that counts—most importantly in retaining that bodily safety from harm that has come to sig-nify a western identity regardless of where it is found in the global sphere—and which has become, in the process of representation, the foundation of that very identity.

Slow Pain: Cinematic Time and the Invitation to Imagine

The relative power of more recent cinematic narratives as devices that enable audiences to imagine the suffering of others beyond the illusory universality of western subjectivity often lies in narrative experimentation—innovations in voice narration, point of view, temporality, and a sensory realism com-bined with outré flights of fancy increasingly mainstreamed in the twenty-first century. While literary narratives may imaginatively evoke all five senses in the magical leap from page to an imagined textual universe that tran-scends real time, space, and experience, cinematic narratives present explicit material that enters viewers' consciousnesses through two power senses: sight and sound. If done well, viewers may feel that a film brings the cine-matic world to life so vividly that, seeing and hearing, they also can virtually feel, smell, and taste it. Unfortunately, however, much of the stuff of Holly-wood action/adventure cinema presents scenes of explicit pain to deflect such connection. Still, Saul Friedlander's prescription for a "distanced real-ism," a realism ethically moderated by a narrative "margin," may be taken up by directors and cinematographers to effectively portray another's pain as an other's, as opposed to producing the obliterating effect of transference common in the counterhistorical dramatic film (17).

Judith Butler's recent ruminations on what might be made of the shock to the collective U.S. system upon the fall of the twin towers are based upon this recognition of one's own (individual and/or national) vulnerability, and of the vulnerability of the other (individual, national, or supranational entity) as distinct and distinctly valued, equally important in its consequence. Butler's turn to Emmanuel Levinas's reading of the face of the other is instructive: "To respond to the face, to understand its meaning, means to be awake to what is precarious in another life, or rather the precariousness of life itself. This cannot be an "awakeness," to use [Levinas's] word, to my own life, and then an extrapolation from an understanding of my own precariousness to an understanding of another's precarious life. It has to be an understanding of the precariousness of the Other" (*Precarious Life* 134). This distinction prompts a complex mental process dependent upon the acknowledgment of the other's distinct life as other, not as trace of or proxy for self, as Hartman's work on abolitionist literature revealed. Indeed, the specific ethical charge depends upon our ability to find traces of the other in the self, as opposed to looking for traces of the self in others. Butler locates the ground for this mental process in "the domain of representation where humanization and dehumanization occur ceaselessly" (135), with "representation" referring in this context to its various manifestations in the realms of politics, law, media, and community life. Describing her attempts to "approach the question of a nonviolent ethics," Butler explains her turn to Levinas, and how his philosophy may be interpreted specifically by cultural theory: "Through a cultural transposition of [Levinas's] philosophy, it is possible to see how dominant forms of representations can and must be disrupted for something about the precariousness of life to be apprehended" (xviii).

A disruption of dominant forms of representation: experimentation, not for experimentation's sake, not for the ruse of an avant-garde aestheticism, but for the ethicopolitical project of countering the massive accumulation of imagery that confirms the globally uneven distribution of human characterization, consideration, and corporeal safety. David O. Russell's chronicle of the end of the 1991 Gulf War, *Three Kings*, offers a vehicle for examining the common misreading of generic disruption—e.g., innovation—as aesthetic bombast or as impenetrable elitism. The film's technique strategically innovates to intervene in the quite specific dehumanization of Iraqi people enacted in

U.S. foreign policy, as well as in media coverage of the war, staging an ethical counternarrative to the official version of that history in two ways. First, Russell dramatizes the suppressed narrative of U.S. incitement of a Shi'a uprising in southern Iraq, matched by the uprising of Kurdish people in northern Iraq, and the subsequent abandonment of those involved in the uprising to their fates under Saddam Hussein's hypertorturous regime. (Significantly, these bodily violations, long suppressed in mainstream western news media, surfaced twelve years later as evidence of Saddam's brutality and as one thread of the retrospective rhetorical justification by the United States for its invasion of Iraq after accusations of Iraq's development of weapons of mass destruction were disproved). Second, the film counters in slow motion what Martha Nussbaum has termed the "besetting [human] vice" of "obtuseness and a refusal to see" (148). In the case of the 1991 invasion of the Gulf, what we, with the help of our media, refused to see was the wounding and death that accompanied this televised war. *Three Kings* refocuses audience vision upon the ubiquitous wounding that is occasion, goal, modus operandi, and legacy of war.[23]

Three Kings is ambitious by way of narrative margins. Reading a stack of mainstream reviews of the film, I count at least six generic designations, including "action-adventure," "war movie," "satire," "caper flick," "heist movie," and "morality play." It is to the filmmaker's credit that the film manages to embody this range of arguably pleasurable generic designations without allowing its message to be swallowed by the demands of any one of them. It is also to the filmmaker's credit that he was able to make a mainstream action-adventure-war movie—a film that earned a respectable $60,652,036 at the box office— while still delivering a counter-cultural message about war in general, the first Gulf war in particular, the role of the U.S. military in both, and the parts played by varying brands of masculinity in all three (Nash Information Services). Not insignificantly, the Muslim Public Affairs Council Foundation in 2000 honored the film's director and producers with the Entertainment Media Award, which honors individuals whose work contributes to developing "a better understanding of Islam." *Three Kings* earned it for "being the first in the movie industry to expose the real suffering of the Iraqi people" and for "going beyond stereotypes and insisting upon portraying Iraqis as sensitive humans" (Twair and Twair 55). Both elements of this citation focus upon the success of the film in portraying the human capacity for emotional and corporeal suffering—arguably the source of energy for the entire project of human rights—of Iraqi people for western viewers.

The film's strategy for equalizing the humanity of U.S. and Iraqi people by elucidating shared human qualities and dramatizing human connection across identity difference begins by foregrounding two contextual points; both relate to the metatopics of media representation and identity formation, effectively juxtaposing irony with its dominant realistic mode. The film opens with a clip that plays like an outtake, camera angle askew in a long shot of an armed Arab man rising from a bunker in a surreal desert landscape, waving at the camera in what may be an act of either surrender or aggression, accompanied by a soundtrack of running feet. The runner turns out to be Troy Barlow (Mark Wahlberg), one of the titular three kings, who appears in the lower right corner of the frame and asks over his shoulder, as if of the camera operator, "Are we shooting?" Several moments pass as the actor attempts to get a grain of sand out of his eye, the invasive foreign landscape captured in this seeming outtake as a disruption of the film's production. Then he asks, "Are we shooting people or what?" The additional words, fleshing out both the meaning and the implication of the question, relocate the viewer from what may have felt like a privileged position outside the mechanics of the film production to her proper place inside its story line, as blood spurts in close-up from the neck of the Iraqi man and his gurgles are caught on the soundtrack along with the celebratory remark of one of Barlow's colleagues: "Congratulations! You shot yourself a raghead! I didn't think I'd see anybody get shot in this war!"

This prelude is no cagey joke serving the narrative purpose of exposition for the film's plot (which opens with the official end of the first Gulf War in the company of a group of reservists who "didn't see any action"). It cuts quickly to a deeply masculinist scene of celebration confirming the end of the war and acts as an extratextual comment upon the complicity of media with violence—not simply in recording it, but in the far more dangerous activities of authorizing, packaging, and distributing it. This metacomment upon the role and function of the media (including feature films) as a global contributor to violence and its consciousness is one way in which the film foregrounds existing modes of connection between the peoples of the United States and Iraq—the two peoples linked by their stakes in a war that came to be known by its reception via sanitized high-tech media imagery as "virtual."[24] The film's ongoing critique of racism, the other featured undesirable mode of connection between these peoples, shows racism both in its distinctly U.S. manifestation within national borders against African American citizens, and externally in the material form of sanctions and bombs aimed at Arab and Muslim people.

This latter critique is particularly effective in its nonincidental quality, sustained over the course of the script in a variety of contexts. It too is introduced early as an ironic metacomment, via the protests of African American soldier Chief Elgin against terms like "sand nigger" and "dune coon"; he suggests that "'towel head' and 'camel jockey' are perfectly good substitutes." The link between U.S.-brand racism and the violent practices and identity politics of war in the Middle East receive reinforcement from a quick shot of members of the Los Angeles Police Department beating Rodney King in a video playing on a TV in an Iraqi Republican Guard torture chamber; by the ongoing race-based argument between Chief Elgin and Conrad Vig, the stereotypically undereducated enlisted white man from the rural South, over whether there are "any good black quarterbacks"; and in questions posed by the Iraqi torturer of Troy Barlow about Michael Jackson's cosmetic surgery as a sign of pervasive internalized racism in the United States.

This is in part a film about the ways that humans can transcend given roles in real interactions—as the three kings end up transcending their roles as U.S. military representatives in the massive wasteland of the Iraqi postwar landscape, placing their own bodies in harm's way to save a group of Iraqi refugees from certain torture and death at the hands of Saddam's Royal Guard. That transcendence is no flight of fancy or illogical outcome of emplotment. Rather, it is sustained realistically as the deep structure of the plot occasions the development of modes of identification across established lines of difference. Over the course of the film, powerfully drawn human connections replace the parallel prejudices delineated against African American people at home and Arab people abroad. Connections between Chief Elgin and Conrad Vig, and between the U.S. military men and the Iraqi refugees under their protection, are forged around the specter of the wounded body and the desire on the part of protagonists (and presumably, by extension, the film's audiences) to relieve its suffering.

In contradistinction to criticisms of the film's jarring pace, I understand one of Russell's primary narrative strategies to be a temporal modulation, an episodic slowing of narrative time within an overarching linear chronology, according to which the mechanism of human connection actualized through rising consciousness of the precariousness of the other, to borrow from Butler, is made visible. Similar to Boorman's slowing of filmic time to capture the massacre of pro-democracy students in *Beyond Rangoon*, Russell pairs a suspension of narrative time with visual depth to refocus viewer attention on the wound *as* wound, or on the wound as vehicle of connection among otherwise institutionally disconnected humans. The strategic difference is in the combination of temporal cinematic innovation with that other modal giant, point of view: *Three Kings* refuses to locate its tripartite protagonists as mediating presences in the action of others (as, for instance, the screaming Laura Bowman witnessing the massacre of Burmese people or the palpably relieved Woods family flying out of South African airspace to the beat of the Soweto riots). Rather, the film foregrounds the process by which its protagonists are removed from one world order, the military-industrial arm of global capitalist exploitation, to another, the radically alternative realm of globally interconnected agents in all their flawed humanity. It is precisely the deep flaws in these drawn characters, the resistance to pure heroism, that heightens the film's realism and therefore its potential to activate an ethical imagination in a broad viewing public.[25]

The film schools viewers in the consequences of the action adventure that is war by directing our identification to the naïvely zealous, inexperienced characters of the reservists as they learn the same lesson from military superhero Archie Gates (George Clooney). Thus, when Troy Barlow—who has been distinctly humanized in terms of bodily vulnerability (he is more fearful than the others of the consequences of engaging in military action) and desire (he is a new father, deeply committed to his wife and infant daughter, eager to return home to them in one well-functioning piece)—lays eyes on an Iraqi resistor being tortured by the Royal Guard, we register with Barlow the shock of seeing this man with bloodied face, slab of wood between his teeth, arms bound with wire, clearly the victim of beating and electrocution, and we endure with Barlow the horror of watching as this man's wife and daughter witness his condition. However, we also perceive that Barlow's ability to focus his vision upon this man and the atrocity being wrought upon his body is fleeting, his face recording shock synchronically as his buddy, Vig, asks: "Did you see the gold? How much?" The shot is masterful in its capture of the slow turning of Barlow's head: away from the corporeal effects of U.S. betrayal and failed policy in Iraq toward which he had momentarily been drawn as a human witness, and back toward the masculine militarist-materialist economy of Saddam's gold bullion that he has come to steal using his U.S. military uniform as a literal desert shield.

This turn—the momentary suspension of the character between the two economies that structure the film's dramaturgy—makes manifest for viewers the aporetic time of emerging consciousness that structures both the action of the film and the transformation of the characters' mission from the unlikely heist of millions in gold bullion to their more interesting fulfillment of the U.S. promise to defend those it incited to rise up against Hussein in the wake of the war. In fact, the plot hinges on the actualization of the three soldiers' cynical posturing as agents of the U.S. government come to retrieve the stolen Kuwaiti gold as they are transformed into surrogates for the U.S. government, finishing what it started, fulfilling its obligations in protecting the Shi'a and Kurdish people who rose against Saddam and were now suffering the brutal consequences. The result is the opening of a narrative space able to hold the otherwise utopic possibility, dismissed by the status quo cynicism of modern realpolitik, of truth and accountability in a political policy grounded in ethical attention to the experiences of persons caught in its crossfire.

This glimpse of the otherwise imperceptible movement toward identification with the wounded body, normatively precluded by the deep structure of identity in the context of war, is expedited in the film with its innovations of narrative and cinematographic temporality, the same innovations dismissed by many critics as unsuccessfully edgy aesthetic experiments. The *New Yorker*'s David Denby describes the film as "rash[ly] disorder[ed]," "an irresponsible, infuriating mess," and accuses Russell of "diddl[ing] with film technique, as if he were making some sort of experimental Western, and the diddling is borderline offensive." Denby reads the ending of the film as a reversion away from "moral investigation" to a "conventional movie fable," which, while "brave," is still ruined: "Russell tries on too many moods and plays too many games. By the time we understand what he's saying, we're too exhausted to care" (117). Yet the film's cinematographic play suggests that it is precisely orientation rather than disorientation that Russell is after, resulting in a deepened capacity to care for others in ways that are often foreclosed in Hollywood cinema. The "tricks" used most often in the film involve shifts in film speed, or brief plot interruptions that *re*orient audience attention to the process and effects of bodily wounding—arguably the authentic heart of this story—away from the frenetic action of war that so infamously leaves bodies strewn in its wake without a lingering glance by the camera. The shifts in film speed almost without exception correspond to the violent conflict sequences of the film. This technique constitutes a reversal of the common convention for filming such scenes, in which the camera maximizes wounding and destruction, accentuating the chaos of battle as a linear, digestible sequence interrupted only by multiple camera perspectives of individual events such as a falling body or exploding building. Instead, Russell periodically arrests the camera to slow-motion speed during the film's first battle scene—which is, importantly, unmediated in terms of point of view—forcing viewers to engage with the process of human injuring, capturing the flow of blood as an emphatic and not incidental consequence of wounding.

It is only after this prolonged battle that the reservists begin to consider risking their own lives in connection with saving the refugees their presence has created. As the soldiers collect themselves to leave the scene, abandoning the Iraqi rebels to their fates in a microcosmic replica of U.S. policy, the wife of the torture survivor with whom Barlow began to identify earlier is shot at point-blank range in front of her husband and daughter. Archie asks the men to "imagine if that was you." Even as close-up witnesses to this bodily wound, however, these men, cocooned in the safety constructed by and for the United States as an organic, inherent aspect of citizenship, are unable to form an identification powerful enough to change their actions. It is necessary that Gates iterate, "Imagine if that was you without Kevlar," the prepositional functioning as metonym for the uneven distribution of power and safety (and its technological apparatuses) in the age of global militaristic capitalism. With this prompting, the men show a glimmer of recognition of the humanity and bodily vulnerability of the (unarmored) other—enough to change their course of action and help these people to escape.

This new visibility of the process of deepening consciousness has been forecast by another moment in the film's structure that surely contributed to its critical reception as "disordered" and strange: the interruption of the story line by the camera's pursuit of an imaginary bullet through a body and past its point of exit as visual accompaniment to a lecture Archie Gates delivers to his action-hungry reservists. The journey away from U.S. base camp into the Iraqi theatre of battle is also Gates's education of Vig, Barlow, and Elgin in the consequences of war, which always centers upon the vulnerability of the body: when the three reservists rig a football as a grenade, watching it explode midair, Gates asks: "You want to see action?" At their affirmative response, Gates points out a decomposed body, half hidden by sand, wearing a U.S. military uniform. "This what you mean by action?" It is as a corrective to Vig's congratulatory announcement that Barlow "saw action" when he shot the man in the film's opening scene—to which the film now flashes back in close crop to the blood spurting from the bullet's entry—that Gates describes a bullet's journey through the body.

The camera acts as visual aid for the lecture, documenting the impossible: the interior of the human body as the bullet enters and as the cavity it opens fills with bile. Rather than constituting a trick in the pack of cards that comprises the sensationalized flash-cutting of the music video, as critic Janet Maslin asserts, the effect is of defamiliarization through literalization, a technique made famous in Gabriel García Márquez's brand of magic realism in *One Hundred Years of Solitude*.[26] In that text, when the monumental José Arcadio Buendía is mysteriously and suddenly shot dead, his blood flows out the front door of his house, trickles down the street, and makes a left turn into the house of his mother, stopping at her feet in the kitchen as she stirs a pot of soup. The literalization of the ineffable—in this case the spiritual connection between mother and son that would inform her knowledge of his death at the precise moment of its occurrence, regardless of her physical location—is one of Márquez's narratological techniques for illuminating that deeper, impossible real hidden by the mundane realism or outright erasure that characterizes official accounts of things. Paul Ricoeur conceptualizes the function of the metaphor similarly in terms of defamiliarization: "Metaphorical reference frees a more radical power of reference to those aspects of our being-in-the-world that cannot be talked about directly" (15). And while the suspended time of this cinematic moment that uses sound and sight to trace an imaginary bullet on its path through a body is the antithesis of metaphor in its scientific contours, it accomplishes the same "radical power of reference" in forcing us to abandon our besetting vice of a refusal to *see*. In this scene, the irreducible fact of wounding in all its infected unglory is restored precisely in opposition to the constructed masculinist-militaristic discourses that depend upon its elision.

In her meditation upon cinematic time, Mary Ann Doane argues that "modernity is conceptualized as an increase in the speed and intensity of stimuli. Time emerges as a problem intimately linked to the theorization of modernity as trauma or shock" (33). If we accept this aspect of a definition of modernity, then the postmodern, with its overload of stimuli (often of the traumatic sort), is not a break from but rather a continuation and intensification of the modern. In this context, Russell's ruptured narrative responds to that condition that has been called empathic overload in postmodern western culture, in which tragedy after tragedy blurs and fades within the onslaught of received media and cultural images. Susan Sontag identifies this experience of overload as an example of the unethical pseudo-universalism claimed by the West: "To speak of reality becoming a spectacle is a breathtaking provincialism. It universalizes the viewing habits of a small, educated population living in the rich part of the world, where news has been converted into entertainment. . . . It assumes that everyone is a spectator. It suggests, perversely, unseriously, that there is no real suffering in the world" (105). Precisely through its cinematographic innovations, *Three Kings* counters this provincialism, the same that informed the broadcasting of the 1991 Gulf War from inside the scopes of bombers and fighter jets in night vision on CNN as, not ironically, a video-game spectacle for western viewers.

In fact, the film holds up the moment of wounding, the penetration of flesh, and ultimately redirects it onto the body of the perennially safe U.S. protagonist-hero, not in an evocation of tragic pathos via a mortal wound, nor as a retributive reversal of the standard distribution of safety and harm in the global arena, but rather as a redistribution of the visceral experience of torture and wounding reserved for others in the cinematic codes of Hollywood. It is crucial to the film's emplotment that it is Barlow (Wahlberg) whose body the bullet enters in this shot, and that Barlow bear the initial commitment of the shifting consciousness of Iraqi humanity, as Barlow is the only reservist who has killed a man—and, given the ironic presentation of that first scene, we are led to experience this act as a thoughtless blunder, the natural and inconsequential mistake of a revved-up masculine military machine. Barlow is the first to register the real consequence of U.S. policy in that early scene of witnessing the torture of a Shi'a rebel by members of the Iraqi Royal Guard, and it is Barlow who will himself be tortured by an Iraqi man. In each case, the violence that Barlow inflicts or ignores is reinscribed upon the terrain of his body, not as revenge but as a function of the plot, which serves to broaden his ability to integrate the precariousness of the other into his own actions and commitments. Moreover, the redirection onto Barlow's body during his capture by Royal Guard soldiers of the experience of torture from which he turned away earlier in the film is used to humanize the figure of the torturer. This humanizing has been a central goal of the human rights movement since Hannah Arendt's insistence upon the capacity shared by all humans to engage in evil acts, her resistance to the idea that such perpetrators as Hitler and Eichmann were monstrous aberrations.[27] From a human rights perspective, to dismiss perpetrators of mass atrocity as aberrant, inhuman monsters is a counterintuitive, ahistorical means of redirecting the knowledge that all such acts are conceived and perpetrated by otherwise ordinary human beings—in other words, by ourselves.

Various theories and narratives have attempted to account for the actions of the torturer: some consider torture the result of a pathological sadism, or evidence of an insatiable drive to power; most explanations focus upon the tenets of hierarchical or authoritarian systems such as the military or, in a more banal sense, education, which teach pure adherence to authority. One of the effects that fictional narrative, in particular, can achieve is to add to these explanations representations of what we might call reciprocal wounding, dramatizations that enable characters (and, by extension, readers or viewers) to imagine the mutual processes of pain, suffering, disempowerment, desire, ambition, fear, or obedience that may contribute to a human's participation in the torture of another human. Isabel Allende's *House of the Spirits* contains a powerful example of reciprocal wounding (see chapter 4); the central torture scene in *Three Kings* also rises to an ethical examination of the forces that contribute to the birth of the torturer in the soul of an otherwise humane human.

The depiction of the interrogation in *Three Kings* rather purposefully lacks verisimilitude. The torture victim makes a variety of responses that do more to advance an idea of the humanity of the torturer than to create a realistic scene of torture with its relentlessly one-sided mode of interrogation. Indeed, the interrogation becomes a dialogue between torturer and tortured to reveal the similarities between the two men—both are fathers and both joined the military in order to support their families, although the Iraqi torturer's child has been killed and his wife crippled by a bomb. As each man speaks his pain, fear, and desire about the situation of his family in relation to his participation in war, the film flashes back to dramatize scenes enacting their fears for or the actual losses of those family members (for example, the roof of the torturer's home caving in on the crib of his infant son after the house is bombed). These scenes empower each character to imagine the other's humanity across their identity divides; perhaps more to the point, they empower audiences to better understand the dynamics and origins of the scene of torture. In this way, corporeal vulnerability is balanced. Safety—one's own or one's family's—is neither exclusionary nor taken for granted in association with a particular identity position. By the end of the film, Barlow's rise to consciousness through a cognitive, physiological, and affective identification with the victim/survivor of torture is complete, a rare and narratologically powerful reversal of conventional generic codes.

Criticism of the film's experimentation notwithstanding, its narrative structure successfully advances the argument that the elision of bodily wounding in the dominant narrative of the 1991 Gulf War is parallel to and figure for the larger elision of the story of U.S. betrayal of Shi'a and Kurdish people incited to stage a rebellion against Saddam Hussein at the close of the war. In the course of staging this parallel, both narrative elisions are reversed and restored. In this way, some critics read the film as a courageous message movie that happens also to be a great, original action flick. (These critics generally represent less-highbrow press organs—an interesting paradox, that those who might be most oriented toward postmodern pyrotechnics are least willing to sacrifice the story to them.) The achievement is no small thing: a film able to package and deliver the masculine thrill of the war-adventure genre using a group of highly watchable stars, and also to issue an unapologetic critique of U.S. betrayal of Iraqi people at the end of the first Gulf War and to deliver on the promise of cross-cultural identification among people otherwise linked only by the prepackaged and preordained experience of global violence.

Signs of a cinema that encourages audience identification and pleasure even while bearing ethical, coherent witness to gross violations of rights are emerging on a broader scale. Consider the release of Terry George's *Hotel Rwanda* (2004), the first counterhistorical dramatic film to refuse to split characterization and plot, which consolidates audience identification around the family of Rwandan hotelier Paul Rusesabagina during the genocide. Consider the near-simultaneous release of Raoul Peck's *Sometimes in April* (2004), also a major mainstream release (HBO), which ventures further into the realm of dramatic witness in its presentation of the story of the genocide through the lens of the Rwanda Tribunal in Arusha, Tanzania. Refusing even to provide a hero figure for audience identification, Peck's film shows the effects of a family torn apart by the hatred at the heart of the genocide, incorporating historically accurate material from the Arusha Tribunals into its emplotment, dialogue, and characterization. The tremendous potential of film to dramatize for mass audiences the stakes of the unfolding, immeasurably consequential narrative of human rights and their violations is finally being unleashed with the kind of experiments in point of view and temporality that put to the test the old truism that every story is a hero story.

2

TORTURE II
CITIZENSHIP

Early in Oliver Stone's *Salvador* (1987), protagonist Richard Boyle (James Woods) and his sidekick, Doc (James Belushi), both U.S. citizens, are stopped at an army roadblock as they cross the border into El Salvador. Lying beside them in the road is a body engulfed in flames. Increasingly nervous about entering this seemingly lawless—or, perhaps more accurately, extraordinarily lawful—land, Doc whispers fearfully, "Jesus, Boyle." "Relax man, it's just some guy," Boyle responds. Here, as in John Boorman's *Beyond Rangoon*, the tortured body stakes out a danger zone through which the western protagonist will travel, a zone that in terms of narrative emplotment heightens audience suspense regarding the protagonist's physical safety. The burning body signifies a double margin: first, between bodily safety (the United States) and bodily vulnerability (El Salvador), and second, between relative narrative calm and the rising action of the linear Hollywood adventure plot. The image evokes the consumptive link between emplotment and national identity that shapes the subtext of safety in the counterhistorical drama.

Seized by the military, Doc and Boyle are confined and transported to San Salvador, their entrance to the city marked by more signs of military power: a body hanging backward over the side of a pickup truck in the square, a student shot point-blank in the street as a "subversive." The death of this student triggers a shift in Boyle's perspective on the tortured body inasmuch as it signifies his own possible subjection to authoritarian force. Rather than dismissing the body as amorphous and unremarkable, the men now acknowledge its symbolic weight. Transcending the obscuring appellation "just some guy," the student's body, while still not considered in terms of its woundedness, destabilizes U.S. immunity from such violence, as Boyle now exclaims, "Shit! They're going to kill us."

The execution of the Salvadoran student momentarily dissolves the protective cloak of difference that separates the U.S. protagonist from the native bodies upon whom such violences are routinely enacted—differentials based upon Boyle's U.S. citizenship, his role as journalist with contacts in the Salvadoran government, and his ability to move safely within this unsafe space using his dollars, broken Spanish, and smarmy streetwise authority to bribe and flatter soldiers. At this moment of dissolution, the film simultaneously begins to construct a kind of definition: what it means to be North American in an international context, what it means to be not North American. Viewers are made to experience the fear and vulnerability endured by nonwestern people as Boyle and Doc are stripped of their protection in the international danger zone. The erasure of difference is momentary and plot driven; regeneration of national difference converges with the relief of suspense as the western characters regain the safety that will be theirs for the remainder of the film, a safety delivered to viewers neatly packaged in *Salvador*'s masculinist adventure narrative.

Jon Avnet's *Red Corner* (1995) stages a similar moment of cultural/ national/ideological distinction, also based upon the image of the tortured body. Amidst the chaos of his arrest in China for a murder he did not commit, international businessman Jack Moore (Richard Gere) shouts, "I'm an American," a disclosure meant to trump accusations made or evidence found against him on Chinese soil and to create a kind of geopolitical shield against nondemocratic governmental violence. Moore utters these words again after his arrest, this time quietly to himself as he is forced to watch video footage of kneeling, blindfolded Chinese prisoners shot in the head at close range by soldiers who bend over their bodies to shoot them again. And while the utterance "I'm an American" fails to activate the protection implied by U.S. citizenship in the international arena, leaving Moore subject to imprisonment and torture, the pain and indignity he suffers while in custody are rendered with a pathos absent from the dull gunfire and falling bodies used to represent the executions of Chinese prisoners, directing viewers to identify with this body in pain more deeply than with the others'. This racially inflected differentiation of characters renders nonwestern bodies so irreducibly alien *by nature* from western bodies that their bodies become *natural* vessels for the pain inflicted by authoritarian governments, surrogates who absorb the threat of such pain from (white) western bodies. Safety, then, is not simply one symbolic contour of the identity position marked by "the West" but is foundational to it. The stock myth of western bodily safety in the counterhistorical dramatic film emanates paradoxically from the hegemonic prerogative of the (nominal) constitutional democracy of the United States, rather than from the internationalist narrative of human rights that is such a film's putative subject.

Indeed, belying the advocacy of international human rights agendas which is the premise for most counterhistorical dramatic film, the argument for international adoption of a democratic constitutionality mirroring the U.S. political system as a remedy for (perceived or actual) political chaos, authoritarianism, or brutality consolidates a nationalist-patriotic ideal of western or U.S. identity. With the advent of the war on terror, it has become nearly impossible to overstate the force of this cultural work.[1] While democratic constitutionality (i.e., the allegiance to a recorded law, not to human beings) is often the desired end for people and groups resistant to oppressive governmental regimes, its representation in counterhistorical dramatic film is overdetermined, not only signifying a desirable political alternative but also constituting the symbolic capital of the imperialist brand of U.S. patriotism embedded in the films' narrative schema. That symbolic capital is then exchanged for a measure of safety for western characters in the global danger zone.

If the evocation of the international serves paradoxically to iterate the privileged national in the counterhistorical dramatic film, the ascendant identity in this genre is, not surprisingly, most often white, male, heterosexual, and in possession of means to move freely about the world. In this way, fantasies of universal freedom and safety evoked by the human rights discourses in the films might more accurately be located according to their initial distribution in early constitutional democracies (notably the United States and France): that is, among white, Christian, male, property-owning constituents presumed to be heterosexual. These gaps in the national distribution of the rights of citizenship as represented in the counterhistorical dramatic film parallel the exclusion of some nonwestern citizens from global narratives of freedom and safety. They also reveal the extent to which gender operates both as a limit case set out by the Enlightenment narrative of masculine mobility, progress, and action that informs the ideal of citizenship, and as an a priori challenge to its legitimacy. These stories of exclusion are old and familiar, exhaustively researched and critiqued; clearly, however, the realms of both the real and the representational remain saturated with their effects. Illuminating their deep structures in a particular generic cultural form, I believe, contributes to broad efforts in scholarly and activist communities to disrupt them, here in a study of the exclusionary nationalist-patriotic rhetoric and imagery in *Salvador* and *Red Corner*, and via an argument about the convergence of nationalist, racial, and gendered exclusions in Gil Courtemanche's fictionalized eyewitness account of the Rwandan genocide, *A Sunday at the Pool in Kigali* (2003).

Considering gender in the counterhistorical dramatic film, I rely upon Teresa de Lauretis's distinction in cinematic terms between the figure of woman, "constituted as the ground of representation, the looking-glass held up to man," and women, referring to "the historical individual[s]" (*Alice Doesn't* 15). De Lauretis's distinction presages a question posed by Judith Butler twenty years later regarding the location of normalizing operations on gender: "Is the symbolic eligible for social intervention?" (*Undoing Gender* 43). While I cannot fully answer Butler's provocative question, my analyses in this and other chapters flirt with it in the hope of finding a path to an affirmative response. Most nearly approximated by the term "semiotic," the figure of woman under analysis casts a glance in the direction of each realm implicated in Butler's discussion of the source and function of gender norms: on the one hand, toward the Lacanian symbolic, sphere of binaristic sexual difference codified in the Law of the Father upon which the sexual exchange of women is premised; and on the other, to the domain of social practices governing and informed by gender norms experienced by differently gendered bodies in a changing historical world. While the figure of woman bears historically specific representational burdens derived from identity politics of race, ethnicity, nationality, class, and sexuality, I contend that images of woman as "ground of representation" cross these borders of identity in something close to a dystopic universal: diverse oppressions of women within the tenacious reach of patriarchalism across cultures. Let me be clear: I do not take the cross-cultural oppression of women to be the foundation of a politics of victimization that "makes shared victimization the basis for woman-bonding" (hooks 397); rather, for the purposes of this analysis I bring to light the compulsive instrumentalization of the figure of woman both at the scene of torture and in many of the cultural texts that attempt its representation. The structure of scenes of human rights violation, and of many cultural texts that represent such violation, depends upon dominant gender norms linked to exclusionary practices of citizenship and human rights, and therefore gender as an analytical category must be afforded space at the very center of the study of and struggle to maintain international human rights. This effort presumes a feminist struggle that refuses to restrict its focus to gender, but rather highlights the connection between dominant gender normalization and the brutalities of racism and economic imbalance in global and local contexts.

Constitutional Limits: The Faces of Freedom and Safety

The ideal of safety holds the philosophical center of U.S. constitutional principles. To the extent that the ideology of democratic freedom in the West is grounded in the rule of law, the sites protected by that law are national and individual bodies, and the measure of its success is the degree to which it secures the safety and autonomy of those bodies. Ensuring the safety of bodies protected by constitutional law, however, implies leaving other national bodies, as well as bodies in other nations, insecure and lacking autonomy; as Stathis Gourgouris points out: "Constitutional law is always an act of nationalization, no matter what might be its claim to the universality of rights" (125). This constitutional tension between the specificity of nationhood and the universality of rights results in part from material limits that constrain the universal. The most persistent critique of human rights discourse, by nature universalist, has been the preordained failure of its universal application in national and local contexts.[2] The counterhistorical dramatic film contributes to this limit: rather than emphasizing the radical transcultural potential of current international human rights conventions and critiquing the limits and exclusions in their application, images of tortured bodies often foreground the absolute difference of nonwestern cultural and political practices and, by extension, nonwestern people, marking them as relatively primitive, atavistic, and premodern in global context. Such images then provide a subtle syllogism that justifies the exclusion in these cultural texts of some bodies from "universal" human rights protection: if torture is a lawless and uncivilized practice, and culture X practices torture, then members of culture X are lawless and uncivilized—and therefore not protected under the rule of law.

This logic is bolstered by the films' derivation of U.S. identity from a politic designed to secure bodily safety. That is, U.S. identity is grounded in democratic constitutionality, and democratic constitutionality guarantees safety from state and military violence.[3] Such logic creates a cordon sanitaire around the western bodies viewing the films, reassuring them of their immunity to chaotic or authoritarian forces represented as antithetical to the guaranteed liberty and order of the democratic West, and thereby weakening the potential for cross-cultural identification invited by the films' international settings and politics. Moreover, the select safety implied by the films' construction of western political identity is further compromised by their violent exclusion of women from that contract. As one viewer articulated her take on the distribution of safety in *Salvador*: "I felt fear not as an American in El Salvador, but as a woman in the film."[4]

Despite these gendered gaps, the seduction of the counterhistorical dramatic film's representational reassurances of bodily safety may account in part for its popularity as a genre with western audiences. Before freedom, before democracy, was the primal human desire for physical safety. After Vietnam, after 9/11, and after the advent of the war on terror, we witness the convergence of desire for individual and capitalist-nationalist modes of safety, respectively, within the global arena. Bodily safety is the ground of Enlightenment thought regarding individual autonomy, rights, and the consent to be governed. Bodily safety and conditions conducive to the acquisition of capital motivated imperial-era rhetoric of *la missione civilizatrice* and dictate contemporary conditions of interaction among world powers and the division of geopolitical space into different worlds. Bodily safety is in large part the object of the rule of law, although the threat of force embedded in the idea of the law exposes the often capricious incongruity between the body as site of the law's enforcement (whether by violent means or via ideological interpolation as discipline) and body as subject of the law's protection. Even aside from the problem of human fallibility in application, the idea of law as protective force is circumscribed by the violent enforcement intrinsic to the idea of law itself. The violence repressed in the definition of the law introduces an arbitrariness—or at least a resistance to determination by objective criteria—to the idea of justice that obscures a clear sense of the law as either "regulative or coercive"; that is, as legitimate and necessary to the maintenance of a free democratic order, or brutal and disruptive of it (Derrida, "Force of Law" 6). One person's law and order is another person's human rights violation. This slippage in meaning often emerges in discussions about state responses to criminal violence. For instance, the flogging of two U.S. students accused of vandalism in Singapore in 1994 occasioned international outrage; however, a counterdiscourse emerged to the effect that such violently authoritarian responses to minor criminal transgressions were a good to be sought in the lowering of the crime rate in such terminally free (read: lax) cultures as the United States.[5]

Ultimately, then, the materialization of law as protective of the body depends upon whether one is at a given moment a subject of the law or its object. Already slippery in the constitutional order, the paradoxical nature of the law (both in the abstract and in practice) is further confounded in the authoritarian governmental systems critiqued by the counterhistorical dramatic film, wherein adherence to (or, perhaps more precisely, the naming of) a state of excessive lawfulness actually causes reversion to a state of absolute lawlessness, of being without the law and subject to the arbitrary rule of violent people. Without the gravity of a constitutional document to steady the force of law, individual consent to or denial of governance is irrelevant. According to this tautological schema, nonwestern people are culturally and politically atavistic because they are not members of the tradition of civility and progress that includes democratic constitutionality, and they will continue to be excluded from this tradition (lending the counterhistorical dramatic film's quest for international democratic reform an air of ironic futility) because of their demonstrated cultural and political atavism.

Admittedly, representation of the exclusion of certain people from the law's protection in the counterhistorical dramatic film is as complicated as that exclusion in the practice of daily life: individuals are excluded by virtue of membership in ethnic, social, or political groups; adherence to particular belief systems; relationships with people suspected of belonging to banned political groups; or, in the great majority of cases, for arbitrary reasons unknown and unjustified to anyone except the authoritarian government and its agents. Despite such attention to particular instances, the umbrella term under which such exclusions may be placed in the ideological work of the counterhistorical dramatic film is "citizenship"—specifically, citizenship in a country without a democratic government. It is a sign of the force and intractability of the power differential between the global North and South that, in spite of the protective function meant to be served by the state as conceived in the western philosophical and political tradition, human rights discourse has so strenuously had to address and to account for the role of states in harming their own citizens in the twentieth century. The massive shift from early Greco-Roman notions of human rights protections afforded quite specifically to strangers, outsiders, noncitizens (a.k.a. "barbarians") is iconified in the repetitive image of the evacuation of western citizens from danger zones around the world, leaving the state's own endangered citizens to suffer at the hands of government agents or rebels.[6] The passport is the privileged signifier of safety in this context, as evidenced in Roland Joffe's *The Killing Fields* (1984), which tracks the divergent paths of *New York Times* reporter Sydney Schanberg and his Cambodian photographer, Dith Pran, after the conquest of Phnom Penh by the Khmer Rouge in 1975. In a scene that takes place just after the fall of the city, all the remaining foreigners are holed up in the French embassy when Khmer soldiers order all Cambodian nationals, many of whom were linked to the ousted ruling party, out of this safe haven to certain death. Panicked, Schanberg and his western colleagues attempt to create a British passport for Dith, snapping and developing a photo for the forgery without proper photographic paper or ink. The image of an official opening the passport in the rain only to have Dith's photo run in rivulets of ink until his image washes away is paradigmatic of the vulnerability and ultimate invisibility of nonwestern (non)citizens in the international narrative of access to human rights.[7]

Freedom and Populism in *Red Corner* and *Salvador*

Although *Red Corner* diverges in some ways from the generic conventions of the counterhistorical dramatic film, it uses similar representational strategies. Additionally, the conditions of its circulation and publicity locate it in the mode of protest against international human rights. While its plot is not split between the foreground of the individual western protagonist and the collective background of a nation in struggle, its politics are perhaps more egregious, given that representations of Chinese human rights violations, while providing requisite suspense for the fate of protagonist-hero Jack Moore (Richard Gere), are underdeveloped to such an extent that they might more accurately be described as setting than context or plot. *Red Corner* is indeed a fairly straight courtroom drama, with little of the historically based documentary material that characterizes most counterhistorical dramatic film. No historic clues accompany the video of state-sponsored executions witnessed by Moore, for instance: while date-stamped 1992, its location, political context, and victims' or perpetrators' identities are not disclosed. In one sense, this lack contributes to an argument regarding the ubiquity of human rights abuses and their disavowal: they are both everywhere and nowhere. On the other hand, the only real reference to a struggle in China against human rights violations comes late in the film, when Moore's lawyer, Shen Yuelin, reveals her guilt regarding what she considers her complicity with the oppressive politics of Chairman Mao's Cultural Revolution. This guilt, stemming from her inability to defend her father against vilification by government agents, results rather inexplicably in her decision to risk her life defending a U.S. citizen accused of murder, rather than being moved to do the same for one of the countless Chinese dissidents or prisoners of conscience referenced by the film as victims of regular government brutality. Indeed, the only comprehensive violation of rights *Red Corner*'s audiences witness are those of the American Jack Moore, although the film presents evidence of the brutal totalitarianism of the Chinese penal and justice systems to heighten fear for his fate.

In addition to its setting, *Red Corner* is worth examining in the context of the counterhistorical dramatic film genre because of its politicized distribution. Its release was timed to coincide with then Chinese president Jiang Zemin's 1994 visit to the United States, which was marked by heated protests against the Chinese record of human rights violations. In one of the more blatant demonstrations of celebrity politics cum self-promotion, also receiving wide publicity were the association of the film's star, Richard Gere, with the Dalai Lama; his activism in Tibet's independence movement; and his protests against Chinese violation of Tibetan human rights. The official MGM *Red Corner* Web site emphasized this aspect of the film's history, structuring Gere's bio to include both a list of his acting/producing credits as well as a description of his human rights activism regarding "the tragedy that has been unfolding in Tibet under Chinese occupation." One of the site's main links, listed under the heading "Human Rights," detailed other cases of international human rights abuses and provided direct links to the Web sites of Amnesty International, Human Rights Watch, and Human Rights in China.[8] The discourse of human rights may be understood in this context as part of the Hollywood promotional machine that provides viewers with tools for consuming the film, increases potential box-office figures by seamlessly matching Gere's personality to that of the character he plays, and offers audiences access to the star's virtual approval by way of their own Web-based activism.

Given these conditions of production, circulation, and publicity, the film participates in protest discourse against human rights, even if its protest is delivered in a less overt form (without captions referencing historical facts, for instance) and uses slightly different generic conventions than other counterhistorical dramatic films under analysis here. Its human rights discourse is compromised in a manner similar to the counterhistorical dramatic film more generally by the process of national and cultural differentiation, which depends upon, among other things, images of torture. Consider Avnet's decision to situate *Red Corner*'s arguments about democracy and justice in the context of conflicts regarding cultural identity and globalization. The film opens at Beijing's Ministry of Radio, Film, and Television during a screening of *Beachside* (modeled on *Baywatch*, one of U.S. television's most widely circulated programs in foreign markets at the time) by a group of Chinese media executives and government officials, and the western businessmen attempting to sell them a western media programming package. After viewing the program, one of the Chinese executives remarks: "The director has real concerns about your programming package. He says your programs are pornographic, violent, and superstitious." Moore responds: "They are, of course. As the great Chairman Mao said, 'Use the west for Chinese purposes.' If western programming is pornographic, violent, and superstitious, wouldn't it tend to discourage the pursuit of western values?" Lurking beneath the cover of Moore's ironic assertion is an implication regarding Chinese state control of its citizens, here figured as relatively benign ideological interpellation through state-approved entertainment. While acknowledging the violent extremity of much western entertainment, Moore's comment also contains the medium by which the terms of this cultural debate will be switched, so that the violent, pornographic nature of western culture is ultimately construed as a sign of western cultural superiority—equated with its adherence to the rule of law—in a global context. In this new rhetorical schema, Chinese culture acquires the negative charge in the dichotomy because of its authoritarian nature; however, we might also interpret the film as a symptom of growing fear of the Chinese becoming capitalists, of not being the right kind of capitalists, or of that massive populace wresting market control from the West, as the Japanese were in process of doing at the time of the film's release.[9]

The film's argument then turns to political ideology, employing paradoxical conceptions of first-world criminal violence as compared with third-world state violence. Criminal violence in the first world is treated as a necessary characteristic of freedom and democracy, a signal that the democratic tenets of a free society are in working order, while authoritarian state violence—which can produce the societal side effect of drastically reduced individual criminal violence—is condemned as the mark of a morally corrupt society.

Arguments made by Chinese characters in defense of the Chinese political system reinforce this logical turn. Early on, the procurator general presiding over Moore's trial admonishes him: "We hold the welfare of the state above the welfare of the individual. We have six times the population of your country, Mr. Moore, and one-tenth the crime rate. Tell me. Who is right?" This seemingly serious question—potentially an occasion for sober consideration by audiences—is rendered ironic in light of the images audiences have already seen of Moore's subjection to brutality in prison, mass executions of Chinese citizens by military/police officials, and the nondemocratic operation of Chinese law-enforcement and judicial processes. So ironic, in fact, that in this film's narrative landscape the question reads as rhetorical, its answer predetermined for audiences who, properly horrified at Chinese authoritarian barbarity, already know who (what) is right: U.S. democratic constitutionality, even with its necessary evil, the inflated individual crime rate. The film's position in this regard is related to its romanticization of U.S. democratic individualism as opposed to Chinese Communist collectivism. Generally, modern westernized Chinese characters, constructed as good guys, approve of recognizing the individual over the collective. A young Chinese man who helps Shen Yuelin in her investigation, and who displays a funky western chic with his Doc Marten boots and bleached-blond hair, explains his willingness to put himself at risk to help Moore: "I have a certain sympathy for your American. One guy against everyone . . . very cool." The individualism he admires here evokes both the heroic tradition of the John Wayne western and that of the maverick global capitalist, which is, after all, the role that landed Moore in a Chinese jail.

Moore's rhetorical reliance upon an East-West dichotomy—one that bolsters the film's process of cultural differentiation—is complicated by the premise that structures the film's conflict: a typical old- and new-guard split among the Chinese executives regarding the business deal by which this western programming package would be sold to the Chinese government Ministry of Radio, Film, and Television. The younger of these executives wax hopeful about maintaining a compromise, a balance between tradition and modernization, or westernization—although their desire for modernization is clearly motivated by self-interest in economic terms, with none of the ideological purity of the old Maoists. The material demonstration of such compromise appears in *Red Corner*'s next scene, when the executives attend a Chinese fashion show of western haute couture staged in the mise-en-scène of traditional Chinese opera, in which the balance represented by the staging is marked as deeply conflicted. Shots of the models in scanty western dress are rendered through the quick click of camera shutters that the soundtrack delivers as gunshots, and are interspersed with black-and-white images of opera actors in traditional Chinese dress, dueling with swords. The film's heavy-handed symbolism identifies the conflict between tradition and modernization, or westernization, as a violent one, with violent consequences. Importantly, the equation of modernization with westernization shifts the debate from a discourse about time to a discourse about geopolitical space. This slippage in the term "modernization," which implies a move away from a certain time period characterized by the concept of tradition, signifies a move into a certain geopolitical, technological, and ideological space characterized as the West. This close identification of modernization with westernization in cultural terms also characterizes the film's representation of torture. Atavistic disciplinary practices designate China chronologically as premodern and therefore by definition nonwestern, if modernity is understood to coincide with the introduction of Enlightenment notions of individual autonomy under the rule of law.

In the context of this conflict between national, ideologically based tradition and cultural globalization, *Red Corner*'s western protagonist seems to favor globalization, originally for economic reasons, but later in the progressive hope that China will adopt a just democratic system. Accompanying this shift is a change in Moore's position: his glib argument that the Ministry of Culture use western media programming to fix negative perceptions of the West in a collective Chinese consciousness evolves into a nationalist-patriotic apology for the supremacy of western political systems in the same global context. Coupled with his demand for immunity from violence based upon national difference ("I'm an American"), the contrast of Chinese with U.S. citizens resulting from the film's early construction of cultural differences deflects audience absorption of its argument against human rights violations in China. *Red Corner*'s protest against human rights in an international context uses the Chinese struggle with human rights violations—the relative lack of freedom of the Chinese people—as a counterpoint to differentiate and strengthen a western identity based upon political ideals of freedom, democracy, and a resulting bodily safety.

Capitalizing upon international publicity of the gross human rights violations perpetrated against Chinese and Tibetan nationals to construct the story of one American man who fights the stony bureaucracy of China's judicial system and wins, the film essentially subverts any potential protest against human rights violations, becoming a document of U.S. political superiority and an apology for western cultural imperialism. Ultimately, the safety it advocates is for the capitalist system, the entrepreneurial venture, the basic right to buy and sell. Although the film delays gratification of the promise of safety contained in the phrase "I'm an American," offering viewers the image of a U.S. citizen experiencing (limited) state-sponsored torture, it finally endorses western security from such horrors by manipulating the genre of courtroom drama to allow not only for the extremely unlikely acquittal of Jack Moore, the American, but also for the triumph of U.S. legal and political ideology over a (Chinese) totalitarianism exposed as hypocritical, corrupt, and illogical—and left wholly intact within the film's narrative scheme.

The same brand of narrative and ideological discord cripples Oliver Stone's *Salvador*. The force of the film's critique of state-sponsored terror and U.S. intervention in El Salvador in the early 1980s is eroded by its submersion in a masculinist adventure narrative oblivious to its own violences and inconsistencies.[10] Stone also uses the process of cultural differentiation employed in *Red Corner*, presenting a composite of El Salvador as politically and culturally alien from the United States on the one hand, and a land primed and ready for constitutional democracy on the other ("a United States in a nascent stage," in a description by John F. Stone [184]). The director figures the "legitimate peasant revolution" of the Salvadoran people (language used by *Salvador*'s protagonist, Richard Boyle, as he argues against U.S. intervention in support of the Salvadoran military junta) led by the socialist reform group FMLN as a movement closer to U.S. political ideals of constitutional democracy. In actuality, such democratic ideals had little to do with the politics of that historical moment in El Salvador, which featured a struggle between an oligarchic-military ruling class and a grass-roots socialist reform opposition. Indeed, in the climactic dialogue between Boyle and a conservative U.S. military aide, Boyle's discursive ingredients—constitutional patriotism folded into the universalism of human rights rhetoric—turn out an ideological mix reminiscent of nineteenth-century western Enlightenment philosophy to justify its civilizing mission. Not surprisingly, his argument rests squarely on the symbol of the constitutional document: "All you're doing is bringing misery to these people, Jack. I don't want to see another Vietnam. I don't want to see America get another bad rap. I lost my hearing in this ear in Vietnam. What do you think I did that for? . . . I did it because I believe in America. I believe that we stand for something. For a Constitution. For human rights, not just for a few people, but for everybody on this planet. Jack, you've got to think of the people first. In the name of human decency, something that we Americans are supposed to believe in, you've got to at least try to make something of a just society here." Even in this ostensibly radical critique, the power to "make" a just society remains in the hands of the Americans—even as the power to unmake the FMLN's revolution depended upon the U.S. intervention that Stone critiques here. However, Stone has offered audiences such brutal images of El Salvador's lawlessness, degradation of human life, and lack of the kind of "human decency" attributed to U.S. citizens, that cultural and national differentiation between U.S. American and Latin American (or, perhaps more accurately, between first- and third-world) actors solidifies into the classic Manichean binary. As a result, Boyle's ardent hope that U.S. constitutionality will trickle down (diplomatically or by force) to El Salvador is a foregone impossibility—especially since neither the military government nor the peasant rebels indicate interest in constructing a constitutional document. The universalism that marks Boyle's utopic dream of human rights for "everybody on this planet" is restricted to U.S. citizens protected by the film's generic manipulations, unavailable to racial/cultural/national others who, unprotected by a constitutional document, are confined to the violent background designated by the film's narrative split.

The cultural differentiation of Salvadoran from U.S. characters that represents Salvador as a primitive national entity hovering just outside the modernity of the law also organizes the neat classification of the Salvadoran people as either good or evil that the cowboy-style adventure genre demands. The lawlessness associated with Salvadoran military rule manifests in a string of seemingly monstrous characters, mostly military personnel and right-wing civilians portrayed as drunk, lecherous, threatening, and cruel. These characterizations are countered by idealized images of the peasant and rebel groups that recall the orderly utopias of mythic early U.S. populism—stripped, however, of its revolutionary military aspect.[11] While some images in this montage depict guerrilla soldiers training on horseback with a small arsenal of handguns, most of the images are of revolutionaries engaged in various activities in keeping with an idealized vision of a collective peasant lifestyle: cooking over open fires; learning to read in an open-air schoolroom; sewing;

pounding tortillas. Indeed, the greatest store of artillery depicted in these shots is found in sashes worn around the chests and shoulders of elderly women, signifying the material weakness of the rebel army in military terms.

Rendering FMLN rebels benign by neutralizing representations of their military capability coincides with the film's erasure of the FMLN's identity as a revolutionary socialist movement whose goals did not include a U.S.-style constitutional democracy.[12] By veiling the group's socialist ideology with images reminiscent of U.S. populism, precursor to constitutional democracy, Stone effectively co-opts the repressed Salvadoran history his film claims to unearth—particularly the history of the FMLN rebels and the *desaparecidos* who fell victim to the U.S.-supported military regime in El Salvador—replacing it with a document of the supremacy of U.S. constitutional democracy in international context. Indeed, Stone situates Boyle's didactic-patriotic monologue within a denial of accusations from the U.S. commander in El Salvador that Boyle is a Communist, a denial that waters down Boyle's protest rhetoric to the limp idealism of an adamantly patriotic liberal: "I may be left wing, but I'm not a Communist. And you guys never seem to be able to tell the difference. . . . I love my country too." Such repudiation of Communist political ideology by the film's designated defender of El Salvadoran rebels diverts focus from the material history of the socialist-based FMLN, replacing it with the patriotism espoused by Boyle, who offers his bodily injury, sustained while fighting Communist North Vietnamese in the Vietnam War, as proof of his national dedication. Given the U.S. definition of itself in cold war terms as diametrically opposed to Communism's red threat, even the film's minimal support for the FMLN as an alternative to the Salvadoran military junta is remade into another piece of imperialist U.S. identity.

The Female as Limit Case

The understanding of western identity as constitutionally protected from corporeal harm is grounded in another condition of freedom in the Enlightenment philosophical tradition that led to constitutional democracy: freedom of movement. Elaine Scarry has argued that the ideals of freedom and individual autonomy enshrined in national constitutional documents may be defined precisely as the ability to move: "Discussions of freedom are almost invariably couched in terms of physical movement. . . . Movement locates, rather than merely illustrates, the will" ("Consent" 875). An understanding of freedom as movement is instructive in considering the failure of the counterhistorical dramatic film to disrupt dominant narratives or to restore repressed historical accounts of atrocity. The western protagonist in the counterhistorical dramatic film is free because he or she can move out of one state into another, "state" meaning both nation and state of being safe. Laura Bowman in *Beyond Rangoon* can travel to the exotic (dangerous) East to heal the trauma of individual violence in the West and can choose, when her adventure is over, either to stay or to go. Richard Boyle can cross the border into El Salvador seeking a good time and a better photo opportunity, crossing back to the safety of U.S. territory while his Salvadoran girlfriend is remanded to the danger zone. Donald Woods orchestrates a safe escape to inform the western world of the terror of apartheid South Africa epitomized by the torture and murder of Steve Biko in a Port Elizabeth jail. Sydney Schanberg returns to New York to accept a Pulitzer Prize for his reporting on Cambodia while Dith Pran is tortured and starved for years before escaping from a Khmer Rouge camp.

While these representations may be classified as historically correct, faithful to the political and geographic organization of the world and even to actual events, the collective action—chase scenes, courtroom brawls, adventure sequences, even romantic interludes—of the foreground plot composes in their dramatization an aria of movement for western characters on-screen, opposed by the ensemble stagnation of nonwestern characters, teleologically stuck in place and (anachronistic) time. Given that closure in the counterhistorical dramatic film means fulfillment of the excessive generic requirements of the foreground plot, nonwestern characters are literally left behind in the suspended time-without-resolution of narrative danger. This leaving behind is also a chronologically appropriate terminology, as nonwestern characters and nations are positioned at the embryonic edges of the western progress narrative that confers the modernity of Enlightenment freedom of movement, and thereby of safety and escape, upon the western characters. In this way, western characters wear their citizenships (not to mention their skins) like protective wraps in faraway places, allowing them to move safely and to command help from natives willing to expose themselves to danger in order to save the western protagonist. The surprise of disbelief when they do confront peril or pain—even in spaces clearly demarcated by falling and fallen bodies—echoes in the cry: "I'm an American."

The difference of the female represented on-screen consummates this narrative passion for national opposition. That is, movement through narrative space and time, as well as movement through the historical space and time of the referent (the privileged freedom of individual movement toward and away from real danger posed in global conflicts), are also gendered. If national bodies are differentiated by their relative safety from harm and ability to move, then bodies gendered female epitomize such oppositions. Excluded from the western progress narrative of citizenship, female characters in the narrative scheme act either as generic by-products or as pure signs of difference. As such, women are almost without exception relegated to the premodern time of the counterhistorical dramatic film's danger zone. This narrative containment of the female evokes the ideology of woman as subversive that, as I shall argue in greater detail in chapter 3, informs the repressive structure of state-approved torture and further undermines any universalist, transcultural potential of the human rights protest attempted by the counterhistorical dramatic film.

Let us return to the moment when *Salvador*'s masculinist adventure narrative with its typical road-trip conventions is disturbed by the image of burning, mutilated bodies littering the road. Audience contemplation of the pain and terror these humans experienced before their deaths is mitigated by the plot-directed fear that the same fate is in store for the American heroes; however, fear for the bodily safety of Boyle and Doc is abruptly relieved when the action of the film takes a turn in the direction of an eroticized masculine fantasy. Rather than being tortured or killed, the prisoners are taken to the underground headquarters of Colonel Julio Figueroa, the leader of a military death squad, who is well disposed toward Boyle because of a complimentary profile Boyle once published about him in a right-wing Salvadoran newspaper. The tension of Boyle's and Doc's imprisonment (heightened by Doc's disbelief that this could "actually happen—to *Americans!*") is released with backslapping and guffawing among the men, followed by a meal served by prostitutes who enthusiastically wash Boyle's and Doc's sweating bodies. The threat of bodily harm has been waylaid in a manner particularly satisfying to the film's travel-adventure genre emplotment; that is, through the sexual relief provided by nameless Salvadoran women.

It is not irrelevant that the threat of wounding to male bodies in the film is often posed in terms of castration anxiety: as an alternative to the requisite phallic display of automatic weaponry, everyone threatens to cut off everyone else's balls. In this scene, in which Boyle's and Doc's anticipation of the sexual pleasure offered by Salvadoran women is about to be fulfilled, Colonel Figueroa greets Boyle by chortling, only partly in jest, "You're lucky you've still got your balls." In this phrasing, relief of the threat to the male body signifies both freedom (safety) from torture by the state apparatus (prerogative of the western male) and freedom to fulfill sexual desire (with Salvadoran women, also prerogative of the western male) according to the sexual contract grounded in the Oedipal story of kinship relations and solidified in the Lacanian symbolic. Castration anxiety doubles back as the excessive, normatively violent and denigrating male sexuality Boyle and Doc exhibit, and reappears as negative commentary upon the physical and professional mobility claimed by (western) women who enter the public sphere. Specifically, the protagonists' early description of "forward-thinking" women—that is, women moving forward in the public sphere of progress traditionally reserved for male subjects—as "yuppies who would rather get dressed up and go to jazz aerobics class than fuck" is reiterated in the juxtaposition of a female character with Boyle in the professional arena.

While Boyle's masculine-model photojournalist is constructed as honorable—that is, self-righteously unspoiled by network pandering and unafraid to get dirty covering the war the right way—his female colleague is well dressed, coiffed and manicured, and dishonorable, meaning that she represents the conservative status quo, giving U.S. audiences what they want to hear with regard to Reagan's military intervention. Boyle rails at this very blonde (very employed) reporter with barbs that take sexual form, mostly insinuations that she has slept her way to the top. Meanwhile, Doc, who has made an unsuccessful pass at her, gets her back (quite literally, as it turns out) by putting a tab of LSD in her drink. The camera cuts to the female put back in her place: the woman who refused Doc's sexual advances is now in a state of erotic disarray, with her blouse unbuttoned and falling off one shoulder, her hair sexily mussed as she tries to deliver a news report. Her composure completely undone, she screams with laughter and falls in a heap on the ground, literally a fallen woman, taken down for her movement in(to) the public sphere.

In actuality, this woman has fallen precipitously onto the turf of woman, that spectral sign against which the narrative domain measures masculine progress, experience, and mobility, the intractable figure denied full subjectivity. This is the turf delineated by de Lauretis in 1984 in *Alice Doesn't*, the persistent division she identifies in the disciplinary perspectives of linguistics and semiotics (Saussure); psychoanalysis (Freud, Lacan); and anthropology (Levi-Strauss), the grounds upon which women stand as "signs in social communication" (19). Twenty years later, we are still looking for evidence of the expansion of the feminist cinematic praxis that de Lauretis hoped could disrupt the conditions by which the female spectator is so often made "complicit in the production of (her) woman-ness" (15).

Before more fully iterating my own call for a renewed feminist struggle in response to the persistent gender norms that continue to structure the perpetration and representation of human rights violations, I will describe an encounter with the figure of woman in Canadian writer Gil Courtemanche's massively successful—if success is measured in sales figures, international awards, and film deals—novel about the 1994 Rwandan genocide, *A Sunday at the Pool in Kigali* (2003).[13] Over years of thinking about the counterhistorical dramatic film, I have considered the question of a fictional counterpart in the trade book market. I hypothesized that genre novels or journalistic memoirs might approximate some of its narrative conventions of setting, point of view, and emplotment. I had not, however, fully ruminated upon the extent to which the global gender politics of the cinematic genre might also inform a fictional analogue. The pornotropics (to borrow from Anne McClintock) of Courtemanche's book came then as that kind of paradoxical surprise characteristic of the postmillennial political despair that resonates as persistent disbelief (Can this be?) and then surfaces as utter familiarity (of course: the intransigent, deteriorating status quo). Without succumbing to the naïve idealism that wills a historically insupportable transformative aura onto this notoriously gradual globe, in addressing Courtemanche's text I invite readers to follow Toni Morrison in refusing to relinquish the capacity for an old-fashioned sense of shock at what is base, violent, and corrupt among us, no matter how statistically commonplace it becomes. As Morrison asserts: "I insist on being shocked. I'm never going to become immune. I think that's a kind of failure, to see so much [human barbarism] that you die inside. I want to be surprised and shocked every time."[14]

I admit to experiencing that state of disbelief at Courtemanche's narrative, a shock that threatens yet to devolve into the usual sense of familiarity, leaving only a trace disturbance regarding the figures that announce the book's success not only in pecuniary terms, but also in terms of its distribution of a "historical" account of the Rwandan genocide of 1994 to millions of readers and film viewers. Like the counterhistorical dramatic film, Courtemanche's text presents an ambivalent relation to historical veracity and to the work of mourning and memorializing real persons that it claims to perform. The ambivalence is manifest in the ardent sentimentality of the text's inscription to Courtemanche's Rwandan friends—"I have tried to speak for you / I hope I have not failed you"—juxtaposed with its *pornographic* emplotment, a term I use deliberately, emphatically to evoke the convergence of racial and class-based imbalances reified in a violently sexualized image system.[15] No occasion for the deterministic heterosexual erotics isolated in earlier polemics against pornography (*e.g.*, Dworkin, MacKinnon), Courtemanche's novel remaps the foundational racialism that structures global sexual exchange onto the specific scene of international politics in a Rwanda boiling toward genocide.[16]

In her delineation of the pornotropic, McClintock traces Europe's repetitive historical figuration of Africa (and the other "uncertain" continents: the Americas, Asia) as monstrously eroticized, "a fantastic magic lantern of the mind onto which Europe projected its forbidden sexual desires and fears" (22). Specifically, as McClintock demonstrates, the land, locus of imperialist male desire, is figured by the (native) woman. Particularly trenchant with regard to Africa, the tradition framed the argument that "it was as impossible . . . 'to be an *African* and not lascivious, as it was to be born in *Africa* and not be an African'" (22, emphasis in original). *A Sunday at the Pool in Kigali* presents a narrator who projects this ambivalent psychic response to Africa's eroticized landscape: the desire to engulf the other economically, culturally, and sexually, and the reflexive fear of being engulfed by that same monstrously lush, erotic, violent other.

The pornotropic ambivalence of the novel is produced in part by its fractured relation to historical events, persons, and its own mode of production. Courtemanche's preface produces a splitting such that readers understand the figure "author" to account for two distinct subjectivities: "This novel is fiction. But it is also a chronicle and eyewitness report. The characters existed, and in almost every case *I* have used their real names. The *novelist* has given them lives, acts, and words that summarize or symbolize what the *journalist* observed while in their company" (i, emphasis mine). The tautology "this novel is fiction" is cancelled by the claim that "it is also a chronicle and eye-witness report," leaving readers to guess who has produced a given scene. This fracture creates a problem with gendered ethical contours, given the novel's insistence upon preceding images of particular human deaths from genocide and AIDS—the two specifically African specters of eroticized mortality that haunt the novel's narrative/historical schema—with moments of ejaculatory ecstasy for the male characters. Was it the journalist who witnessed or the novelist who imagined the spray of ejaculate from a character upon the genocidal militiamen who gang-raped his wife and then macheted him while he "made love" to her in front of them? (98–99). Where in the text might a reader locate a point of view upon this scene from which to refuse the fantastical omniscience of male pleasure in the face of racialized female sexual ruin?

The problem of authorship indeed pivots upon the omniscience of the narrative voice, which, while appearing to occupy the point of view of protagonist Bernard Valcourt, a jaded Canadian journalist working in Kigali to set up a television station, also has total access to the thoughts, desires, and sexual lives of all the characters. The speciousness of the viewpoint is revealed in the many instances in which this narrator succumbs to the temptation of judgment forbidden an omniscient narrator in the literary sense. Our narrator, ultimately, is and is not the protagonist, the Canadian journalist Valcourt, who is and is not the author, Canadian journalist Gil Courtemanche—and this perpetual slippage in point of view compromises both literary and ethical claims to value that the text and its distribution materials assert. This masculine narrator delivers judgments about first- and third-world politics of sexuality, economics, diplomacy, aid, and AIDS that aggrandize Valcourt as an authentic white with sincere motives and unadulterated access to real Rwandans, while critiquing the rest of the theatre of white diplomats, soldiers, journalists, aid workers, and tourists as inauthentic, racist, and sexually exploitative. (I gender the narrator in this statement to mark its obsessively heterosexist masculine temperament; what else are we to make of a third-person indirect narrative voice informing readers that "Leo is not a moderate, it's just that *he's got a bone on* for Immaculee, Raphael's sister"? [12–13, emphasis mine]). It is neither possible nor desirable to analyze the many such incongruous moments of narrator intervention in the text, but here is one set of representative examples: "This is how the Whites at the hotel, instant minor gods, hear and figure Africa. Close enough to talk about it, even to write about it. But at the same time so isolated with their portable computers in their antiseptic rooms, and in their air-conditioned Toyotas, so surrounded with little Blacks trying to be like Whites that they think Black is the smell of the perfumes and cheap ointments sold in the Nairobi duty-free shop" (46). Consider, by contrast, this description of Valcourt: "He had approached [Rwandans living with HIV/AIDS] and questioned them with such patience and respect that these cautious, even secretive people now confided in him with a familiarity and candour that made his heart glow" (82). While the mass of capital-W whites are pathetically out of touch in their distance, privilege, and benighted susceptibility to the subversive mimicry of Courtemanche's genuflecting "little Blacks," Valcourt has managed to bridge the divides of race and nation, and even the objectivity gap of journalistic distancing, to achieve genuine human closeness with this otherwise inscrutable demographic. This putative third-person voice provides far too flimsy a cover for a first-person narrative from the perspective of Valcourt/Courtemanche, highlighting the incompatibility of the text with its claims to veracity and with the act of memorialization it purports to effect. The erotics of the violent spectacle and the violent spectacle of erotics are, finally, the subjects of this book.

Thus, the pervasive specter of death that haunts Rwanda from the double angle of imminent genocidal violence, on the one hand, and AIDS, on the other, is figured through an endlessly killing desire to fuck. Sex is paired early with death in the figure of the relentless buzzards, ravens, and vultures that clutter the landscape and symbolize the predatory paratroopers and diplomats who graze the pool at the Hotel des Milles Collines for "carcasses"— women who, "if they knew what danger stalked them, would drown in anticipation of ecstasy or else get themselves to a nunnery" (5). The expression of desire by these European women is tethered between the poles of a promiscuous desire for what will amount to rape and a proscribed celibacy (and the Shakespearean allusion does nothing to dispel the sense that this musing is precisely the male proscription upon female subjectivity that a cursory reading indicates). Both options confirm and extend the fatal emptiness represented in the novel as the core of European existence and epitomized in the European woman. African women, on the other hand, are in this Manichean rendering likely to be either prostitutes who use their "opulent bod[ies] the way others use their chequebooks" (50), as currency for a range of opportunities and exchanges, or shy young girls accustomed to sexual violence both at home and in the Kigali society in which Rwandan and European powerbrokers mix.[17] In both cases, erotic human connection in this global meeting ground is figured as a function of death, with purely physical pleasure gaining a small foothold just before death engulfs the landscape.

This, then, is the backdrop for a reader's introduction to the novel's heroine, Gentille, who has known only sexual abuse in both the familial and public spheres. Her relationship with Valcourt, however, delivers her from a state of silence and fear to a romantic citadel, which produces the novel's primary tension: how and when will Valcourt remove Gentille from Kigali, given the portentous signs that she is vulnerable to the genocidal forces unleashing themselves upon Tutsis and moderate Hutus even as she is courted by, and then engaged to marry, Valcourt? The failure of Valcourt to act upon these warnings and to extend the protective umbrella of a Canadian visa—"He could do it, today, tomorrow, with no trouble" (144), our omniscient narrator informs us—ensures the convergence of gender and national identity (woman/citizen) in the pornotropic danger zone as a space of immobility and certain death. The romantic narrative of Gentille and Valcourt ends with Gentille's death from HIV/AIDS after she has survived multiple gang rapes as the sexual prisoner of a Hutu Interahamwe.[18] In this context, the figure of woman is purposefully excluded from the safety of human rights protection on the basis of a citizenship that signifies both a literal, national orientation (Rwandan) and a mythical, feminine burden (African woman) from which there is neither textual nor material escape.

Courtemanche's romantic narrative is complicated by its development to the rhythms of the love poetry of Paul Eluard, signifier in this text of the western tradition of romantic love revered by Valcourt and ultimately inaccessible within the Rwandan sexual landscape that contains Gentille. Eluard's lines also function synechdochically in the text as one aspect of western civilization, the strain developed through the French romantic literary and philosophical traditions that includes a primary document of human rights (specifically, the Declaration of Rights of Man and Citizen, 1789), as well as the political trajectory of resistance signified by Eluard's participation in the French Resistance to Nazi occupation in World War II. Gentille attempts first to access the figurative space of that tradition through Eluard as an escape from the sordid manifestations of love as rape to which she is accustomed in the Rwandan context. Later, her physical survival urgently demands access to the geographical space of the neutral Canadian land to which Valcourt could transport her. In both cases, Gentille is refused access, her containment in the pornotropic region of Rwandan/womanhood disfiguring and dismembering her so irreversibly that she ceases to belong in either the category of human/citizen or the category of woman. As she states at novel's end: "I'm not a woman anymore. Do you understand what they've done to me? I'm not human anymore" (259).

Gentille's inductive logic moves from the particular inability to locate herself as woman to the more general exclusion from the category human.

Resulting in this case from her perception of herself as diseased, disfigured, and wholly given over to the degradation of sexual slavery and AIDS that her Rwandan womanhood seemed teleologically to produce, this logic is in a broader sense the logical economy that continues to limit the category of human in the narrative of human rights. It is this logic that the human rights movement has sought to defeat in the last fifteen years through campaigns that address the human rights of particular identity categories: replacing the inductive path that failed to lead from *woman* to *human* with the deductive move from the *human* to an inclusive attention to the particular manifestations of that condition.[19] Still, the neat supposition of the transitive verb in the slogan "Women's rights are human rights" remains a utopic gesture, its certainty yet unfulfilled. Gentille's end is a measure of the distance from such certainty, punctuated by narrative forms that predict the failed induction from woman to human.

There are two ways in which Gentille is refused access to the western romantic/democratic tradition. The first refusal—of entry into the narrative of ethical romantic love projected onto the signifying body of Eluard's poetry—is presaged by her essentially inappropriate response to a recitation of love by Valcourt. In one of the more fantastical erotic moments of contemporary literature (notwithstanding that which announces itself as explicitly erotic—or, perhaps better, parodic), the only female orgasm that warrants description in the novel is Gentille's, phantasmically induced when Valcourt announces that he loves her. This spontaneous orgasm verifies the heretofore unverifiable idea cultivated for Gentille at school that "words could lead to ecstasy" (90). Rather than exemplifying the metaphysical ecstasy described by intellectuals from Augustine onward as the result of access to bodies of knowledge in textual form, Gentille's ecstasy remains zoned in the carnal district of the strenuous partition of mind and body in the western tradition, substantiated in the "wetness of her crotch" (91) as passive emission rather than as creative expression. Rather than affirming the affective power of the word, Gentille, constrained by the pornotropic tradition in which she has been imagined as African woman, can respond only with the physical evidence and expression of her desire, which, in turn, will only ever be embodied (not minded).

The second refusal of access—to the geographic safety zone that a western visa would ensure—is clinched by the belatedness of Valcourt's decision to marry Gentille and take her to Nairobi to escape the genocide. Over the course of the novel, the visa takes on the weight of a test of the legitimacy of the romantic narrative, much like the compulsory virginity tests which would not apply in this distinctly African case—at least not in the context in which Courtemanche has represented Rwandan sexual mores. The idea that Gentille bestows the great gift of her physical beauty upon Valcourt in a mercenary bid for access to the geopolitical opportunity of the West haunts this relationship, as Valcourt wonders whether she is truly after "a White, a White like any other. A promise of wealth, maybe a visa for somewhere else; and if the blessed Holy Virgin answered her prayer, marriage with a White and a house in a cold country, a clean one" (37). The masculine imperialist fantasy of an improbably reciprocated desire projected onto Gentille/Rwanda cannot withstand the threat of such pragmatism rooted in the global sexual economy, and Valcourt is unable to resolve his fear of being instrumentalized as a means to the end of Gentille's escape. Even more improbably, however, Valcourt is reluctant to leave the landscape of Rwanda, to which he feels increasingly connected, for the cold expanse of Canada—even, it would seem, for the brief time it would take to protect Gentille from impending doom. The equation of woman with land in this two-pronged desire and in the plot maneuver of a militia checkpoint at which Valcourt is sent on to Nairobi while Gentille is detained, her narrative reverting to its predestination within the pornotrope, evoke the very worst of the iconic Conradian figuring of African woman as immobile, vulnerable marker of space, left keening on the shore as Kurtz is carried away on the steamer. Sadly, we must differentiate between Conrad's reflexive racism in a novel that, in its critique of imperialism if nothing else, transcended its historical moment, and Courtemanche's uncritical reproduction of pornotropes to dramatize global racism and violence. And while readers never learn the fate of Conrad's African woman, we witness Gentille as she endures the slowly doubled death of genocide and AIDS that becomes the figure for Rwanda itself, unprotected by the prophylactic of a Canadian visa or passport that would have enabled her to move out of the racial-sexual danger zone.

Significantly, the novel ends with a truncated expression of *écriture feminine*, the rise of woman to the symbolic realm of language and writing proscribed within the family structure presumed by the psychoanalytic model. The subjectivity implied in the term *"woman"* remains unavailable to Gentille, who briefly glimpsed its possibility in the colonial education that proved incapable of leading to a destiny other than the service industry reserved for most women of color within the global economy; however, she does create two records of herself at the end of her life. The workbook that records her experience, found after her imprisonment by Hutu militia, is literally marked in the novel as a feminine writing: "The words lined up obediently, like fine lacework made of tall loops and steady, round curves. Valcourt recognized this writing. It was his mother's and his four sisters', the airy, fragile hand that Quebecois nuns had taught and that had been learned by all the young Rwandan girls who, like Gentille, had gone to Butare's Social Service School" (241–242). This writing is linked imagistically to the kind of products educated women were formerly restricted to creating for circulation outside the realm of economic exchange—decorative lace, embroidery, and other such abridged expressions of women's creative impulses. More significantly, this description links women from the first and third worlds through the figure of woman produced as and producing object(s) of beauty and display, rather than of substance and access, in the global economy. However, in the African woman's case, the narrative written in that fragile hand is an account of the dehumanization of rape: "I'm not human anymore. I have no name and even less soul. I'm a thing . . . I'm a vagina. I'm a hole" (246). It is also the pornographic narrative, addressed to Valcourt, of yet another improbable search for desire, in this case, with one's rapist: "Since I'm going to die, I'd rather my rapist remind me of my husband and give me pleasure. . . . I have to get some pleasure out of dying" (245, 247).

The first-person account of rape Gentille records in her workbook is a record of her stasis in the realm of genocidal death, which is not the sudden death of bullet or machete but rather the agonizingly protracted death of HIV infection. And so it is that Valcourt finally locates her in the marketplace reading the familiar copy of Eluard and "transcribing his most beautiful lines into another school workbook" (260). This woman, who accessed the symbolic long enough to write the story of her most brutal exclusion from it via the age-old story that is rape, has now fallen back to the silence that is her existential condition, doomed to copy over and again the words of the tradition of romantic love and ethical citizenship in the family of humans from which she was excluded. Gentille's death is, finally, a literalization of *la petite morte*, the little death of the orgasm that, in the text, marked her desire not for sexual pleasure, but for the romantic signifier of citizenship engendering the human rights protection that could not in its current definition or practice extend to her. At the climactic heart of the love story, just before Gentille's abduction by Interahamwe forces, both Valcourt and Gentille "die with ecstasy . . . together" (202–203). Crucially, only Gentille will literally die. Valcourt will close the novel in Kigali, living with a Swedish Red Cross physician with whom he has adopted an orphaned Hutu girl, "at peace with himself" (260). The capital O of Gentille's original orgasmic response to the word is, tragically, an ode to the French tradition of literature, philosophy, and political protection to which she has no access, compulsively transcribed as her own elegy on the pages of her workbook.

Postscript

If Gentille reveals the teleological exclusion of African/woman from the narrative of safety that is citizenship in a constitutional democracy, the woman who anchors the plot in *Red Corner* carries the spectral quality of woman as pure symbol, rendered thus because of and at the expense of her desire. While Gentille reveals the historical woman frustrated in her desire for access to a narrative of love/desire outside the penetrative economy of rape, Hong Ling, Chinese model with whom Jack Moore spends his first night in Beijing, is the woman punished for her expression of sexual desire. Her murdered body bears the full weight both of the film's plot and of its ideological debates: it is in the chaos of his arrest in the hotel room where Hong Ling was murdered that Moore cries out, "I'm an American," and it is for her murder that he is put on trial. In spite of its narrative centrality, however, the body of Hong Ling remains purely phantom—pure plot device—in both its desire and its pain, as her murder is interpreted and reinterpreted upon demand of plot and genre.

De Lauretis, again, has theorized this equation of woman with space in plot typology:

> Opposite pairs such as inside/outside, the raw/the cooked, or life/death appear to be merely derivatives of the fundamental opposition between boundary and passage; and if passage may be in either direction from inside to outside or vice versa, from life to death or vice versa, nonetheless all these terms are predicated on the *single* figure of the hero who crosses the boundary and penetrates the other space. In so doing the hero, the mythical subject, is constructed as human being and as male; he is the active principle of culture, the establisher of distinction, the creator of differences. Female is what is not susceptible to transformation, to life or death; she (it) is an element of plot-space, a topos, a resistance, matrix and matter. (119, emphasis in original)

This use of woman as background/other excludes her from the narrative of law and freedom; in the case of Hong Ling, such exclusion further undermines

Jack Moore's already unstable arguments regarding the safety democratic constitutionality provides.

In her first meeting with Jack Moore, Hong Ling, star model of the film's early western-style fashion show, boldly returns the desiring gaze of Jack Moore from the runway. Reversal of the traditional direction of the look in both cinematic relations and in the normative scheme of the fashion show is emphasized here, as Hong Ling not only stares back at Moore, but also photographs him from the runway and later sketches a portrait of his face. This reversal of imaging/imagining relations might be read as part of the film's arguments about modernization and westernization: Hong Ling is a particularly westernized Chinese woman, fully interpolated by western practices via clothing, technological apparatus (cell phone and camera), and, most importantly, cultural manners. Her capture of Moore's image, along with her sexual overtures to him, are marked as particularly dangerous western characteristics, especially within the context of cultural differentiation that marks Chinese women as demure, modest, and deferential in the presence of men. Hong Ling's body is symbol for the excesses of western culture, as well as for its manipulation or constraint in the Chinese market—but it remains symbol, rather than body (embodied).

As the film progresses, flashback shots of Moore's evening with Hong Ling demonstrate Moore's interior process of reconstructing her murder as a means of freeing himself from prison. Some sort of ghostly helpmate, she is conjured upon plot demand to aid audience suspense in the form of Moore's slow cognition in piecing together the events of the evening after he had been drugged. In the end, when all the pieces are in place, audiences are gratified to learn the identity of Hong Ling's murderer: Dan Lin, her boyfriend, whom she was jilting by cell phone in the last scene Moore remembered from before his arrest for her murder. It seems that Dan Lin used his girlfriend to lure Moore into a sexually compromising position with a Chinese woman (dramatizing the minister of culture's fear of western culture as a sexually corrupt force for Chinese citizens) but was then angered by her obvious pleasure in the encounter. Upon her refusal to follow through with their conspiracy against Moore, Dan Lin sent a Chinese military officer to stage her murder scene with evidence implicating Moore. And so the murdered body of Hong Ling is reread: out of the story of international capitalist competition and desire, and into the story of male competition and desire (perhaps these are, in the end, the same). Originally understood to signify the problem of jealousy (competition) between nations in the context of global exchange, the deep structure of Hong Ling's symbolic currency in *Red Corner* is jealousy between men in the exchange of women. As de Lauretis notes with regard to Freud's story of Dora: "And so the story, like any other story, is a question of his desire" (*Alice Doesn't* 133).

And so it is, but it is also more: the story of the deadly repression of her desire as subversive, dangerous, in need of containment. Like Gentille's desire for a romantic conception of love, which can never transcend its physical limit within the pornotropics of Courtemanche's narrative, Hong Ling's desire is unaccountable, uncanny, wrong. The record of human history thrums with the unaccounted-for pulse of female desire, and with the violent narrative of its suppression in the name of masculinist power and privilege, safety and mobility, access and opportunity. There is, then, hope for narrative forms in which the subnarrative emplotment of this repressed female desire—which, in her analysis of plot typology, de Lauretis reveals as foundational to narrative's mythical deep-structure—might surface as the subject of narrative address. Or better, that the narrative zoning which constrains both national and gendered others in the counterhistorical dramatic film, fatally limiting the potentially inclusive transculturality of universal human rights protests, might be disrupted, as it is in *Three Kings* and *Hotel Rwanda*, rather than simply reversed. Acknowledging the parallel of racist-imperialist and patriarchal representations at work in the linear plot typology, the project of ethically representing the pain experienced by nonwestern bodies merges with the process of opening representations of gender to allow for women to be represented as desiring historical subjects rather than as narrative signs or symbols.

This is not to say that only novels and films foregrounding gender and sexuality according to feminist principles will offer ethical representations of international human rights violations; however, a certain kind of feminist intervention in the narrative process might open ground to restore nonwestern actors to the position of historical subjects in the universal story of international human rights protest. Indeed, feminist narrative or cinema need not be restricted to a category of gender-specific projects; rather, as de Lauretis argues: "Feminist cinema . . . is the notation for a *process* of reinterpretation and retextualization of cultural images and narratives whose strategies of coherence engage the spectator's identification through narrative and visual pleasure and yet succeed in drawing 'the Real' into the film's texture" (de Lauretis, *Technologies* 115, emphasis mine). This process addresses *how* rather than *what* (form rather than—or as connected with—content) in narrative terms. The process of feminist cinema that de Lauretis evokes—which might also be examined in literary narrative—attempts to meet the demands of both historical witness ("the Real") and narrative pleasure in the process of telling the story, without compromising either. It is precisely this process which, laboring toward a representational ethic that avoids the ideological pitfalls of the classical Hollywood film and its linear novelistic counterparts, might be equal not only to recuperating the mobility, emotion, and experience—indeed, the subjectivity—of women such as Hong Ling and Gentille, but also to revealing the largely overlooked potential of gender as a major theoretical tool for the study of representations of the scene and act of torture.

3

TORTURE III

DESIRE

Consider the assertion that women's desire is repressed on a global scale.[1]
One can support this statement with a seemingly endless litany of evidence:
the repression of sexual desire enforced by laws and customs related to sexual
expression and "adultery," including the perpetration of honor killing, forced
marriage, child marriage, sexual slavery, genital cutting; the desire for self-
actualization limited by laws and customs around dress, work, career, public
visibility, driving, voting, inheritance, divorce, custody; the desire for safety
forestalled by constant global exposure to harm through poverty, domestic
abuse, trafficking, rape, war. What does this massive repression have to do
with the practice of torture (of and by either men or women)? What would a
methodology that foregrounds gender and desire as analytic tools in the fight
against torture and in the study of its cultural representation do? When one
investigates these problems by exploring the category of subversion in its
function as rationale for the perpetration of torture, one finds that the term
"subversion" in its political manifestation is thoroughly gendered—if not
sexed—and that this gendering is performed with a variety of consequences
both at the scene of torture and in its literary and cinematic representation.
Reading Stephen Frears's *Sammy and Rosie Get Laid* (1985) alongside selected
events of public record, I follow this line of argument to address three questions related to the link between gender and torture:

> How is a rhetorical parallel between political and sexual subversion estab-
> lished and represented, and how does this parallel bear upon practices
> and discourses of torture?
> What do we make of the woman as torturer (most notably, for instance, at
> Abu Ghraib prison in Iraq in 2004)?

What has the feminist response to the gendered nature of torture looked
like and how might it be strengthened?

An appropriate starting place for this investigation is an auditorium at the
City University of New York Graduate Center, 24 October 2003. On this day,
academics, activists, and students gathered to address questions related to torture in the post-9/11 world. The first and arguably central speaker was Harvard
University professor of law Alan Dershowitz, defending his idea that a system
of legal warrants for the use of torture be instituted as part of the global "war
on terror." In brief, Dershowitz posits that officials who believe that torturing a
suspect will produce information that could potentially save innocent lives
endangered by an imminent act of terrorism—the so-called ticking-bomb scenario—ought to be obligated to obtain a "torture warrant" to authorize the use
of torture.[2] Such warrants would, according to Dershowitz, regulate the practice of torture, providing it with "accountability, recordkeeping, standards and
limitations."[3] This idea, unfortunately, has too often become the starting point
for debates about the use of torture in the war on terror in legal, governmental,
and even scholarly forums, subsuming the tacit pre-9/11 consensus upon its
prohibition. The post-9/11 presumption that torture is in some cases either
necessary, morally acceptable, or both has taken the place of the formerly transcultural drive for torture's abolition, once considered a near universal good in
public and academic discourses, particularly in the United States.[4]

Apparently unbeknownst to Dershowitz, Sister Dianna Ortiz, a U.S. nun
and founder and director of the Washington, D.C.–based nongovernmental
organization TASSC International (Torture Abolition and Survivor Support
Coalition International), was to deliver the forum's keynote speech just prior
to his talk. Ortiz herself was tortured in Guatemala by the Guatemalan military in collaboration with one man whom she has identified as a North American CIA operative.[5]

I have come to perceive the events at the CUNY conference as paradigmatic
of several of the major strains of a gendered theory of torture: the strength of
masculinist desire to perform and reproduce the spectacularly persistent splits
of mind/body, rational/irrational modes of being, and public/private spaces—
the very splits that inform such behemoths as patriarchy, human rights convention and law, and narrative structure across the range of their historically
and culturally specific manifestations.[6] My choice to describe the proceedings
of that morning in print is in some ways a gesture toward muddying the illusory slashes that mark the binaries as such: what I divulge here feels intensely

private (embarrassingly so), although the events I describe took place in a public forum and Dershowitz himself recounts them in print.[7]

It would be difficult to overstate the discomfort Dershowitz exhibited at the presence of Ortiz, a discomfort I bear witness to here to illuminate some ideas about gender and torture. Sister Dianna Ortiz made three oratorical moves to which Dershowitz took exception, and which reveal the gendered paradigm characterizing the phenomenon of torture and its discourses. First, she drew attention to her body as representative of the collective body of torture victims and survivors by clothing herself in modes of dress from around the world and informing her audience of that choice as symbolic of both the ubiquity of torture as a global practice, and of her role as spokesperson for hundreds of torture survivors. Second, she evoked both sacred and affective realms by lighting a candle in memoriam for persons lost to torture, a symbolic act that, she informed her audience, was for her an ethical precondition for engagement in public discourse about torture victims and survivors. Third, in her talk she combined rhetorical styles and generic forms, a miscegenational coupling of the substance and methods of testimonial speech and of logical and empirical proof. Indeed, Ortiz announced that part of her role speaking as a survivor of torture was to "rescue the conference from the rational, that is, the abstract." She indicated that she meant to offer empirical evidence of torture's excess, of its highly irrational proclivity for leaping the bounds of any and all rationalized justifications for its use, particularly in light of the post-9/11 resurgence of arguments that theorize torture via cost-benefit analysis of its results. Ortiz further indicated that this empirical evidence had been derived from both her own experience of torture and her experience directing an NGO devoted to providing support and pursuing justice for survivors of torture worldwide.

When Dershowitz entered the auditorium, he moved to the front row reserved for speakers. Ortiz gestured to the seat beside her and he took it. After Ortiz had been introduced and had taken the stage, Dershowitz exhibited a range of explicitly irrational behaviors for the duration of her talk. Situated within several feet of the podium where Sister Ortiz was speaking, and directly in her line of vision, Dershowitz noisily rustled a stack of papers, made notations upon the pages, and passed them back and forth with a colleague in the row behind him, exchanging whispered comments. After a time, Dershowitz gestured to his colleague to move into the seat next to him—the seat Ortiz had occupied, so that upon completion of her talk, she returned to find she had been, quite literally, displaced. Immediately thereafter, Dershowitz took the stage, prefacing his remarks with a disclaimer: "Unlike the last speaker, I will not apologize for limiting my discourse to the rational." At the end of the session, I approached Dershowitz and asked why he had invoked a separation between rational and irrational spheres with regard to Ortiz' presentation, especially given his disruptive behavior during her talk. His response: "Had I known that she would be here, I would not have attended."

Dershowitz's claim to the rational as a clearly defined mode of thought and manner of being relegated to the irrational, by way of contrast, Ortiz' remarks (and, by extension, Ortiz herself). The claim was based upon Ortiz' decision to foreground her body not only in an individual sense but also as symbol for a globally tortured corpus. In my reading, her decision was predicated upon two points. First, survivors commonly believe that when it comes to torture, an individual subjectivity from which to speak can be tenuous. Rather, the ubiquity and similarity of torture experiences across spaces and times means that when one speaks of one's torture, one often speaks in a plural voice haunted by the suffering of others who survived and, more urgently, who did not survive similar experiences. In her capacity as founder and director of an organization comprised of hundreds of torture survivors, each of whom also represents others lost to the torture that he or she managed to withstand, Sister Ortiz' rhetorical and visual moves are not only theoretically reasonable but also comprise an ethically charged stance from which to publicly articulate a position upon the subject of torture.

Second, a central tenet of testimonial literature and speech is that the narrative "I" may be conceived as a symbolic voice for a collective of persons precluded from speaking publicly and/or unable to be heard and acknowledged (witnessed).[8] Taken together, these points foreground one of witness literature's central problematics: the western desire or need for a unified, bounded, narrative "I" as it encounters the survivor's need to account for the "we" that is often the subject of representation/expression. This problematic was perhaps most famously witnessed in debates about the veracity of Nobel Laureate Rigoberta Menchu Tum's narrative *I, Rigoberta Menchu*, but it has also characterized debates about Shoah testimony and literature.[9] The use of the term "rational" in this encounter reveals the equation of reason with the disembodied subject and the construction of the rational as the opposite of affective or sacral.

Both these constructions have long and troubled histories in western thought, starting with Augustine's agonized disavowal of the body and Descartes' equally emphatic refusal of the affective.

Dershowitz's defensive postulation of Sister Dianna Ortiz as "irrational" in her purposefully embodied vulnerability recalls the deep structure of the term "subversive," so often historically mobilized to mark a group of persons as dangerous and in need of rehabilitation or removal. Etymologically referring to the act of "turning" (Latin: *vertere*), according to the online *Oxford English Dictionary*, the subversive "upset[s], overturn[s], break[s] up, disturb[s], or overthrow[s] the immaterial condition of things." Perhaps not surprisingly, the term is etymologically related to "torture," which originates in the Latin *tortura*, meaning "twisting," and the French *torquere*, "to twist, or torment," If the subversive is imagined to turn away from or disturb the order of things, torture as antidote constitutes a forcible turning back—a twisting—to a legitimated arrangement, within authority's reach. The immaterial condition the subversive overturns may be likened to the abstract (yet, paradoxically, hyperpragmatic) nature of Dershowitz's argument, which can play to a crowd versed in the alarm of the war on terror only so long as the spectators' attention is not turned toward the bodies who might receive the regulated torture that is the subject of Dershowitz's proposal.

More disturbing than Dershowitz's literal calling out of Sister Ortiz' embodiment was his virtual disappearance of her. I use this term mindfully to evoke the history of *desaparecidos* in the Latin American context, of which Ortiz' experience in Guatemala is part.[10] By declining to listen to or hear Ortiz (rustling papers, conversing during her talk), physically displacing her (taking her seat), and refusing to refer to her by name ("the last speaker"; "she"), Dershowitz revealed the drive to render anonymous and invisible the corporeal, human consequence—that is, the victim's or survivor's unique body and identity—of the argument that supports lifting the prohibition against torture, a move that characterizes the broader discourse currently addressing the use of torture in the war on terror.[11] In an essay chronicling responses to his proposal, Dershowitz again refuses to address Ortiz by name, stating that "the conference [at John Jay College] began with an emotional speech—replete with candles—delivered by a victim of torture" ("Tortured Reasoning" 264).[12] Dershowitz's sardonic tone unmasks his ad hominem annoyance at the invasion of a public sphere in which he claims a proprietary right to proscribe affective or sacral speech or thought, to set the terms of the debate, and to deride those who do not accept those terms. He complains that Ortiz' speech was "calculated to make it difficult, if not impossible, to conduct a rational discussion about the ways of limiting and regulating the use of nonlethal torture in the context of terrorism prevention" (265). Indeed, the warrant of Dershowitz's argument—since torture is currently a widespread practice, it is obligatory to legislate its practice—presumes that torture is acceptable under certain well-defined circumstances. While claiming that Sister Ortiz limits the debate in her call for abolition, Dershowitz purposefully excludes her and others who argue for the abolition of torture from the dialogue, making it "difficult, if not impossible" to discuss the a priori subject of whether torture is ever permissible, no matter what the circumstances.[13]

His remark also clarifies two problems related to the gendered aspect of knowledge and discourse related to torture. First, the presumption that Ortiz' speech was "calculated" to do anything other than to persuasively express her perspective on and arguments about the problem under discussion is an unwarranted projection closely related to the second problem, that is, a refusal to acknowledge Ortiz as a professional agent carrying out her work in a public sphere, with or without the consent of those who have historically laid claim to such space.[14] Indeed, the term "calculated" is telling, given its deep structural connection to the rational: the "irrational" (e.g., Sister Dianna Ortiz) is in this case rational enough to attempt to foreclose the functioning of logos but not rational enough to advance legitimate arguments. Notwithstanding his own protestations, Dershowitz in his response to Ortiz communicates the irrational core at the heart of unfettered reason's performance, an anxiety historically treated with an (over)dose of rationalism.[15]

Crucially, in the speech Sister Dianna Ortiz delivered that morning, she did not explicitly describe her own experience of torture. Rather, she spoke as—and we might presume that her invitation to speak was predicated upon her position as—director of a functioning NGO working on issues directly related to those under discussion in the forum. Further, Ortiz is by profession a working member of a religious order for whom the act of lighting a candle in memoriam may be considered more accurately from the vantage point of her vocation than from the perspective of the trivialized play to pathos Dershowitz registers. Was it inappropriate for Sister Ortiz, a member of the Ursuline order, to light this candle at an academic conference? Would Dershowitz object to being compelled to refrain from citing jurisprudence in his remarks as a lawyer to this multidisciplinary professional audience? The remainder of Ortiz' remarks was restricted to arguments (the mode of logos, not pathos) against the practice of torture, some of which incorporated testimonial accounts as evidence to support her claims. Given its inherently brutal nature, such testimonial evidence may have evoked emotional response in the audience; however, it falls squarely within the realm of the empirical upon which Dershowitz bases not only his argument, but also the drive to make such an argument in the first place. Dershowitz resists the charge of "sadism" leveled at his argument in support of torture warrants by asserting a distinction between his "*normative* preference (that torture *should not* be employed and that its use *should* be reduced or eliminated)" and his "*empirical* descriptions and predictions (that torture *is* being practiced by democracies in extreme situations" ("Tortured Reasoning" 274, emphasis in original). Ortiz and Dershowitz are aligned, then, in the rhetorical grounding of their arguments in empirical evidence, that is, confirmed descriptions of the widespread use of torture. Ultimately, Dershowitz's response to Ortiz in print and in person illustrates anxiety toward, misreading of, and finally refusal to accommodate certain qualities or presences gendered female in the broader arena we might term the public sphere: the female professional entering this space; the female professional in the public sphere who calls attention to herself as embodied; the embodied female professional who engages any combination of physical, affective, sacral, and/or intellectual/rational modes of being as part of her professional performance.

In this context, if Ortiz must needs be present, then Dershowitz demonstrated—in a combination of nonverbal cues, body language, and veiled insinuations that fell under the rubric neither of rational discussion nor of logical debate—his preference that she not mark herself as a survivor, a representative of torture's elongated reach. In this case, that reach extended to a U.S. citizen acting in a politically unstable country under the auspices of the Ursuline order teaching underprivileged children to read. The reading of Ortiz' body as sign of torture's reach past those legitimate targets most often characterized by Dershowitz's own infamous ticking-bomb scenario (although since 9/11 also more nebulously encompassing anyone labeled a potential or proven "terrorist") is consequential for the purposes of this chapter.[16] The success of any argument regarding the efficacy of torture, in time of war or otherwise, depends heavily upon the global invisibility of survivors of the practice, most of whom are neither terrorists nor enemy combatants but prisoners of conscience tortured for their opposition to (often repressive, abusive, or dictatorial) governments; or for their membership in a particular ethnic, gendered, sexual, religious, or political group or their perceived relationship to such members; or as examples meant to invoke fear and compliance in the community.

Or by mistake, as is the case with many prisoners held in and tortured at Guantánamo and Abu Ghraib prisons. Or for no *reason* at all (pun intended). In this way, torture itself is supremely irrational: the act of purposefully inflicting pain to achieve a desired end is finally license to commit sadistic acts without limit or censure, always already an excess in form and content (object).

To argue for the limited, legislated use of torture as a necessary evil, one must buy into two states of mind and being: first, a denial of the effects of the practice—that is, of pain—the very denial that is central to the frame and act of torture itself and that is, at its core, the will to power; and second, a division of persons into those vulnerable to torture's reach (subversives; terrorists) and those who do not expect to find themselves strapped to a table while an official applies electric shock to their nipples or needles under their nails (innocents). To make his argument, Dershowitz must refuse prompts that could produce an image of himself engulfed in the narrative of pain/death that accompanies the slide from the terrorist to the terrorist's comrade, to his brother, to a neighbor, to a person who lives in his village, to a person suspected of sympathizing with his cause, to a person who happens to look like or be proximate to any of these, to a person. Dershowitz—and others who advance the argument—must be convinced of their status in the benign, innocent, noncomplicit, anonymous polity ostensibly protected by the injection of those sterile needles precisely three centimeters under someone else's finger nails. The appearance of Sister Dianna Ortiz on a stage, her body a sworn testimony to torture's excess—both in its objects and in its methodologies—gives the lie to this heavily rationalized division of persons into guilty and innocent.

Finally, then, Alan Dershowitz was less disturbed by Sister Dianna Ortiz herself or the substance of her argument than by what she signifies: the concrete challenge to his abstract argument, the return of torture's irrational excess to haunt the sphere of rational debate about its policies and procedures. Sister Ortiz did "make it . . . impossible . . . to conduct a rational discussion" about torture, not because, as Dershowitz would have it, she appealed to pathos in an effort to foreclose upon logic, but because her presence and her remarks unmask the prior evacuation of reason, not to mention linguistic and epistemological order, from the space marked by torture. Considered in a certain light, the drama is not new: the conflict produced by a multicultural female body claiming intellectual, affective, and sacred space at an academic conference staged and centered upon white male judges, lawyers, and academics accustomed to holding the line of abstract intellectual engagement.

In her performance as collective, affective, unbounded corporeal sign of the moral failure of a putatively rational argument, Sister Dianna Ortiz signifies the intrusion upon and potential collapse of the discourse itself. It is the response of Alan Dershowitz to this woman as a signifier, rather than as a subject, that is most interesting. Which brings me to the first question under address in this chapter: how is a parallel between political and sexual subversion established, and what are some consequences of this parallel for human rights?

Signifyin': *Sammy and Rosie Get Laid*

I ended chapter 2 by investigating how the mythological trope of the feminine that reduces woman to sign and refuses to note the reality of her subjectivity and desire impacts narratives of human rights violations delivered in dominant generic forms. The foregoing analysis of the CUNY conference further suggests the way in which public discourse around torture is gendered. One etymological aspect of the term "rational" is that it "exist[s] (only) in the mind (opposed to the *real*)," according to the *Oxford English Dictionary*. This aspect connects the reductive misreading of Sister Dianna Ortiz as woman—sign of threat to the public sphere; to logos; or, in psychoanalytic terms, to the symbolic—with the refusal in larger cultural and narrative contexts of the female as real, historical, thinking, desiring being. It also evokes the repudiation of the body in favor of the mind that genders the discourse of torture, as opposed to the practice of torture, which savagely magnifies the body in its attempt to repudiate—or to possess—the mind.

One way in which the drive to torture is sexed is the way in which political subversion, motivator and rationale for torture's disciplinary charge, is figured by the threat of sexual subversion within patriarchy—in simpler terms, by the threat of female sexual desire. Screenwriter Hanif Kureishi's and director Stephen Frears's parodic turn on the romance in the film *Sammy and Rosie Get Laid* shows how the sexing of subversion triggers the torturer's desire to reinforce the heterosexually legitimated order of things. Kureishi tells the story of Sammy (Samir), a Pakistani-British accountant, and Rosie, a white British social worker, who live in South London during a series of riots resulting from race and class conflicts. Both are enlightened, anticapitalist liberals who believe passionately in social justice and nonmonogamy, and who equate (sexual and national) order with death. Enter Sammy's father, Rafi, a Pakistani politician returning to London to escape persecution from the "opposition" at home, a man trying to recapture something of his lost youth in England, "the bosom of civilization." As the film progresses, torture is revealed to have been Rafi's coercive governing method of choice, and the story becomes in part an exploration of his psyche and of the responses of others to him. In structural terms, *Sammy and Rosie Get Laid* as a narrative might fall into Teresa de Lauretis's provocative category "Oedipal with a vengeance": "The most exciting work in cinema and in feminism today is not anti-narrative or anti-Oedipal; quite the opposite. It is narrative and Oedipal with a vengeance, for it seeks to stress the duplicity of that scenario and the specific contradiction of the female subject in it, the contradiction by which historical women must work with and against Oedipus" (*Alice Doesn't* 157). By foregrounding and, in some measure, subverting traditional romance narrative conventions, and by high-lighting the Oedipal contours of the family drama, Kureishi demonstrates the ways in which the use of and justification for torture in a political, often nationalist, context is directly related to and supported by that foundational (though certainly, following de Lauretis, duplicitous) narrative of order, progress, and civility. Specifically, Rafi equates the sexual indeterminacy wit-nessed in Sammy and Rosie's flat with a lesbianism which stands for that which is extra-Oedipal, and therefore chaotic, disordered, out of (male) con-trol—and which exists in perfectly disordered synchronicity with the chaos he meets and deplores in riotous urban London.

As Rafi tries to bind his vengeful Oedipal prescriptions to the chaos and indeterminacy of 1980s London, a chaos he experiences in both national and sexual terms, Kureishi and Frears show how the disorder the torturer reads as a sign of female desire is in fact the collapse of his own pretension to power, accompanied by his discovery that the abjection he assigns to others is most unbearably to be found within. This revelation emerges in a snippet during a brisk montage sequence depicting the weekend cultural lives of these forward-thinking Londoners, a stylistic homage to Woody Allen's signature filmic paeans to Manhattan. In the last image of the sequence, Sammy and Rosie attend a "seminar at the ICA" during which the soundtrack swells to reveal—appropriately—a *fragment* of Colin McCabe's lecture: "the same fear of losing control of meaning as the father's fear of losing control of female desire" (Kureishi 32). This seeming throwaway line, this easily missed frag-ment, cues the figuring of political by sexual subversion that is central to practices and discourses of torture. In the film, the loss of control of meaning and of female desire results in a nightmare of unintelligibility that neither pater nor patria can withstand, as the two monoliths undergo a fatal collision in the abjected figure of Rafi. Working from the site of that impending crash, Kureishi stages an argument about the motivations of the torturer, exposing the ironies and inconsistencies in the rhetorics of national order and progress used to justify state-sponsored torture. Specifically, having documented the gendering of subversion and chaos, this argument reveals the dependence of national narratives of order and progress upon the repression of that which is labeled chaotic, which refuses to take a place or to stay in its place, ultimately exposing the placelessness of the author of such narratives within the identity politics of a changing postcolonial world. At issue in the film, significantly, are not so much the subversive expressions of sexuality or nationhood revealed in the lesbian embrace or broken bottles thrown in a burning street, but that the signifiers themselves are openly contested. In this way, Rafi's ultimate psychic destruction (like Alan Dershowitz's academic annoyance) results as much from the linguistic chaos which has usurped his control over the process of signification as from the visual, epistemological chaos of nation and gender which he experiences daily in this new London.

As feminist scholars of nationalism have asserted for some time, woman has historically carried several tropic burdens in relation to nation, including, in her chastity, symbol of the nation's honor, and in her maternity, culture bearer for the nation.[17] The tropological implications of "nation" contain an implicit paradox in that, despite its construction through female icons (mother or virgin) in need of protection, the nation as patria in its practical functioning and power relations is decidedly gendered male, epitomized in the figure of the male official or soldier intent upon retaining the sanctity of male power against the threat of feminized subversives. As such, the urge to contain and repress female desire figures the urge to repress other subversive elements that threaten the sanctity and strength of the nation.

In her analysis of gender as spectacle in Argentina's "dirty war," Diana Taylor traces the mythology of woman as degraded other that underwrote the Argentine military junta's gendered spectacularization of their war on subversion: the proud male patria, anthropomorphized in its soldiery, waging war on feminine/feminized subversives (leftists, labor organizers, students, professors, health and church workers, etc.). Taylor's description of the Argentine state's interpretation of subversion resonates unmistakably with hegemonic tropes used to demarcate the feminine: "'Subversion' (*i.e.* any and all opposition to the armed forces) was thus transgressive, hidden, dangerous, and dirty" (67). This definition provides a point of convergence between discourses of gender and nation as related to the practice of torture, for the female—woman, if not historical women—has also been constructed as transgressive (respecting no borders or boundaries); dangerous (potentially threatening to social and national order and honor); dirty (unclean, impure, requiring patriarchal and state constraints upon her person and her sexuality); and, perhaps most importantly, hidden (unknowable, obscure, mysterious, uncontrollable). The literature—feminist and otherwise—addressing these constructions of the feminine is too abundant to document here, but one or two relevant theoretical threads will identify these four descriptors of subversion as the warp and weave of a most artfully feminized tapestry of abjection.

I raise the specter of abjection at this point because, historically speaking, much of the world's (that is, both western and nonwestern) mythology of woman has its source in the female body—particularly its sexual and maternal aspects, which are also, as Julia Kristeva argues, the principal sites of the abject. And what better place to begin examining the abject female body than in Stallybrass and White's musings upon the transgressive quality of the grotesque body as celebrated by Rabelais and re-presented by Bakhtin? If Rabelais experienced a certain flagrant *jouissance* in the boundless grotesquerie of the carnivalesque body, the flip side of its ability to transgress is its abjection, as Stallybrass and White articulate:

> The grotesque body, as Bakhtin makes clear, has *its* discursive norms too: impurity (both in the sense of dirt and mixed categories), heterogeneity, masking, protuberant distension, disproportion, exorbitancy, clamour, decentred or eccentric arrangements, a focus upon gaps, orifices and symbolic filth (what Mary Douglas calls 'matter out of place'), physical needs and pleasures of the 'lower bodily stratum,' materiality and parody. The opposition between classical and grotesque in this sense is invoked as automatically and unconsciously by Charcot in his description of the female hysteric as it is by the police spokesperson in a description of pickets or Auberon Waugh in his description of the women encamped at Greenham Common ('smelling of fish paste and bad oysters'). The grotesque physical body is invoked both defensively and offensively because it is not simply a powerful image but fundamentally constitutive of the categorical sets through which we live and make sense of the world. (23)[18]

Of note in this lengthy exposition is the presence in gendered, corporeal form of Taylor's four descriptors of the political, ideological subversive: transgressive, dangerous, dirty, and hidden. Also of note is the identification of the grotesque body as female (although oddly absent from these examples are the racialized female bodies immortalized in the early nineteenth-century figure of Saartjie Baartman, the so-called Hottentot Venus).[19] Important to my argument is Stallybrass and White's contention that the grotesque (female) body historically has not been invoked simply as an image, but rather is used in a tropic sense to make and remake the "categorical sets" which structure our world. As these sets vary from culture to culture, so do the limits of the normative and deviant, rational and irrational, classical and grotesque or abject. What remains fixed is the fear that the (feminine) grotesque will cross the bounds of the (masculine) norm, indeed that the feminine is always located outside the order of things because of its inherent inability to be contained.

This desire for containment, which might alternately be understood as a desire to see and to know and to control, is equally significant to Elisabeth Bronfen's examination of the history of western art as marked by its aesthetic inclination toward the dead female body. If the female body contains traces of the abject, then the dead female body is its apogee; as Kristeva argues: "The corpse, seen without God and outside of science, is the utmost of abjection" (4). Bronfen interprets the aestheticizing of the female corpse as a means of renouncing the mortality associated with woman in cultural myths of femininity: "It is crucial . . . that the production of beautiful images (aesthetics) and the construction of femininity are culturally equated because they are analogously positioned in relation to death. The beauty of Woman and the beauty of the image both give the illusion of intactness and unity, cover the insupportable signs of lack, deficiency, transiency" (64). The "intactness and unity" of the aestheticized female body gained by representing her in the stillness of a beautiful death renders woman sign, ruptured from real historical women whom, in their grotesqueness, she refuses to signify.

Keeping in mind the connection between meaning and desire in McCabe's haunting fragment, let us examine Bronfen's equation of the beautiful (dead) woman with the beautiful image: both signify intactness, wholeness. Could this beautiful image be equated with the beautiful wholeness of the sign before poststructuralism's discontents? Of rational discourse without the specter of its gross bodily effects? Could we consider the satisfaction resulting from this intactness of image in terms of the meanings traditionally assigned to those gargantuan signifiers of the twentieth century: pater, patria, . . . and phallus? For the phrase hidden by ellipses in my earlier quotation of Bronfen raises the sign of the phallus in relation to these discourses of nation, sex, death, and the body: "The beauty of Woman and the beauty of the image both give the illusion of intactness and unity, cover the insupportable signs of lack, deficiency, transiency and promise their spectators the impossible—an obliteration of death's ubiquitous 'castrative' threat to the subject" (64). While Bronfen admonishes readers in a footnote that she means the word "castrative" "in a global, 'non-gendered' sense to indicate an act of depriving of vitality, of cutting up a unity, of severment that curtails power, or loss" (74n.23), it seems impossible to dispute the vitality, unity, and power to which she refers as tropically and constitutively gendered male, which has, beginning with Freud, been symbolized by the phallus.

Thus the phallus in its unity as sign for the order of things stands in opposition to the abject, which, in spite of its link to the body's manifestations and excretions, is not caused simply by "lack of cleanliness or health" but rather by "what disturbs identity, system, order. What does not respect borders, positions, rules. The in-between, the ambiguous" (Kristeva 4). Exposure to this kind of living, feminized abject disturbance threatens the phallus, which (like patriarchy and nation) is predicated upon, stands for, and demands familial, social, linguistic, and political order. And perhaps the most threatening disturbance of all in this regard, as Lee Edelman argues in his meditation upon the sociocultural significance of the men's room, is homosexuality. Edelman traces the "cold war equation of homosexuality with Communist infiltration and subversion" (an equation which also haunts the postcolonial London of *Sammy and Rosie*), arguing that "when homosexuality enters the field of vision . . . it occasions a powerful disruption of that field by virtue of its uncontrollably figuralizing effects; and that disruption of the field of vision is precisely what homosexuality comes to represent: so radical a fracturing of the linguistic and epistemic order that it figures futurity imperiled, it figures history as apocalypse, by gesturing toward the precariousness of familial and national survival; . . . it is seen as enacting the destabilization of borders" (277). In other words, it is not so much the practice of homosexuality that disturbs the social order as what it stands for: a shattered epistemology and muddied, nebulous borders. A central irony of *Sammy and Rosie* is that, for all its arch hints at the unconventional and/or homosexual desires of its characters (including drag, same-sex flirting, etc.), the only sex audiences witness in the film— aside from a couple of kisses between out lesbians—is practiced heterosexually, missionary style. This irony recalls the paradox that the "figuralizing effect" of Ortiz' presence, rather than the substance of her remarks, produced the defensiveness Dershowitz displayed. Far from being irrational or excessively reliant upon pathos, Ortiz' remarks formed an argument based upon logic and proof—in other words, the very empirical argument that Dershowitz himself relies upon in staging his claim for the limited use of torture.

The problem, then, is precisely the unknowability, the uncontainability signified by such threatening presences as the embodied female intellectual or the overt expression of female—sexual, intellectual, emotional, or political—desire. Homosexuality is in this construction intrinsically subversive, "a threat to the interpretive certainty invested in the phallus as the privileged signifier of that identity upon which patriarchal epistemology definitionally depends" (Edelman 274).[20] Rafi glimpses evidence of the mirroring of political by sexual subversion when he reaches London: national subversion made visible in wrecked city streets aflame with people of all shades of color; sexual subversion signified by Rosie's lesbian and cross-dressing friends, and by her nonmonogamy.

Which brings me to the provocative idea that *Sammy and Rosie Get Laid* answers de Lauretis's call to be "Oedipal with a vengeance." In the film, Kureishi neither subverts nor overtly critiques this Oedipal foundation of the patriarchal order and its political spawn (conservatism and extreme nationalism). Rather, he highlights the Oedipal process itself, constructing his family drama upon the points of its most spectacular moments: the ascension of the son into the paternal order; the legitimation of that order through lineage and inheritance; the affirmation and solidification of the incest taboo. Kureishi further complicates this psychosocial drama by locating it within the dynamics of race and nation, such that audiences may reflect upon the Oedipal order as it has been translated into the patriarchal state, put to authoritarian purpose in the twentieth century to cleanse the body politic of its subversive elements.

Let us then examine Rosie's place—or, better perhaps, her refusal to take her place—in this Oedipal drama. For Freud, predictably, "the girl's Oedipus complex is simpler than that of the small bearer of the penis." He explains: "In my experience, it seldom goes beyond the taking of her mother's place and the adopting of a feminine attitude towards her father. Renunciation of the penis is not tolerated by the girl without some attempt at compensation. She slips—along the line of a symbolic equation, one might say—from the penis to a baby. Her Oedipus complex is then gradually given up because this wish is never fulfilled. The two wishes—to possess a penis and a child—remain strongly cathected in the unconscious and help to prepare the female creature for her later sexual role" ("Dissolution" 665). One element of Rafi's manipulation of the Oedipal drama is his attempt to fulfill Rosie's compensatory Oedipal wish for a baby by placing her in the role of his daughter and prescribing that she bear *him* a child through his surrogate, Sammy. In addition to serving Rafi's general need to reestablish a conservative patriarchal order, this scenario also expedites his more specific desire to keep Rosie in her place, that monogamous heterosexual/maternal post for which progress through her own variety of Oedipus conflict should prepare her. In this regard, Rosie's complete disengagement from her own father is relevant, for, rather than moving through the Oedipal phase to a place of healthy identification with the paternal order in the form of the father figure, she dissociates completely from him: "I'd happily die without seeing him again. I changed my name and became myself" (Kureishi 39). She later clarifies this dissociation, stating that, having been beaten by her father, "I've had difficulty in coming to terms with men's minds. Their bodies are all right" (40). This distinction demonstrates Rosie's rejection of the patriarchal order (and patrilineage, given that she has changed her name) while allowing her object-choice to remain male, in a purely sexual identification that confirms her threat to the paternal order as representative of aggressive (transgressive) female desire.

Part of the problem with Rosie's place in the Oedipal triangle she shares with Rafi and Sammy is the slipperiness of the incest taboo within its borders. If the primary developmental purpose of the Oedipus conflict is the instantiation of the incest taboo, then the ambiguity of Rafi's desire for a child borne by Rosie, his overt desire to contain her within a heterosexual maternal universe of his making, is tinged with incestuous desire, a first hint of the abjection of the patriarchal order that, clearly linked in the film with the political abjection of the torturer, ultimately engulfs him. Kureishi highlights this incest anxiety throughout the film:

RAFI: (*Pats her arse as she laughs.*) Rosie, one thing more. What about the sound of little footsteps, eh? Isn't it about time?

ROSIE: (*Having to control herself*) Rafi . . .

RAFI: Eh? I know you're a kind of feminist, but you're not a lesbian too, are you?

ROSIE: I'm thinking about having a child.

RAFI: (*Taking her hand*) It would give me so much happiness.

ROSIE: And that's exactly what I want, Rafi (16).

This exchange parodies a conversation between husband and wife about the prospect of children: the wife confessing her desire to have a child; the husband, taking her hand, professing his happiness at the thought. (To ensure that the point is not lost on the audience, Kureishi pointedly includes Rafi's pat on Rosie's "arse.") The threat of lesbianism to the (reproductive) patriarchal order is foregrounded inasmuch as Rafi's articulation of his otherwise covert anxiety about Rosie's "lesbianism" coincides with his expression of desire that she accept the traditional, heterosexual mantle of motherhood.

Rosie's threat to the incest prohibition is part of her more general disruption of both sexual and national orders, obviated in her refusal to comply with her given roles as wife and mother. Rosie's ambivalence about bearing a child—and her refusal to leave the chaos of the city behind to start her family under a civilized suburban sky that still bears some resemblance to the "unity" and "civilization" of Rafi's England—signifies her disdain for the ordered developmental progression Rafi craves, a disdain that has direct implications in terms of the order and cohesion of the nation. For woman's symbolic function vis-à-vis the nation, especially in sexual and maternal terms, cannot be overstated. On the most basic, physical level, Nira Yuval-Davis points out: "As the biological 'producers' of children/people, women are also, therefore, 'bearers of the collective' within these boundaries" (26). Greater still, however, is their symbolic role in terms of that collective: "A figure of a woman, often a mother, symbolizes in many cultures the spirit of the collectivity" (45). Yuval-Davis describes this process of symbolization as a "burden of representation on women of the collectivity's identity and future destiny" (45), a burden Rafi intends Rosie to bear unquestioningly—and Rosie rejects unequivocally. As the "decay of British civilization" and the decay of sexual "normalcy" confront Rafi more and more concretely throughout the film, he hopes to reestablish his psychic stability by (re)enforcing the normative sex/gender hierarchy and traditionally sanctified familial structure he associates with the "bosom of civilization" (London) and "mother country" (England).[21]

The volatility of Sammy's and Rafi's responses to Rosie demonstrate how readily idyllic constructions of the heterosexual-maternal feminine turn rancid when historic women refuse these roles. That is, the construction of the feminine as hidden, dangerous, dirty, and transgressive lies just beneath the surface of the image of the selfless maternal culture-bearer, the symbol of pure womanhood for whose protection a nation's men must fight to retain order. Not surprisingly, then, Rafi's venerating descriptions of Rosie as "favorite daughter-in-law" and "decent woman" are recast as the venomous "damn dyke" as Rosie alternately plays along with or challenges Rafi's place and his politics. In this regard, Rosie represents the threat posed by women who refuse to follow order, to stay in their places, and who thereby signify both familial and national disintegration.

I must stress that in spite of the subversive signification of Rosie's positioning outside the Oedipal contract, the film's argument about the relationship between narratives of sexual order and narratives of political order—about the gendering of torture—is complicated by the simple truth that Rosie does not, in fact, engage in lesbian sexual practices. All representations of her lesbianism— her association with lesbians, her flirtation with a drag queen, her obvious joy in the pleasures of nonmonogamous sex, and, not least, her Marxist-Feminist politics—quite simply remain unpursued hints, created by the machinery of Rafi's mind, a point Kureishi ironically underscores by rendering Rosie's only (hetero)sexual encounter in straight, domesticated, missionary style. Her radical politics are similarly domesticated by her refusal to act upon her growing knowledge of Rafi's atrocities, as well as by the unabashed racial, sexual, and class tourism characterizing her affair with the Afro-British squatter Danny. Rather than any actual practice, it is the defiant unintelligibility, the flagrant transgression of the patriarchal epistemology and order of signification, that most threatens Rafi. Perhaps the greatest symbol of this unintelligibility is Rosie's only response to Rafi's worried interrogation of her sexuality during their exchange about childbearing: a wry smile that in its cryptic Mona-Lisa detachment, held by the camera in tight headshot for a painfully long interval, frustrates and deflects his every attempt to know her.

SEXUALITY AND THE SIGN: UP FOR GRABS

Upon his arrival in London, Rafi is transported by a Pakistani cabdriver, who turns out to be the representative ghost of Rafi's Pakistani torture victims, to Sammy and Rosie's apartment in a neighborhood which has just erupted in revolt against the wrongful shooting of a black West Indian woman by white police. The streets are aflame, packed with rioters and looters; Rafi is "rescued" by Rosie, who takes him upstairs. Rafi's hope that this domestic space will be "safe" (ordered, civilized) is dashed, however, when he enters the room and finds several of Rosie's friends, lesbians, demonstrating the use of a condom on a large carrot, the tip of which they subsequently bite off in a droll literalization of male castration anxiety. Rafi's anxiety turns to visible horror as two of the women (Rani, a Pakistani woman, and Vivia, a black Londoner) exchange a series of erotic kisses.

Beginning with this scene, the film stages a struggle over meaning of the phallus, which culminates in Rafi's abjectification and suicide—an event that might also be read allegorically as a form of Oedipal patricide. For these women call into question what Cathy Griggers refers to as the "natural link between the cultural power organized under the sign of the phallus and the penis as biological power" (181), not only by irreverently representing the penis in this bit of performative display with a "knobbly carrot" (Kureishi 7), but also by debating the organ's relative attractiveness and utility as compared with said carrot.[22]

Later, during an argument with Rosie about the authorization of torture in his postcolonial government, Rafi bites into a breadstick only to find a fingernail embedded there. The image of the breadstick, mimicking the phallic carrot presented earlier, is conjured here as evidence of the phallic underwriting of torture's practice of power. The contamination of Rafi's body with this abject signifier of torture, his horror as he plucks the fingernail from his mouth, indicate the dual processes of bodily and psychic abjectification which, signifying both the consequences of his abuses of others as well as the instability of the phallic sign (and thereby the phallic order), afflict Rafi with increasing intensity as the movie progresses. At a later party scene, in a further invocation of the abjectified phallic image conjured by the carrot and breadstick, Rosie and her lover Danny lick one another's outstretched fingers in a brazen display of extramarital sensuality. These free-floating phallic signifiers haunt the film, revealing Rafi's increasing anxiety in the face of their instability and their undeniable implication in terms of his practice of torture.

This interrogation of the sign of the phallus—which, in order to retain its cultural power must not be linked with anything so tangible or fallible as its materialization in the penis—represents a challenge to the patriarchal orders of both family and nation such that Rafi finds himself unable to control the process of signification, not only within Britain, but also of Britain itself as signifier of civilization, progress, the "bosom." This phallic uncertainty signifies the disequilibrium of his own place in Britain as what Homi Bhabha would describe as the "mimic man," a colonial figure who "problematizes the signs of racial and cultural purity, so that the 'national' is no longer naturalizable" (Kureishi 87). Displacing his own internalized racism, Rafi interprets the threat to the "natural" construction of England as nation in terms of the threat to patriarchal order posed by such phenomena as lesbian erotics occurring within the conjugal domestic space of Sammy and Rosie's London apartment. As such, he objects more to the indeterminacy of Rosie's sexual identity, and that of her lover Danny, than to anything he knows about their actual sexual practices.

Perhaps the film's most effective representation of epistemological disorder symbolized by signification gone mad—or as McCabe would have it, loss of control of meaning, especially as connected with the father's loss of control of female desire—is the image of Danny/Victoria's trailer in the squatter community, to which he and Rosie retire for their night of passion. This trailer is covered with graffiti, a graffiti that constitutes, like much else in the film's landscape, an ironic contradiction. For this is not the riotous, colorful scrawl of traditional urban graffiti art, but a measured, even printing in neat block letters of T. S. Eliot's masterpiece, "The Wasteland."[23] Kureishi's inclusion of this monument to high modernist mastery of language and form is symbolically important not simply for its content, imaging London as wasted urban wilderness, but also for the fragmentation of that monument in its representation here; in other words, the utter loss of control of meaning of the linguistic sign, offered to viewers precisely at the moment when the daughter-figure, Rosie, indulges her desire for her extramarital lover. For the words are visible to us only in pieces: as the interior of the trailer rocks to Rosie and Danny/Victoria's lovemaking, the exterior rocks to the Ghetto Lite Band's performance of Smokey Robinson's "My Girl," the possessive thrust of the song emphasizing the relocation of the female body out of the paternal order into the transgressive domain of desire. The bodies of these ragtag black musicians, emblematic of the vibrant, anarchic youth whom Kureishi celebrates throughout the film, dance in front of the words, hiding and then exposing them in bits and pieces and, in their movement, making the letters almost seem to come alive, dancing themselves. The combination of (young, black, poor, artistic, anarchistic) bodies dancing in front of—and thereby literally splitting apart, at least from the audiences' perspective—the words of perhaps the quintessential modernist poem, in this moment of illicit interracial sex, on the Marxist underbelly of civilized, capitalist Thatcherite London, jubilantly symbolizes the fate of such foundational signs as pater, patria and phallus in general, and of paternal control of female desire in particular.

This juxtaposition of upper-crust London with the chaos of rioters and derelict city streets also dramatizes the consequences of the reversal of migrancy after the collapse of empire, a reversal that allowed a flood of colonial immigrants into the nation in what John Clement Ball calls "a reinvasion of the centre" (17). This (re)invasion causes Rafi's great dismay as he no longer encounters the civility and freedom of an enlightened England, confronting instead a London that is violent doppelganger to the revolutionary Pakistan he was forced to flee. Indeed, these London streets conjure ever more vividly for Rafi that now-global chaos and violence as he realizes that there is no place outside of it and, further, that he has helped create it. Indeed, this return—made possible only by the postcolonial nationalism Rafi espoused in fighting "200 years of imperialism" (Kureishi 29)—is also the surfacing of Rafi's sense of marginalization within the national narrative of Britishness. In this reading, his torture victims bear the brunt of his racial and national ambivalence. Kureishi's critique, then, addresses both the tragedy of Rafi's desire for the mythological Britishness and the consequences of his violent imposition of this myth of unity and wholeness upon a nation bursting at the seams of its own difference.

WHOSE FILM IS IT, ANYWAY?

In her review of *Sammy and Rosie Get Laid*, bell hooks asserts: "When I left the film, tightly clutching my ticket stub, I felt wound up, tight inside, disturbed. I noticed that the ticket simply said 'Rosie.' And I thought it was finally Rosie's film." Although the film's rifle-quick intercutting of scenes exceeds the conventional classic Hollywood plot splitting characteristic of the counterhistorical dramatic film, bell hooks asserts the same basic claim in her reading of *Sammy and Rosie Get Laid* that I have made with regard to that genre; namely, that the filmmakers put the black characters (especially, in this case, black women) to narrative use as "donors," fodder, or in hooks's words, "backdrop" to the white and South Asian characters. Hooks argues: "In *Sammy and Rosie Get Laid* and other contemporary films by white directors that focus on black characters or people of color in general, the experiences of the oppressed black people, specifically dark-skinned black people are appropriated as colorful exciting backdrop, included in a way that stimulates interest, . . . yet often their reality is submerged, obscured, deflected away from, so that we will focus our attention even more intensely on the characters whose reality really matters" (158–159). Hooks is in one way correct in her assertion, especially with regard to the black woman whose death opens the film, upon which the entirety of its plot rests.[24] For while this woman's murder (based upon the real-life accidental shooting by police of a woman named Cherry Croce) is ground and cause for the film's riots, as well as for the meeting of two of the central characters, Danny and Rosie, neither her life nor her death, and certainly not the agony she experiences as she is shot at point-blank range, are explored in any detail by Kureishi/Frears.[25] The question is, is this film meant to be Croce's story in the same way that, for instance, *Salvador* is the Salvadoran people's, *Cry Freedom* is Steven Biko's and apartheid-era blacks' in South Africa, or *Beyond Rangoon* is Burmese pro-democracy protesters'?

If Kureishi and Frears might rightly be taken to task for using the pain and death, indeed the body, of this black woman as the ground upon which to build a largely unrelated plot, hooks's assertion about the use as backdrop of women of color, such as Rosie's friends Vivia and Rani, does not begin to account for the complexity with which Kureishi renders these characters to highlight and challenge the very ways in which women, people of color, and especially lesbians are read through their "figuralizing effects" as threatening, and as object of torture's repressive desire: transgressive, hidden, dangerous, and dirty. In short, subversive. Kureishi's inclusion and representation of these women, far from being an act of appropriation wherein "two men (one brown, one white) create yet another patriarchal text, where a woman, in this case a white woman, and all the brown and black people who act as colorful backdrop, are powerless stars" (hooks 163), is precisely the dramatization of the figuralizing effects of such women and people of color, and the consequences of such effects within the patriarchal context. This dramatization calls into question the Oedipally based patriarchal system, as audiences witness its collapse under the weight of its own inconsistencies and as its representative, Rafi, becomes increasingly aware that his desperate endeavor to prove the abjection of others only, in the end, proves his own. Thus, rather than being Rosie's story, as hooks claims, the story of this film is most emphatically Rafi's, and the other people populating the film are put to narrative purpose not to aid attention and suspense regarding this main character, but to confront the complex sociopolitical and ideological network that informs his career as torturer, as well as his demise. In the process, the film makes an argument about the dependence of torture as system and practice upon intransigent constructions of gender and sexuality.

Rafi's increasing abjectification over the course of the movie, which ends in his suicide by hanging, is represented to audiences as a series of wounds accumulated in time to the crescendo of magic realist-style appearances by the ghostly figure of a victim of torture ordered by Rafi. Most often, the visibility of

lesbian women triggers the appearance of the ghost, as Rafi interprets lesbianism as a sexual parallel to the political disorder and anarchy he experiences in
both the riotous urban London where Sammy and Rosie live and the riotous
Pakistan of union organizers and political reformists which he has just fled. As
each of these threatening factors—the decay and indeterminacy of British civilization and the decay and indeterminacy of sexual normalcy—confront Rafi
more concretely, the memories of the Pakistani victims of his torture become
proportionately more vivid and haunting. Indeed, one might say that Rafi is
equally haunted by the women around him, whose sexuality he is increasingly
unable to contain. To trace the timing and nature of the ghost's appearances,
which most often coincide with conflict over women's sexuality, is to construct
a map of Rafi's route to abjection, a map in which all paths lead to the intolerable figure of woman subversive who shatters the unity and coherence of the
loose brew of postcolonial and enlightenment philosophies that have
informed Rafi's personal life and politics.

The ghost's early appearances are subtle and almost undisturbing. Introduced to him as the benign cabbie who drives Rafi from the airport, audiences
next meet the ghost after the restaurant scene staging Rosie's confrontation of
Rafi regarding his human rights abuses. Significantly, the subject of torture is
linked with lesbian sexuality when the drag queen flirts with Rosie, who calls
her a "star." At this, Rafi tells Rosie, "Now you're acting like a damn dyke!" The
word "dyke," used as an epithet by Rafi, acts as a prompt: Rosie immediately
switches the direction of the confrontation to the subject of torture: "When
you were in the government, people—opposition people—were murdered and
tortured. . . . Didn't they have to drink the urine of their gaolers?" (Kureishi
27–28). Rafi's self-justification takes the form of anti-imperialist nationalism,
which implicates Rosie (an upper-middle-class British woman) as complicit in
the events framing the abuses she accuses him of, but which also reveals the
inconsistency in his adulation of Britishness: "Our government awoke the
down-trodden and expelled Western imperialists. . . . The man who sacrifices
the others to benefit the whole is in a terrible position. But he is essential! . . .
I come from a land ground into dust by 200 years of imperialism. We are still
dominated by the West and you reproach us for using the methods that you
taught us" (28–29).

As the ghost's appearances become increasingly threatening to Rafi, Rafi
becomes more wounded, delirious, hysterical, abjected. He is next haunted
upon returning home to find that Rani and Vivia have appropriated the space

reserved for conjugal domesticity: Sammy and Rosie's marital bed. In the first real indication of Rafi's abjectification, he becomes hysterical in the manner traditionally attributed to women, screaming, slamming things around, and cursing in his native tongue: "What are you doing, you perverted half-sexed lesbians cursed by God?" (Kureishi 46). This reversion to (subtitled) Punjabi at the moment of overt threat from the lesbian women signifies his loss of control of language (at yet another moment of loss of control of female desire), a slip of his hold upon the myth of (English) nationness to which he has clung since arriving in Britain. Rani responds in equally hysterical form, also in Punjabi, using language mimicking that of the torturer in a rant of sexualized threats to—What else?—the penis: "Come here and let me bite your balls off with my teeth and swallow them! I'll rip off your prick with a tin opener! . . . That pigshit bastard, I'll crush his testicles right now! . . . Let me get at that withered sperm-factory with this [large phallic-looking weapon] and put the world out of its misery!" (46). The threat to the phallus/penis that has haunted Rafi from the moment he entered the space of this flat has materialized, just as he always knew it would, in the form of this "God-accursed" lesbian woman. In a reversal of roles that leaves Rafi terrified victim rather than omnipotent torturer, he climbs out the window and slides down the drainpipe, landing with an injured arm in a heap on the street, the first physical sign of his abjection, as the ghost looks on.

The symbols of sexual subversion and of the threatening heterogeneity of the city that confront Rafi in this scene dramatize the extent to which he finds himself—along with all the normalizing codes and symbols which define his world—out of place. Having appropriated the power of the phallic weapon to threaten Rafi with precisely the sort of torture he used to repress such subversives, Rani, the Pakistani lesbian, is in a sense a ghost, inspiring in Rafi the same terror as does the film's real ghost. Rafi has already articulated that, in an attempt to combat the kind of "decadence" characterizing the West: "I shut all the nightclubs and casinos. The women have gone back in their places. There is restriction. There is order" (Kureishi 42). Believing that he has successfully put Pakistani women "back in their places," he now finds himself haunted by just such a woman, an escapee who not only refuses to remain invisible, in her place, but also torments him by violently flaunting her grotesque, subversive sexuality and politics. It is Rani who digs up the facts on Rafi, including the explicit testimony of his torture victims. It might be argued that Rani, not Rosie, disrupts the Oedipal contract between Sammy and Rafi.

Kureishi highlights the threat of the grotesque inherent in the female body—especially the sexualized, lesbian female body—in terms similar to those delineated by Stallybrass and White, dressing Rani and Vivia in short nightshirts that, during this confrontation with Rafi, barely cover their genitalia, leaving them menacingly close to exposure as the women move about. As Rani and Vivia run downstairs, the other forces of subversion converge *tout court* on Rafi: the lesbian couple who have formed a nuclear family structure complete with the baby Rafi wishes Rosie would bear; Rosie, who arrives on the back of her black anarchist boyfriend's motorcycle after a night of extramarital passion; even the police, guardians of civility and order, who look on and do nothing while Rafi is threatened by this pack of subversives, throwing into cold relief for Rafi the extent to which there is no place for him in this new world order. As he limps off, Rafi finds himself lost in the London tube, inadvertently caught among a group of Jewish boys being "harangued by a group of young men. They yell: 'Yiddo, yiddo, yiddo!' at the kids, and Rafi is confused and lost" (Kureishi 47). In another reversal of power and demonstration of abjection, Rafi falls in with the relatively weak Jewish boys persecuted by the conservative forces of hatred of the other. Rather than being associated with the Thatcherite forces of governance, progress, and civility, Rafi is increasingly abjected, marked by association as a subversive element in need of repression—or purging.

The process of abjectification and emasculation takes increasingly corporeal form as Rafi makes his way to Danny's trailer in the squatter community for tea. The bandage on his wounded hand has unraveled, and he is soaked by rain. Kureishi's script directions indicate: "Rafi stops under a railway bridge where other wretched rejects are sheltering—the poor, the senile, the insane, the disabled" (Kureishi 50)—in short, the abject. Tripping on the outstretched foot of one of these homeless men, he falls among them, watched by the ghost who follows him constantly now, and who carries a weapon resembling the one wielded by Rani. His foot injured, Rafi takes off his shoe and continues, hobbling through the rain to Danny's squat, where he asks for a cup of tea. The ghost appears, framed in the window outside the trailer, refusing to leave, haunting Rafi as a symbol of degraded Britishness in this mockery of the ritual of afternoon tea. He is also symbol of Rafi's own defilement by his practice of torture; indeed, Rafi has begun to take on the appearance of this most abject ghost of his torture victims, who wears a ratty suit and soiled bandage. Rafi, almost unable to walk, his suit filthy from his slog through the mud and rain and an equally dirty, disheveled bandage covering his wounds, is finally the mirror image of his victim—and of the racialized self emasculated within that narrative of Britishness.

At this point, the film stages the ghost's last appearance, his only confrontation with Rafi and the film's only direct representation of torture. It is the middle of the night and Rafi, unable to sleep, soaks his wounded feet. As the camera moves in for a close-up, the water in the bowl turns bloody, with bits of bone and hair floating in it. The union with his victims' fragmented bodies begun with the fingernail embedded in the breadstick ends here, as Rafi's own wounded body is literally coated with the abject remains of those he tortured. The ghost appears and accuses Rafi: "You said to Rosie that I was the price to be paid for the overall good of our sad country, yes? . . . How could that be possible?" (53). This moment of confrontation of torturer by tortured, the moment when the ghost takes the rubber mask wired for electrical shock treatments from his own crushed skull and places it over Rafi's temples, is more than a symbol of Rafi's failure to repress his tortured conscience, more than a simple act of vengeance on the part of his victim. It demonstrates the utter abjectification of the torturer by his own role in "desecrating" all human life (Kureishi 53).

This transference of the torture apparatus from victim to torturer enacts a different kind of transference for Rafi. When he awakes in the squatter community as it is bulldozed by government-supported property developers, his identification has shifted away from the conservative forces of national order (patria) toward these subversive others, having finally become one himself. He is delirious, wounded, stumbling, crying: "We must not allow these fascist bastards to drive us away! We must fight, fight!" (Kureishi 56). All traces of coherence in his politics, his beliefs, his understanding of himself have been obliterated. When he returns once again to Sammy and Rosie's apartment and finds all the film's women around the kitchen table, discussing the neighborhood riots and the recent eviction of squatters, he is finally unable to deny or repress the extent of his homelessness, his placelessness in the chaotic urban world that he in fact helped create. Specifically, the absence of men and overwhelming presence of women in this domestic space dramatizes the failure of the Oedipal contract to establish a paternal order in which son would succeed father into a realm of ordered heteronormativity. If these women have fully appropriated the sexual/familial realm of the private sphere, they have likewise co-opted the national/political spheres in their discussion—across all manner of racial, sexual, class, and political differ-ences—of the problematics of place in the postcolonial world. Indeed, Rafi's decisive act of suicide occurs directly after Rosie, referring to the squatters with whom Rafi in the end has become identified, argues that "they have no given place in this society!" (57), a statement that hovers in the air, referent no longer clear, perhaps a description of Rafi, the failed mimic man, himself.

Rafi's devastating realization of placelessness is accompanied by his fur-ther understanding that there is finally no way to repress or turn away from the abjection against which he has so zealously struggled. Ultimately, he is that subject described by Kristeva who, "weary of fruitless attempts to iden-tify with something on the outside, finds the impossible within; when it finds that the impossible constitutes its very *being*, that it *is* nothing other than abject" (5, emphasis in original). And so, as if finally giving way to that con-stitutive abjection, Rafi hangs himself. Even this final act is constructed ambivalently by Kureishi as the result of Rafi's loss of control in (either or both) the realms of politics or gender. While it might be argued that he takes his life because he cannot bear the weight of his conscience (signified by his literal torture by the ghost of his victims), a strong argument may also be made that it is his witness of the triumph of this heterogeneous band of women speaking to each other across their differences—and, thereby, refus-ing his containment of them within the Oedipally based technologies of gen-der and sexuality informing the system of torture—that causes his despair.

Complicities: The Case of Lynndie England

One of the most difficult problems facing theorists of gender, sexual differ-ence, and human rights is the spectacle of young women engaged in the tor-ture of detainees at Abu Ghraib prison in Iraq. The confirmation of the worst fears of those concerned with human rights protections in the images of tor-ture released from Abu Ghraib provoked grief and horror in its own right; however, the participation of Specialist Sabrina Harmon, Specialist Megan Ambuhl, and Specialist Lynndie England, often pictured with wide grins and thumbs-up gestures, became the full stop punctuating expressions of disgust in public debate. The image and backstory of Lynndie England complicate her reception in public discourse and reveal the same hysterical trigger for patriarchal repression as the figures discussed earlier in this chapter. While the acknowledgment that women are capable of torturing is worthy of its own discussion, the case of Lynndie England is important for thinking about the gendering of torture and about the contours of a reinvigorated twenty-first-century feminism.

The intrusion of Sister Dianna Ortiz into the public sphere triggered an irrational desire to repress because her presence punctured a predominantly abstract, rationalist space by calling attention to the body and to the role of the affective or sacral in addressing the subject of torture. In Kureishi's and Frears's *Sammy and Rosie Get Laid*, anxiety produced by Rosie's unknowability in both public and private spheres constructs a parallel between her symbolization of the unruly woman and the problem of unruly nations—or, perhaps better, of unruly minority citizens within the hierarchy of established and developing nation-states. In other words, a parallel between sexual and political subversions. Kureishi's genius is to illuminate the threat of this parallel from the perspective of the torturer, and to demonstrate the extent to which the subversion the torturer seeks to repress or disavow is actually located within his own political project. While Lynndie England similarly became an ambiguous, unreadable sign in public discourse about torture and the war on terror, she also reveals to us the ugly underside of the entry of women into the public sphere without accommodation on the part of that public sphere for their presence. The abjection that has been attributed to England as scapegoat located outside the bounds of gender norms and good taste is actually the abjection that "constitutes the very being" (Kristeva) of a public sphere and U.S. culture in which, as Sharon Patricia Holland has persuasively argued, patriarchy has remained essentially unmoved.

While feminist action successfully opened access to the public sphere to women in even such male-dominated arenas as the military, the patriarchal-capitalist public sphere in the West has arguably swallowed the select few women it allows in without recognizing or manifesting traces of their potential divergence from patriarchal norms. Melani McAlister's examination of this phenomenon with regard to dominant responses to multiculturalism in the 1990s provides a relevant parallel. Tracing the emergence of conservative attacks on academic multiculturalism at the onset of the 1991 Gulf War, McAlister argued that "some observers on the Left suggested that a commitment to simplistic nationalism and racism underlay the near-simultaneous launch of the Gulf War and the attack on political correctness. But these critics missed a far more important connection. The concerns of multiculturalism were not, in fact, ignored or undone by the discourse on the Gulf War. They were incorporated by it" (250). McAlister points out that the military's representation of itself in the post-Vietnam era as an organization that embraced cultural and racial difference was part of a larger reaction against proponents of multicultural change in curricula and hiring practices. This campaign constructed the multicultural agenda as unnecessary agitation by downplaying its goal of inclusion as a harmonic fait accompli, at least in the emblematic nationalist context of the military.

Of course, the imagery and narrative circulated by the military of its embrace of diversity ran counter to critiques that identified the military as "a dangerous part of a state apparatus that disproportionately took the lives of people of color and the poor" (McAlister 238–239). This perspective on diversity is echoed in arguments that identify the acceptance by corporations of multiculturalist goals of employment and access to markets by members of minority groups, not for any substantive reasons having to do with equality of opportunity and recognition of diversity, but for the base capitalist needs of supply (of consumers) and demand (for labor).[26] In the contemporary moment, the second Bush administration's willingness to name women and minorities to high-level positions substantiates claims of color-blindness and commitment to a public sphere that reflects a democratic meritocracy rather than an exclusionary or homogeneous state apparatus. In the aftermath of the debates over multiculturalism, the production of such racial or gendered figureheads is a fruitful area for research, particularly into their role in the excessive reproduction of the dominant ethos of the state. Consider the meteoric progress narratives of Secretary of State Condoleezza Rice and Attorney General Alberto Gonzalez, for instance, both of whom ground their success stories in accounts of their marginal racial/ethnic and economic backgrounds and both of whom have exceeded the norms of conservatism in this country in their implementation of George W. Bush's program of constitutional limits, consolidation of power in the executive branch, and destruction of international protocols governing conduct in war and/or times of emergency. Clearly—and contrary to the hopes of many on the Left—membership in historically marginalized groups does not automatically produce more humane ideology or practice when individuals gain power in the public sphere.

In spite of the slow rise of numbers of women in the military to a high of 13 percent in 2006, the military remains a foundationally gender-biased institution. Recall, for instance, the struggle undergone by Shannon Faulkner and those who came after her in her attempt to penetrate the walls of the Citadel, South Carolina's elite military college.[27] In light of rampant allegations and prosecutions for sexual harassment and rape of women in all branches of the armed services, we might further characterize that male-dominated institution as violent in nature.[28] The official silencing perpetuated through the "Don't ask, don't tell" policy of sexual identity contributes to the recipe that produces a culture of misogyny, homophobia, and violence within the military.[29] Now imagine that roiling mix directed outward at the others produced as targets for war, particularly in the pressurized context of the war on terror and the theaters of battle in Iraq. As a matter of public record, it is clear that the pressure is immense to produce "actionable intelligence" in detention centers such as Abu Ghraib in Iraq, Guantánamo in Cuba, and Baghram Air Base in Afghanistan. In addition to sexual and class politics, racial and religious difference play a role in the ways in which prisoners are handled and abused, as we have seen in the many techniques that capitalized on such differences: white European and U.S. men and women forcing Arabic and Muslim men and women to violate their cultural, religious, and moral conventions as part of "softening up" or "fearing up" prisoners for interrogation.[30]

How then can we begin to analyze the role played by Lynndie England, let alone our own highly mediated responses to her? Two general trajectories present themselves: first, the range of anxieties triggered by England's ambiguous signification; and second, England as an object lesson for progressive feminist theory and practice in the realm of human rights.[31]

It seems to me that of the three women convicted of abuse in the Abu Ghraib incident, Lynndie England quickly became the most notorious, the most representative of the scandalous mix of sex, violence, and obscenity that came to define Abu Ghraib prison. Why? Although more images with relatively more shocking content depicted England than either Ambuhl or Harmon, might there not also be something unsettling—indeed, something uncanny— about England's figure, something that the photos both capture and cannot quite account for? Something in excess of her womanhood?

In perhaps the most infamous photo of England, she holds a leash at the other end of which lies a bound, naked man, presumably an Iraqi prisoner. The image is shocking for the degradation it depicts of both torturer and tortured, literally signaling the bestial nature of the entire project of "fearing" or "softening" up prisoners before interrogation. It also shocks because of the androgyny of the person holding the leash. In this pose in particular, England's gender is difficult to read: her boyish haircut, features, and attire seem to contradict the clear outline of her breasts through her military T-shirt. Much of the

Specialist Lynndie England, Abu Ghraib Prison, Iraq, 2003.
AP/World Wide Photos

discourse surrounding images of Sabrina Harmon focuses upon her "pretti-ness," and she is often likened to a cheerleader—partly, to be sure, because of the thumbs-up, smiling pose she adopts near the corpse of a prisoner, but partly because she fits that category of woman in western culture. England, on the other hand, does not fit a mainstream, easily readable category of woman. Instead, she is the image of unreadability: transgendered? butch? boy?

Anecdotally speaking, I have heard England referenced more than once as "that thing"—an expression of disgust at her agency in such dehumanization in the context of an inherently immoral, dehumanizing war, but also an expression of disgust at not being able to place her as a woman. England's gender ambiguity is further complicated when readers came to know that she was four months pregnant at the time the photo was taken. How to assimilate the jumbled signals given by the photo and the story of its referent? England's gender ambiguity stymies the desire to read her as a woman gone wrong by exposure to a brutally corrupted environment—the standard reading of Harmon and Ambuhl. The knowledge that her body was busy creating life stymies the desire to dismiss her as pure monster.[32]

England provides another lens through which we can consider the relation-ship between gender and subversion, between torture and the epistemological inscrutability of the female. In the only major feminist statement that has been published on the issue, Barbara Ehrenreich asserts that the images of England, Harmon, and Ambuhl "broke [her] heart," revealing as they did that "a uterus is not a substitute for a conscience." While I share Ehrenreich's grief at the image, I confess that I do not share her sense of loss at this irrefutable proof that "women can do the unthinkable" (69). Ehrenreich's argument spins on the point of an assumption about the moral superiority of women, and fails to account for the years of feminist writing about the separation of sex and gender, and the idea of gender as performance. Should women ever gain real, proportional access to the echelons of power in this country, one continues to hope, we would begin to see "a lesser inclination toward cruelty and violence" (Ehrenreich 68), in other words, a public sphere transformed in some vaguely proportional sense into the image of those it comprises. In the meantime, however, taking stock of the analytical perspective provided by the separation of gender from sex means that we can continue to identify the gendered nature of social practices, behaviors, and spaces that do not attach themselves to biological sex in predictable ways—particularly when power differentials, or the desire for power, are acknowledged. In this reading—which brings me to my second point of focus, on what we might learn from Lynndie England about how to be progressive feminists in the twenty-first century—the emphasis is upon the performance of gender norms in relation to the distribution of power in particular spaces (in this case, the hyperperformative space of the military prison), not the sex of perpetrators or victims.

Many readings of the scenes of sexual torture at Abu Ghraib refer to the torture specifically as a technique of "sexual humiliation," a humiliation effective in "softening up" prisoners for interrogation because of sexual norms and mores in Islamic culture. The "humiliation" refers both to degrading men in relation to other men—nudity, lack of privacy, and forced sex acts, both simulated and real—and to using women as interrogators to try to humiliate men. Ideas about sexual humiliation as torture in the context of Arab men had their source in *The Arab Mind* (1976), written by anthropologist Ronald Patai and adopted as "the bible of the neocons on Arab behavior" (qtd. in Hersch). Such readings locate the offenses in the realm of culture, failing to recognize the operation of transnational gender norms related to power in the scene of torture. To what extent do such gender norms inform these scenes, and to what extent does the manipulation and performance of such norms reinforce the necessary separation of sex from gender in order to read them? In spite of what seems to be a reliance upon an essentialist female identity in which gender and sex coincide, tactics of female interrogators such as smearing a simulacrum of menstrual blood on male prisoners, or inducing unwanted arousal in the prisoners by stripping down to bra and thong underwear and rubbing against them, allowed these women to occupy the masculine gender position in the context of the interrogation, relegating the feminine position to the prisoners. This reading counters the dominant anxiety in western media about the denigration of western womanhood as the most egregious degradation occasioned by those scenes. Similarly, it should not be surprising to progressive feminists in the postmodern moment that a pregnant woman could occupy the position of the masculine in torturing feminized prisoners, particularly in the context of an institution demonstrably infused with intractable gender norms accruing to positions of relative power. As Joanna Bourke has argued: "In these photographs, England trumps male power, not only in the sense that she claims omnipotence in relation to the male prisoners, but also because she has no need to use the penis to do so" (44). Bourke asserts that "England's cruel triumph resides in the fact that she tortures without consciousness of that vulnerability" of the penis as weapon by which its power is contested by its inherent vulnerability to pain.

In her momentary occupation of the position of absolute power that is the torturer's, Lynndie England reminds us of the unfinished business of patriarchy and can teach us about the troubled relationship between the goal of access embraced by liberal feminism and the goal of radical change too easily abandoned in the wake of the victory of widened access to the public sphere for some women. As Melani McAlister argued with regard to what she calls "military multiculturalism," liberal feminist discourse is also too easily co-opted and put to use in the program of the dominant patriarchal regime. The liberation of Afghani women from the Taliban as a belated justification for the invasion of Afghanistan is a particularly egregious case; the placement of select women in high-level positions that safeguard the status quo is another.[33] As Sharon Patricia Holland reminds us: "Patriarchy has managed to escape our critique, to mask itself, and to survive" (147). It is the patriarchal will to power and dominance that we see performed by the ambiguous Lynndie England in Abu Ghraib prison, in part the consequence of our complacence regarding the perpetuation of a capitalist patriarchy all too happy to engage women as either producers or consumers of a vast, murderous status quo. It is also the feminine and the masculine continuing to "comply with . . . singular norm[s], the norm[s] devised for [them] by phallogocentric means," to borrow from Judith Butler, that we witness in these scenes (*Undoing Gender* 196–197). One goal feminism and human rights can set together, then, is to interrupt the reproduction and repetition of that one brutal strain of possibility for lived, performed, and represented gender identities.

Our complicity with torture is not simply the obvious one related to our (willing or unwilling) participation in an unjust war whose architects have chosen to use torture as a tool, but also involves our unavoidable complicity with intractable gender norms that, if anything, have become more entrenched in the backlash against second-wave feminism. Like Kureishi's imagined torturer, Rafi, if we look closely we find that the abjection we identify and repudiate in the female torturer cannot be isolated in her figure. Lynndie England cannot be disavowed; rather, we must examine the politics of class, race, nation, gender, and sexuality that produced her. And then, as Ehrenreich rightly points out, "we need . . . a tough new kind of feminism with no illusions. Women do not change institutions simply by assimilating into them, only by consciously deciding to fight for change" (70). Without succumbing to what Wendy Brown has termed "Left melancholy," it does seem clear that radicalism, at least in the feminist sense, has been on the decline since the Clinton years. While antiglobalization and anticapitalist movements are heating up, feminism has cooled and been co-opted, much to our collective loss, and violent patriarchy remains. Human rights activists need to identify and fight not only crimes committed at the scene of torture, but also the banal, unyielding gender norms that are intimately bound up with the staging and production of torture, and, indeed, with the conditions that make it imaginable, representable, and debatable.

4

RAPE

THE DIVISION OF SPHERES

One of the greatest challenges for theorists of gender and human rights in the twenty-first century is to make legal, cultural, and political sense of the crime of rape in its various forms and contexts. The struggle over whether and how to define rape as individual (private) crime or mass (public) breach of human rights continues to vex international legal and human rights actors, as does the effort to alleviate the weight of gender norms in interpreting and addressing the act of rape. Cultural representations of rape carry particularly heavy burdens in this regard, as Tanya Horeck has argued: "How can rape, generally thought of as the most personal and private of crimes, be considered a public event? Yet . . . cultural images of rape serve as a means of forging social bonds, and of mapping out public space. It is a crime that has a pervasive effect on the life of the community and the workings of the body politic. And it is a crime that dominates public fantasies regarding sexual and social difference" (4). In addition to the publicity of rape in particular historical contexts, rape has also increasingly been defined as a public event within a shifting body of international law addressing its perpetration as war crime and crime against humanity.[1]

This aspect of public rape lends an even deeper urgency to Horeck's complex questions about the relationship between gender and rape: "What happens to the feminist account of rape as the paradigmatic experience of women under patriarchy when the possibility of male rape is factored into the equation? When feminists have discussed male-on-male rape, they have tended to cast the male body as a substitute for the woman's; . . . if men are raped, they are raped as women" (50). This construction resonates with that of theorists such as Diana Taylor who have discussed the feminization of the torture victim and the hypermasculinity of the torturer, or Kate Millett, who asks in *The Literature of Cruelty* whether, given the power positions that mark the scene of torture, all victims of torture are gendered female. Such inquiries must be pushed even further in the wake of the indictment of a woman, former Rwandan minister of family and women's development Pauline Nyiramasuhuko, on the charge of "genocidal rape" in the Rwanda Tribunal in Arusha, Tanzania, in 1999. Nyiramasuhuko is accused of inciting Hutu men to rape Tutsi women, a scenario that renders ethnicity as important as gender for analyzing the implications of her indictment. It also forces a rethinking of the basic understandings of gender and sexual difference in relation to rape, in much the same way that the case of Lynndie England forces a rethinking of gender and sexual difference in relation to torture. That rethinking, however, must focus upon the destabilization of gender norms related to power and agency as they inform motivations for and perpetration of rape, rather than upon a shift in broad understanding of who typically rapes whom. In other words, in spite of my desire to push for complex analyses of rape and its representation that could capture the realities of changing global contexts, I am deeply uneasy that the indictment of a woman on the charge of rape could decenter our critique of rape as a crime overwhelmingly perpetrated by men against women.

In my own work, I identify the persistence of gender norms in the perpetration of rape and its representation, while I seek models that disrupt these norms to enable more complex analyses of the interplay between gender and power in specific historical and material sites. Such gender norms, particularly as they contribute to the division of space into private and public spheres, are directly connected to temporal modes of experience and representation. As critics from a variety of disciplinary perspectives have argued, human rights violations, and rape in particular, produce what Leigh Gilmore terms a "temporality of violence" or "traumatic simultaneity" (114). In other words, the perpetration, lived legacy, and representation of the event often take shape as temporally paradigmatic and recursive, while progressive modes of chronological time remain elusive in its experience and representation. I find models capable of disrupting these temporal norms most compellingly in narratives that, following Homi Bhabha's reading of Julia Kristeva's work in her essay "Women's Time," I term "exorbitant," in the sense that their structures literally "exceed the bounds of custom, reason, or tradition" (the online *Oxford English Dictionary* definition). In particular, such narratives move beyond basic limits of conventional temporal modes that divide past from present and future, and divide space and persons into public and private.

Three novels illuminate the connection between narrative temporality and the gendered division of space informing analysis and representation of rape. Each figures rape as a central event in a different historical context, and its temporal schema informs the construction of the rape as either private or public, with consequences for the treatment of rape emotionally, socially, and juridically within the narrative. In brief, J. M. Coetzee's *Disgrace* (1999) demonstrates that a linear emplotment—even when part of a narrative of decline, rather than of progress—is ultimately too limited by its own history as narrative form to negotiate the complexities of private and public aspects of rape as a central narrative event. In *Corregidora* (1975) Gayl Jones deploys a circular narrative time that shows how its own radical potential for connection and empowerment is defeated by the repetitive temporality of the traumatic legacy. This narrative temporality also reveals the degradation of the private sphere of individual sexual desire in the contemporary moment by the lingering legacy of the circulation of female bodies as property under slavery. Finally, Isabel Allende's *House of the Spirits* (1978) offers a narrative model that, in embracing both linear (epic) and circular modes of time, illuminates the limits of gendered divisions of space and forms a narrative gesture out of the cyclical time of vengeance. Following Wendy S. Hesford and Wendy Kozol in their challenge to feminist critics to "recognize[e] the interdependence of material and discursive realms" when analyzing human rights discourses, I contextualize each of these representations of rape in terms of related historical and political events, arguing that temporal exorbitance or excess (beyond the strictly linear and chronological) can help create narratives of rape able to account for the complexity of both personal and historical implications in changing global contexts (Hesford and Kozol 13).

Rape and Contract: J. M. Coetzee's *Disgrace*

In a speech delivered at Amnesty International USA's Annual General Meeting in Brooklyn, April 2004, then executive director William Schulz asked members of his audience to turn their thoughts back one decade to 1994, a year in which "two monumental events in the history of human rights occurred, . . . one . . . inspiring and the other enormously tragic."

These events are the end of apartheid and the foundation of the first democratically elected majority government in South Africa (inspiring) and the genocide of Tutsi and moderate Hutu men, women, and children in Rwanda (enormously tragic). Schulz attributed some credit to the international human rights movement for participating in South Africa's triumph and much responsibility to the international human rights movement for the tragedy of the Rwandan genocide, specifically for "fail[ing] to move the hearts of the world's citizens, fail[ing] to activate the strength of the world's armies, fail[ing] to shame the consciences of the United States and United Nations." Schulz's juxtaposition evokes the mind-numbing paradox of the human condition in its highest and best aspect, striving toward freedom and seeking to end oppression, and in its basest and most disgraced, slaughtering individuals for their membership in or perceived sympathy with a group.

This paradox is at the heart of much of South African Nobel Prize—winning author J.M. Coetzee's oeuvre; it certainly claims pride of place in his novel *Disgrace*. In that novel, white romantic literature professor David Lurie is publicly shamed after his pursuit of one of his students, Melanie Isaacs, results in nonconsensual sex (or, not to put too fine a point upon it, rape). Upon losing his academic post, Lurie leaves Cape Town for his daughter, Lucy's, rural farm in time to witness her gang rape by black men who appear to be acting as agents for Petrus, Lucy's farmhand, who has designs upon her land. In a plot move that many readers and critics find both unlikely and disturbing, Lucy, a lesbian, chooses not to report the rape to police and instead accepts the offer of marriage extended by Petrus—who has a kinship relation with one of the rapists—as a gesture of "protection." Lucy explains that this "is what I must learn to accept . . . to start at ground level. With nothing. No cards, no weapons, no property, no rights, no dignity, . . . like a dog" (205).

The ground level that Lucy strives to accept as her historical due is a dramatic restoration of the originary moment of the social contract upon which purportedly egalitarian, democratic civil societies in the western Enlightenment tradition rest. It is the irretrievable moment theorized most famously by Hobbes, Locke, and Rousseau, when humans in their vulnerable individual states, implicitly or explicitly, willingly give up absolute freedom and accept a rule of law that promises to bring the more secure—if mitigated—freedom of individual protection offered by the state. It is also a moment that a trajectory of feminist writing from Susan Brownmiller and Carole Pateman to Laura Tanner and Tanya Horeck has identified as initiated by an act of rape.[2] Among the many narrative and allegorical strains that comprise *Disgrace*, Coetzee embeds an intellectual history of the function of consent and the role of violence in the social contract, ultimately instrumentalizing the rape of Lucy and her subsequent acceptance of a marital contract as an allegory for a pessimistic Hobbesian vision of a consent that can be experienced only as brutal coercion. This, then, is the sociopolitical state of the new South Africa, the subject of Coetzee's book.

The pessimistic vision of brutality underwriting this localized South African version of the social contract is emphasized in the novel by a reversal of the standard progress narrative—a narrative thoroughly tainted by and complicit with the colonial and apartheid systems in South Africa and elsewhere. The historical regression of the novel is presented as inevitable for a land and people so wretchedly scarred by centuries of oppression, racism, and violence; how else to right historical wrongs but to start from scratch? the novel seems to ask.[3] This narrative reversal follows a backward historical trajectory from urban to rural, middle class to peasant, high-brow to earthy, and peaks in the triumvirate of plot points comprising Lucy's rape, her enigmatic response to that rape, and her consent to Petrus's proposal of marriage. Taken together, these plot points create a structural gap that produces meaning—namely, that there is little basis for the widely circulated triumphalist narrative of South Africa as a multiracial democratic beacon lighting the Horn of Africa—precisely through its seeming incomprehensibility.

The novel stages the moment of consent to contract upon which the modern democratic state is based (presumably the state to which the new South Africa aspires, despite the earlier Socialist leanings of the majority ANC party) in repeated textual representations of a return to the state of nature theorized by Hobbes, Locke, and Rousseau. The South Africa evidenced in *Disgrace* shares much in common with the semifeudal, agricultural state of nature based upon the right of the monarch—in other words, upon unearned and mostly coercive power and privilege—that marked the moment of transition to the putatively egalitarian, participatory polity envisioned in the seventeenth and eighteenth centuries via the social contract. This South Africa is essentially lawless, echoing the brutal version of human nature that emerges upon removal of the coercive force of monarch or despot and that necessitates consent to the social contract to establish the democratic polity.

For Locke, only consent to the specific condition of the social contract—of giving up absolute liberty in exchange for protection from the state—will save human beings from themselves and one another, pulling them from the state of nature and relocating them in society (96). However, as the contract theorists themselves—and political theorists interpreting the social contract over the next three hundred years—pointed out, the moment of the "original contract," during which consent was given by "any number of freemen capable of a majority to unite and incorporate into [one political] society," is irretrievably lost (296). Instead, Hobbes and Locke imagine it in predictably different ways: for Locke, consent is tacit, signaled by a man's choice to live peaceably on and cultivate land under the dominion of a government. For Hobbes, consent is an altogether darker force, roughly equivalent to forced submission: "And whether he be of the congregation, or not; and whether his consent be asked, or not, he must either submit to their decrees, or be left in the condition of war he was in before; wherein he might without injustice be destroyed by any man whatsoever" (117).

Importantly, for both theorists the state to which men consent is fraternal (horizontal—Hobbes's "congregation") rather than paternal (vertical, monarchical) in nature. Crucially, the radical reformation of the state in its fraternal structure retains—and, arguably, is based upon—the natural subjugation of women. This contribution to social contract theory, made most notably by feminist theorist Carole Pateman, is that the social contract is preceded by and based upon the sexual contract; however, this "natural foundation" for the civic order is repressed in contract narratives. The patriarchal right of rule over women, which includes access to their bodies, is not, in this account, political; rather, it is derived from the "natural" subjugation of women because of men's "stronger and abler" nature (Locke, qtd. in Pateman 39).

Read in this light, Lucy's decision in *Disgrace* to accept Petrus's marriage proposal conflates the distinct historical moments of the sexual and social contracts into a forced consent equivalent to submission. Forced consent, the text seems to say, describes both the natural status of women in relation to men and the status of the governed within the new civil society of postapartheid South Africa. This new South Africa is, paradoxically, marked by a temporal shift from the structural development and governmental premodernity of apartheid-era South Africa to a structurally premodern (small-scale agricultural, rather than urban industrial) and governmentally modern (contractarian) present. While the text is highly critical of the status of the governed in this new/old South Africa, it also seems content to reproduce as allegory the natural subjugation of women upon which that status is based. The proposal that initiates this simultaneously micro- (private, individual) and macro- (public) level contract is made to Lucy's father after her rape,

dramatizing the traditional exchange of women's bodies among men as foundation for the state. It also is couched as remedy for the bodily vulnerability
that informed the need for the initial social contract: "But here," says Petrus, "it
is dangerous, too dangerous. A woman must be marry" (Coetzee, *Disgrace* 202).

With Petrus's veiled threat / marriage proposal on the table, Lucy literally
"appears not to hear" David's alternative offers of sending her to Holland where
she has family, or setting her up "somewhere safer than here," and seems incapable of conceptualizing an alternative under her own auspices—although this
lack is a function of structural narrative demand, rather than a full fleshing out
of narratological possibility for this character. She replies, "Go back to Petrus . . .
propose the following. Say I accept his protection. Say he can put out whatever
story he likes about our relationship and I won't contradict him. If he wants me
to be known as his third wife, so be it. As his concubine, ditto. But then the
child becomes his too. The child becomes part of his family. As for the land, say
I will sign the land over to him as long as the house remains mine. I will become
a tenant on his land" (204). Through this negotiation, Lucy consents to become
Petrus's wife (with or without legal contract) in order to gain his protection. In
accepting the contract in exchange for such tenuous security, Lucy offers a consent that is both the nonconsent of woman—the naturalized subjugation of the
sexual contract—and an allegory of the informed consent of the governed to
membership in the polity (that is, postapartheid South Africa) in exchange for
protection from harm. Much is made in the text of the historical specificity of
"this place, at this time, . . . South Africa" (112), and Petrus's intimations of danger are always local. In this way, it must be noted that Lucy does not consent to
the monogamous version of Christian marriage in the western tradition, but to
the polygamous, tribal formulation of Petrus's Xhosa tradition. Thus, her status
will be further degraded as a third wife, theoretically subject not only to Petrus's
domination but also to that of his first and second wives, who will be accorded
higher status within the family structure. Moreover, in local South African
terms, her consent signals the reversal by which the white *boervrau* becomes
tenant to the black landowner, a move which constitutes an excessive wish fulfillment of demands for what Zoe Wicomb calls "vulgar reversal"—that is, a land
redistribution that retains the features of power and violence at the heart of
apartheid, the sort showcased to the north by Robert Mugabe's mandated
seizure of white farms in Zimbabwe (213).

Equally significant—and the occasion of another astonishing gap in the
narrative—is Lucy's acknowledgment that accepting the protection of her

rapist's proxy, Petrus (who also safeguards one of the rapists, his "relative," Pollux, under the aegis not of the state but of family), will leave her vulnerable to continued sexual violation by Petrus. When David asks whether there would be a "personal side" to what Lucy has called "an alliance, a deal," Lucy responds: "Do you mean, would Petrus expect me to sleep with him? I'm not sure that Petrus would want to sleep with me, except to drive home his message. But, to be frank, no, I don't want to sleep with Petrus. Definitely not" (Coetzee, *Disgrace* 203). In Coetzee's high-precision prose, Lucy's disavowal does not preclude the possibility that she will find herself in a position of sexual vulnerability to Petrus, who would ostensibly have every right to legitimate their contract, to "drive it home," to borrow from the stunningly unfazed Lucy. The phrase "I don't want" describes a lack of desire, a revulsion even (heightened as it is by the pronouncement "definitely not"); however, what Lucy does not say is that she will not or, more importantly, will not be expected or forced to sleep with Petrus as one signification of his dominion over her.

One question that emerges from this reading concerns the intractability of the sexual contract, even as the social contract is challenged and refined over time as the basis for democracy. Feminist theorists have convincingly shown that this problem has to do at least in part with the tenacity of primeval understandings of the natural states of the genders, that is, the weakness and irrationality of women that originates in their reproductive function and renders them unfit for participation in the public sphere of civil society (these understandings correspond to the distinction made by Teresa de Lauretis between the semiotic figure woman and real, historical women explored in chapters 2 and 3). Pateman identifies a lingering ambiguity with regard to how individuals or groups are considered capable of consent and "so count as full members of the political order." Full acknowledgment of the consequences of this foundational ambiguity within the liberal patriarchal state has been avoided, according to Pateman, by "reducing the concept of consent to meaninglessness. Consent as ideology cannot be distinguished from habitual acquiescence, assent, silent dissent, submission, or even enforced submission" (72).

Lucy's acceptance of Petrus's proposal can best be categorized as "silent dissent" and "enforced submission." While its coercive nature is highlighted through the foil of David's shocked dismay, it is never named as such by Lucy, whose willing (and willful) subjugation dramatizes the extent to which silent dissent and enforced submission are for women natural conditions, ingrained, unspoken. Indeed, her obdurate silence and passivity (one critic calls it "masochism") confirm the aspect of contract theory that refuses to imagine women as capable of giving consent (see J. Woods 45). In this way, Lucy demonstrates the complex and degraded relationship of women more generally to the nature of consent. In addition to dramatizing the consequences of a new South African order constructed with the same brutal tools that built the recently demolished master's house, Lucy's acceptance of her own subjugation marks her as the protowoman imagined by patriarchal political theorists of yore, proven incapable of consent by exercising that power precisely to negate her own ability to consent. By novel's end, with Lucy's declaration that she will give up her land, the original contractarian status of individuation through ownership and participation in the polity has been restored to Petrus, new South African patriarch, figure for a people long excluded on the basis of race.

This reinstatement of black South Africans in the public sphere of civil society is offered here as the violent reversal that so often accompanies political transformation, a reversal complicated by its construction in the ruins of a racialized society. Petrus's initial success comes from the Land Affairs grant that allows him to buy "a hectare and a bit" of land from Lucy. This modest beginning is not furthered through labor, which Locke defines as the sign that the social contract has been accepted. Instead, Petrus reverts to the state of war envisioned by Hobbes as the mark of man in the state of nature, precontract. The end to this state of war comes in the form of the social/sexual contract, Petrus's proposal to Lucy, which also reinstates the gendered separation of spheres upon which civil society in the western tradition rests. And while Lucy can hope for the limited protection of Petrus in their corner of the Eastern Cape, the contract itself delivers the coup de grace where Lucy is concerned, for her consent to governance by Petrus, to becoming Petrus's wife, consigns her to an exaggerated private sphere bounded quite literally by the walls of her home. Importantly, it is Lucy who asserts the terms upon which she will consent to Petrus's proposal of marriage, making a clear distinction between her land and her house (notice that Coetzee does not choose the word "home"): " 'As for the land, say I will sign the land over to him as long as the house remains mine. I will become a tenant on his land. . . . But the house remains mine, I repeat that. No one enters this house without my permission. Including him' " (Coetzee, *Disgrace* 204). This turn to the private sphere, by which Lucy puts herself back in her place, might be read as another instantiation of the female individual proving her irrationality by consenting to slavelike status. It is also a function of the regression embedded in the narrative decline that structures the novel, which will deliver what Derek Attridge has called a "state of grace" for its protagonist, David, at the close of the novel but will leave Lucy silent and unrecuperated in a house owned by her husband/rapist.

Lucy's reasons for refusing to report her rape are even more mystifying than her reasons for consenting to Petrus's proposal, which she accepts as the price she must pay for protection as a woman alone in a dangerous place that she (and this remains rather inexplicable) does not wish to leave. On a macrolevel she seems to consider it her historical due.[4] Regarding reportage of rape, however, the text aligns readers with David in his bewilderment at Lucy's decision, leaving us also shaken by our inability to understand. Lucy presents the clearest explanation she can muster: "The reason is that, as far as I am concerned, what happened to me is a purely private matter. In another time, in another place it might be held to be a public matter. But in this place, at this time, it is not. It is my business, mine alone" (112). Lucy's concern, then, is a matter of expression, of controlling the dissemination of the story of her violation. It is a concern deeply bound up with the politics of the new South Africa: "in this place, at this time." The novel is shot through with oblique references to South Africa's Truth and Reconciliation Commission (TRC), many of which interrogate the nonsecular nature of its proceedings.[5] Read in this light, Lucy's apparent acceptance of a certain role as the historically determined oppressor offering an exaggerated individual gesture of redistribution and balance by refusing to bring her story to the authorities might actually represent something else: an unwillingness to burden the public realm with a story that amounts to a black-peril narrative (trumped-up white male fear of black men raping white women, used to justify the oppression and brutalization of black men), which might well set in motion the wheels of legal or extralegal justice against her rapists—or any likely stand-in, for that matter.[6] Considered in terms of the deeply troubling irony that more than 80 percent of applications for amnesty in the TRC came from black South Africans, perhaps Lucy's individual refusal is a repudiation of the historical narrative of white South African criminalization of black South Africans, obscenely perpetrated in the context of the overwhelming crime against humanity that was apartheid. It is an interesting possibility, a reading that relieves some of the exasperation at her vexing silence.

I am tempted to accept this—or some other—reading of Lucy's motivation, or to consider this aspect of the narrative a defense of the idea of the freedom to remain silent, which the novel explores with regard to both David and

Petrus, and which certainly applies to itself as fictional text. However, as a feminist reader I am drawn to the bodily experience of rape, which is left unnarrated. Aside from the ethical issues raised in the self-sacrificial characterization of Lucy, sign of a long literary and religious tradition originating in Lucy's eponymous foremother, Lucretia, the conflation of meanings of "private" and "public" in the novel's discourse can be redirected from the realm of expression (revealing the details of one's ordeal or, in the case of David and Petrus, of one's infliction of pain or violence onto another) to the division of space in civil society, and the complicity of that division in the recursive temporal construction of rape. Read in this light, Lucy's interpretation of her rape as "private" corresponds to the long judicial history of rape as a private matter: the exclusion of spousal rape from prosecution; the exclusion of rape from prosecution as a war crime (in the precedent-setting Nuremberg and Tokyo Tribunals); the exclusion of rape as a grave breach under international human rights covenants such as the Geneva Conventions. Rape is the teleologic of Lucy's enigmatic decision to remove herself to the private, domestic sphere of her house by novel's end. It is also the unnamed source of the novel's linear narrative of political decline.

The result of contract, then, leaves Lucy as she predicted early on: "With nothing. No cards, no weapons, no property, no rights, no dignity . . . like a dog" (205). Importantly, much of what she repudiates is apartheid apparatus: identity cards, weapons, property. However, Lucy renounces far more than the tools of the old regime, reducing herself to a vehicle for the male penetrative economy by which the exchange value of the act of rape forces her back into a sexual contract she had implicitly rejected as a lesbian, while removing her from the social contract that would provide her agency, autonomy, and voice in the public sphere. The novel thus inscribes Lucy as pure sign: of a newly reconfigured South African land and governance; of one model of being white in postapartheid South Africa; of one way of righting history's wrongs. The decision not to represent the rape itself, but to represent a range of responses to it—including Lucy's own—that border on the "bizarre" and "pathological" (Wicomb 221), leaves Lucy in a realm of dumb silence. Further, the narrative of decline that leaves her quite literally barefoot and pregnant in the house owned by the (newly designated) patriarch inscribes the paradigmatic, recursive time of rape as the moment of origin, festering within the national narrative upon which it is built and which will presumably continue to move—even if that movement leads further into the degraded state critiqued here by Coetzee—while the woman remains still, inside. What can we imagine Lucy to be thinking or doing within those walls as the novel closes?

Even as the revolutionary state occupied by Lucy and David Lurie in Coetzee's novel was being born, the genocidal rape of women in Rwanda over the course of a hundred days took place. The use of rape as a tool of genocide set a major precedent in international law, as the Rwanda Tribunal saw the first indictment of a woman for rape, an event that raises profound questions for analysts of rape and gender, as Sheri Russell-Brown argues:

> It is difficult to argue that "genocidal rape" should be viewed solely as a crime about gender, something that male soldiers commit generally against women during armed conflict, when a Hutu woman . . . can commit "genocidal rape" against a Tutsi woman precisely because of that woman's gender but also because of her ethnic identity; . . . the same can be said about the recent news that transmitting AIDS through rape was part of the Rwandan genocidal campaign. It is yet another example of rape being used as a method of destruction, albeit slow and painful, of not only the individual Tutsi women who were raped but also of the Tutsi group in general. (4)

Consider Lucy, arguably raped because of her ethnic identity and class status as much as for her gender. Consider the child she will contract (double entendre intended) into Petrus's family, for all intents and purposes part of the project of ethnic cleansing. What does it mean that a white, male novelist created such a vessel for ideas about violence, revolution, forgiveness, and state formation in postapartheid South Africa? More significantly, how does this important novelist's decision reinscribe the dangerous narrative of the sacrifice of women's bodies to such projects as the rectification of history, or delusionary ideals of tribal power or state formation? In this moment of international attention to rape as war crime, as crime against humanity, and as an act of torture that transcends biological sex, if not gender typologies and norms, I cannot help but wonder whether it might have been possible to create an allegorical/realist narrative of this place, at this time, without doing gendered violence to a host of women who occupy similarly localized positions, but who also transcend time and place in the moribund übernarrative of rape?

Rape and Slavery: Gayl Jones's *Corregidora*

Although it is committed against an individual, the rape at the heart of *Disgrace* cannot be claimed as a strictly private event from the perspective of either perpetrators (with their larger historical motive of land acquisition) or survivor (who understands the message communicated by the rape and chooses silence as a response with privacy as cover). Another novel concerned with narrating rape that more critically engages what it means for rape to be recursively inscribed as originary moment for familial and historical narratives is Gayl Jones's *Corregidora*. Jones's novel complicates notions of temporality and the division between private and public space by tracing the legacy of slavery through the lives of four generations of women, the last of whom, Ursa, experiences its effects as they surface in her contemporary heterosexual relationships. Female sexual desire in the novel, stuck in the heritage of slavery and rape, finds its parallel in narrative time. That is, inasmuch as the fulfillment of female sexual desire in *Corregidora* remains an impossibility, the narrative structure, rather than surging forward to climax and denouement, remains "like a fist drawn up" (75), unopened, unrelieved. By structuring her novel in a pattern of traumatic repetition, Jones offers neither the closure of a linear narrative (of either progress or decline), nor the redemptive healing of a circular narrative that recalls ancestral strength.

Part of the important work done by the novel is a narration of rape that makes an argument for its status as torture within the context of the international slave trade, although definitions of torture in documents such as the Convention against Torture, codified at around the time the novel was written, seemed to preclude rape by defining the torturer as a person operating in a public capacity, while rape was the paradigmatic private crime. Current feminist human rights theorists and activists have persistently argued that this distinction between systematic or state (public) and arbitrary or individual (private) torture is misleading and have worked to define more specifically what kinds of acts constitute torture. Some contemporary international conventions and treaties have remedied the elisions occasioned by the public/private divide by articulating the ways in which torture is specifically raced, gendered, classed, and nationalized, so to speak, and have, as part of that process, redefined rape as a crime against humanity.[7] Examining the language of the Geneva Conventions, which does not name rape a "grave breach" identifiable as an international crime, Rhonda Copelon argues that "if the egregiousness of rape is to be fully recognized, rape must be explicitly recognized as a form of torture" (201). Copelon historicizes her argument in terms of the shift in torture's paradigm, from being "largely understood as a method of extracting information," to becoming "commensurate with willfully causing great suffering or injury. . . . In the contemporary understanding of torture, degradation is both vehicle and goal" (202). In this regard, rape, an act that is both predicated upon and stages the impulse to "degrade and destroy a woman based on her identity as a woman" (199), is paradigmatic.[8]

In working to redefine rape as a form of torture and a crime against humanity—a move which requires an a priori reconfiguration of the traditional public/private divide in human rights discourse—the point is not simply to broaden the definition of torture to include private as well as public breaches, but more pointedly to denounce such either/or frameworks (which keep the concepts—if not their material effects—intact) so as to account for the ways in which all such breaches are at once one and the same; that is, both private and public. There is an even more complex breakdown of these terms in the case of *Corregidora*: under the public aegis of slavery, the rape/prostitution of Gram and Great Gram would have been excluded as belonging to the private realm and most likely constructed as consensual sex.[9] Further, Ursa's experience of painful penetrative heterosexual sex that ignores and overrides her desire/pleasure and might be characterized as a form of trauma is even further privatized (rendered invisible or unspeakable), as it occurs as part of the ordinary, disavowed oppression of everyday patriarchy rather than under the umbrella of a public event/system such as slavery. Jones's narrative, then, brings to light in the context of historical legacy the doubly imposed privacy of such events.

In a sense, the rhetorical move of bridging the divide between private and public violations simply recapitulates the feminist mantra "The personal is the political," but in the context of feminist human rights discourse it does more: it obliterates the spatial and ideological metaphorics of private and public, or, perhaps more accurately, recognizes the fusion of one with the other. Homi Bhabha's description of the "unhomely moment," part of a larger cultural theory that seeks to account for postcolonial subjectivity, is germane: "The recesses of the domestic space become sites for history's most intricate invasions. In that displacement, the borders between home and world become confused; and uncannily the private and the public become part of each other, forcing upon us a vision that is as divided as it is disorienting" (9).[10] Given the strict dependence of a western worldview upon such obscuring distinctions, calling attention to the displacement of home by world (and of world by home, as in the case of Lucy in *Disgrace*) may, as Bhabha notes, generate an initially "divided" and "disorienting" vision. However, from a feminist analytic perspective, such vision may ultimately be rather clarifying than disorienting, revealing the "private, secret, insidious traumas" that are "more often than not those events in which the dominant culture and its forms and institutions are expressed and perpetuated" (Brown 102). Indeed, citing Carole Pateman, Bhabha identifies the unhomely as a distinctly feminist concept committed to bringing to light that which has been purposefully hidden beneath the mantle of private life: "the 'unhomely' does provide a 'non-continuist' problematic that dramatizes—in the figure of woman—the ambivalent structure of the civil state as it draws its rather paradoxical boundary between the private and public spheres" (10).[11] This conception of the unhomely provides a discourse with which to analyze the separation of private from public that enables and supports torture as repressive mechanism. Acknowledging the danger of imposing further representational baggage on the already burdened figure of woman by rendering her pure symbol of this unhomeliness, we might engage with the life experiences of women such as Ursa and Lucy, who are not figures for, but rather subjects of, an unhomely moment that "relates the traumatic ambivalences of a personal, psychic history to the wider disjunctions of political existence" (Bhabha 11).

Reading Ursa's intergenerational, traumatic experience of the legacy of rape and prostitution under slavery, as well as her experience of a contemporary heterosexual patriarchy uncannily rehearsing that same traumatic experience, is to acknowledge the unhomely as representative of what Bhabha calls a "non-continuist" history; that is, a history that does not smooth itself into easily transmitted tradition but wells up into the present as the kind of literal return that characterizes trauma itself. In this sense, the binaries public/private, state/individual, past/present—supports for torture's repressive structure— bleed together in the everyday experiences of traumatized survivors, unable to articulate themselves as speaking subjects in the shadow of a history that does not pass on. To refuse the categories of private and public is to reconnect individuals with the uncannily current events of collective history, to identify and claim what Leigh Gilmore has called "the long historical arc" of intergenerational trauma resulting from the legacies of colonialism and slavery (99).

Reading rape as torture within the context of *Corregidora*'s specific historic geography means stressing—against the centuries of purposeful misnaming of sex between black female slaves and white slave owners as consensual— the centrality of rape to slavery's system of control. As Catherine Clinton argues, we must understand that "rape was an integral part of slavery, not an aberration or dysfunction" (208). In addition, historians have established that, within the Brazilian slave system, "slave women were used more as prostitutes than as 'breeders,' mostly because the international slave trade continued in Brazil throughout the tenure of slavery, and eradicated the need for the slave population to reproduce itself"; further, "prostitution of female slaves in Brazil amounts to an institutionalized practice of rape" (S. Robinson 153, 154).[12]

Situated within this historical context, female sexuality in *Corregidora* is contoured around the rape of Ursa's great-grandmother and grandmother by nineteenth-century Brazilian slave owner Simon Corregidora and the men to whom he prostituted them, originary violence that produced an incestuous line of women unable to conceive of sexuality apart from the men who "dug up" their genitals (Jones 75). While Ursa is not herself raped, the conflation of Old Man Corregidora with Ursa's husbands Mutt and Tadpole into one figure of violent male sexual expression (effected through an echoing of patterns of speech and desire over the course of the novel) creates a continuum of brutal heterosexuality based upon the violent penetration and consumption of female genitalia characteristic of rape. This continuum is complicated by Jones's careful contextualization of the effects upon Mutt and Tadpole of their traumatic family histories under slavery, revealing their own woundedness in relation to the violence they perpetuate with Ursa. Also, race mediates any simple interpretations of masculine power in the novel, as black men are themselves victims of (sexualized) torture by slave owners such as Corregidora. As Great Gram testifies: "All them beatings and killings [of slave men and women] wasn't nothing but sex circuses, and all them white peoples, mens, womens, and childrens crowding around to see" (125).[13] Still, even consensual heterosexual sex in *Corregidora* is rarely, if ever, figured outside this historical economy, always descriptively echoing the rape / enforced prostitution of Great Gram and Gram, with emphasis on the "magic" of the female genitalia, described alternately as a "gold piece" (profit) or as a "hole" (pleasure), and sex boiled down simply to a woman's "getting fucked."

There are two ways to analyze Ursa's sexual subjectivity through the lens of a temporal paradigm of "traumatic simultaneity." First, she suffers from posttraumatic symptoms, which may be experienced intergenerationally, according to Laura S. Brown, and which are, in Ursa's case, attached to her foremothers' experience of and testifying about rape. Second, Ursa's encounters with violent heterosexuality constitute an "insidious trauma," defined by Maria Root as "the traumatogenic effects of oppression that are not necessarily overtly violent or threatening to bodily well-being at the given moment but that do violence to the soul and spirit" (qtd. in Brown 107). The construction of Ursa's sex as a "hole" by both Mutt and Tadpole is metonym for the overarching violence done to Ursa's "soul and spirit" in her contemporary sexual relationships, yet this designation also circles back to the rape of Ursa's ancestral mothers, whose genitalia were similarly figured as empty vessels to be filled by men for profit and/or pleasure. In both cases, a negation of identity results from that impulse to "degrade and destroy a woman based upon her identity as a woman," which is the cornerstone of understanding rape as an act of torture.

As Gayatri Spivak argues, such a reduction of woman to hole is symptomatic of a pervasive, penetrative "uterine social organization" (152) that denies female sexual subjectivity by repressing (and, in the case of female genital mutilation, actually removing) the clitoris: "In legally defining women as object of exchange, passage, or possession in terms of reproduction, it is not only the womb that is literally 'appropriated'; it is the clitoris as the signifier of the sexed subject that is effaced. All historical and theoretical investigation into the definition of woman as legal *object*—in or out of marriage; or as politico-economic passageway for property and legitimacy would fall within the investigation of the varieties of the effacement of the clitoris" (151, emphasis in original). For Spivak, effacement of the clitoris in both dominant discourse and historical practice situates women within a strictly reproductive economy, repressing both their desires and their subjectivities, often in formal legal terms.[14] Certainly Lucy's subjection to the marital contract in *Disgrace* may be read through this lens. In Ursa's case, such repression is doubled: the effacement of Ursa's clitoris and her desire for pleasure by her reduction to hole would seem to relegate her to a strictly procreative, penetrative, uterine sexuality; however, the loss of her womb in an act of domestic violence by Mutt renders this reduction to hole a literal, rather than figurative, description. There is a hole where her uterus should be, an emptiness that excludes Ursa even from this limited reproductive economy, as well as from the procreative politic of her foremothers' imperative to "make generations." So excluded, she is reduced to a vessel for a phallic pleasure useful in the "field of desire" from which, in de Lauretis's reading, a woman designated as hole is excluded: "Having nothing to lose, . . . women cannot desire; having no phallic capital to invest or speculate on, as men do, women cannot be investors in the marketplace of desire but are instead commodities that circulate in it"

(*Practice* 217). This analysis of women as commodified by their reduction to sexual hole is obviously complicated when applied to texts like *Corregidora* that represent women who are actually circulated as objects of exchange within the economy of the slave trade; still, in the contemporary context, the exclusion of women from the "field of desire" constitutes a negation or denial of full subjectivity, a denial necessary within a certain model of violent heterosexuality to the male accumulation of "phallic capital." Such accumulation approximates in the sexual sphere what Elaine Scarry calls the activity of "world-making"—the expansion of power gained through physical and linguistic control that is central to the torturer's motivation and method—in the scene of torture.[15]

If the narrative remains frustrated, unresolved, it is because a validating witness for the multigenerational experience of sexual violence is never found, and Ursa is ultimately unable to speak either desire or pain. While I do not recognize the redemptive closure which some critics have read in Ursa's final reconciliation with Mutt, the novel does effect two radical representations that indicate an attempt to move out of its circular narrative trajectory, that discursive stasis identified by Hortense Spillers as the historical legacy of captivity: first, the radical representation of the frustration of female desire within a violent heterosexual contract which is, in the system of signs governing representation of women, generally excluded; and second, the representation of Ursa's expression of a measure of desire. For if at novel's end she has not achieved voice with regard to her sexual desire, she is finally able to express the desire not to be hurt of a person who has experienced great pain. There is some promise in the fact that this expression is prompted by Mutt, who similarly is able to express his desire not to be hurt. However, this desire to end the repetitive cycle of wounding contains the impossibility of its own imperative ("I don't want a kind of woman that hurt you. . . . Then you don't want me" [Jones 185]), placing readers in the position of what Cathy Caruth defines as the trauma witness, "witness to an impossibility"—in this case, the impossibility of the desire for a relationship without pain. Rather than providing narrative closure in its call-response blues structure, the novel is purposefully left suspended in the troubled narrative time of historical legacy.

This suspension is logical when considered in terms of the ongoing effects of slavery, and particularly of institutionalized rape and incest within the slave system, which is the origin of the intergenerational wound that marks Ursa. As Leigh Gilmore asks: "How can melancholia end when the effects that produce it cannot be said to be sufficiently past?" (106). Indeed, as Gilmore argues—and contemporary global economic, political, and cultural imbalances demonstrate—"the impact of colonialism and slavery themselves has not ended" (106). In addition to the continued distribution of global power and wealth in patterns that stem directly from colonial enterprise and the slave trade, we might argue that these legacies remain locked in a traumatic temporality partly because of their lack of redress through a public vehicle such as a truth commission, or public gestures such as apology or reparation. Most recently and egregiously, the United States declined to participate in the World Conference on Racism in 2001 in Durban, in part because the topic of apology and reparation for the trade among Europeans and Americans of African people was a slated topic for discussion.[16] While Ursa seeks an individual witness to her pain so that she might express her desire as a woman released from the cyclical reproduction of heterosexual violence in the shadow of slavery, there is also a need for a broader public address, without which the production of humans in the a priori traumatic realm of what Jamaica Kincaid has called "the always conquered" (qtd. in Gilmore 10) will continue unabated. As a case in point, we have the final text of the Durban conference, which "amounted to an apology, calling on those responsible for slavery 'to take appropriate and effective measures to halt and reverse the lasting consequences of those practices'" (Sadasivam).

An interesting comparative note to the official U.S. refusal to address publicly its role in the ongoing legacy of the global slave trade is the recent action of a group called the Lifeline Expedition, based in England, which uses theatrical gestures to try to achieve reconciliation between Europeans and Africans in the wake of the slave trade. In July 2006, Andrew Hawkins, a descendent of Sir John Hawkins, a sea captain alleged to have been one of the first British slave traders, traveled with other members of the Lifeline Expedition to The Gambia, West Africa, where they marched in chains in front of thousands of Gambian citizens. Kneeling on a dais in front of Isatou Njie Saidy, the Gambian vice president, Hawkins asked forgiveness for his ancestor's crimes, at which point Saidy unwrapped Hawkins's chains. Purely symbolic, the gesture was offered in place of a formal apology from the British government which, like that of the United States, is likely not forthcoming precisely because it would imply the need for reparations to be paid to African countries for the destruction wrought by the slave trade. While such gestures cannot provide material reparation, the acknowledgment of wrongdoing and request for forgiveness contribute to healing the historical effects that perpetuate the traumatic repetition of the wound on private/individual and public/historical scales in the postcolonial context.

Rape and Reconciliation: Isabel Allende's *House of the Spirits*

In thinking through the traumatic temporality of Ursa's narrative, I am reminded of the phenomenon of simultaneous, synchronic time explored by Benedict Anderson in his study of the "imagined community" of the nation. Anderson identifies temporal simultaneity as an aspect of linear, calendrical time in which members of the "imagined community" of the nation can, without any real knowledge of their fellow citizens, imagine the actions and events of others' lives happening synchronically with their own. This ideal of synchronicity in turn promotes the idea of a shared linear time marching forward to a collectively identified and identifiable destiny—in other words, a progress narrative.

There is, however, another—almost diametrically opposed—notion of temporal synchrony, or simultaneity, which seems to be the unique aftereffect of (historical) trauma: a sense that, rather than moving forward all of a piece, history repeats itself endlessly over time in events so similar as to come to seem simultaneous. As Michael Ignatieff describes: "Reporters in the Balkan wars often reported that when they were told atrocity stories they were occasionally uncertain whether these stories had occurred yesterday or in 1941 or 1841 or 1441. For the tellers of the tale, yesterday and today were the same" ("Overview" 121). In this construct, synchronous time does not refer to the simultaneity of events within the linear march of calendrical time, but rather to the simultaneity of time itself, of a past, present, and future that take place—literally becoming drawn out, spatialized—all at once and continuously. This is traumatic time: the time of repetition, of the indistinctness of a horror that, folding infinitely into itself, obscures the precision of date or event and leaves only the self-referentiality of its own experience.

In this sense, the configuration of simultaneous time might be drawn as circular, a temporal form that has been celebrated in some feminist circles. The positive charge of such circularity lies in its ability to forge connections with the past as a useful and necessary precursor to the present, a well of strength and experience from which present and future generations might readily draw. This circular notion of time is also represented in the African and Amerindian notions of ancestral and spiritual return, the belief that ancestors linger as spiritual presences in a temporal present or return through the bodily vehicles of their descendants. The conception of time as a circle has been offered as a radical alternative, a form of resistance to the hegemonic shaft of historical narrative taken up by those very groups whose "histories of marginalization," according to Bhabha, "have been most profoundly enmeshed in the antinomies of law and order—the colonized and women" (151–152).

As evidenced in *Corregidora*, however, the experience of time as simultaneous, repetitive, or circular may also indicate the inert time of trauma—and of vengeance. Certainly the dangers of this order of time are readily apparent as manifested in the now proverbial cycle of abuse. In the context of Chile's troubled history, Isabel Allende ends her epic, magical realist novel *The House of the Spirits* with a gesture toward reconciliation which lifts her narrator out of an intergenerational cycle of abuse that is both private and public, familial and political.[17] While Allende offers a positive view of simultaneity as a mode of narrative temporality, her epic is not, in the end, simply circular—even though the novel closes upon the same line with which it opens. As such, it appears that within this narrative frame, history might repeat itself endlessly as the traumatic time of simultaneity. Instead, however, as Sharon Magnarelli argues, the narrative structure is "pseudo-circular": circular because it "begin[s] and end[s] with fictional female voices which attempt to dramatize the fallacies inherent in both the patriarchal discourse and its resultant social institutions," and open-ended since it "posit[s] the possibility, however tenuous, of change, of liberation" (56). In Allende, this possibility for liberatory change is delivered to readers as a gesture concretized in the act of writing which has produced the novel itself.

Allende's narrator, Alba, offers a metatextual comment upon the importance of simultaneity as a mode of representation capable of advancing an understanding of historical extremity: "I write, she wrote, that memory is fragile and the space of a single life is brief, passing so quickly that we never get a chance to see the relationship between events; we cannot gauge the consequences of our acts, and we believe in the fiction of past, present, and future, but it may also be true that everything happens simultaneously—as the three Mora sisters said, who could see the spirits of all eras mingled in space" (432). In this rare moment of textual explanation, Allende theorizes a narrative of simultaneity that does not resemble the vengeful perpetuity of nonserial time, for, given its multiple vocality (that is, its multiple narrative

voices representing a range of points of view), it is both linear and synchronous. More broadly, this is the narrative power of magical realism as a genre:
the ability, in both form and content, to resist the limits of either/or (as in
either linear or synchronic), accepting the complexity, responsibility, and
potential of both/and. Encouraging the perception and experience of time as
progressive, as circular, and as something more, this articulation of narrative
power—spoken by the character belatedly identified to readers as one of the
narrators—constructs temporal simultaneity as a tool specifically for the dis-
cernment of the consequences of our own actions. Allende refers, then, to
responsibility: the responsibility of representation in the face of extreme
events, as well as the admission of personal accountability necessary for reconciliation.

   In addition to operating within a heterogeneous temporality which lays
bare the structures of origin and responsibility for events occurring over the
course of a century, Allende offers a reconciliatory gesture which consciously
labors toward the promise of that retrospective narrative time of simultaneity,
preventing its degeneration into a narrative circle that ceaselessly chronicles
the cycle of abuse. Not a public ritual of atonement offered by a representative of the historic perpetrators, as are most of the rituals and gestures considered useful in the context of public reconciliation, the gesture away from
hatred and vengeance offered at the end of *House* by Alba, a survivor of state-
sponsored rape and torture, is, perhaps, even more meaningful. As Ignatieff
notes: "Sometimes, a gesture of atonement is effective precisely because it
rises above the crimes done to your own side" ("Overview," 122).[18] In spite of
the crimes perpetrated against her, Alba extends a gesture of reconciliation
to her torturer that, we finally see, motivates the writing of the novel itself.
Importantly, this is not exactly a gesture of forgiveness, but a refusal to engage
in the cycle of hatred and vengeance that, beginning generations earlier, has
culminated in the twisted relationship between torturer and tortured. Given
its retrospective temporality, the novel is able to represent the original seeds
of sociopolitical violence as they germinate over several generations into the
crimes committed against Alba, in ways that remain impossible within the
traumatic simultaneity of *Corregidora* and the linear narrative of decline in
Disgrace. Fleshing out the wounds inflicted upon Alba, as well as those sustained by her torturer over the course of his life, and locating them within the
violently repressive structures and ideologies which authorized their perpetration without opportunity for justice or healing, Allende's novel intervenes

in the repetitious cycles of violence and vengeance, laying bare their sociopolitical support structures in an effort to create a reconciliatory future.

Constructed from multiple points of view and multiple temporalities, alternating between the voices of Alba, her grandfather Esteban Trueba, and an unknown third-person narrator, *The House of the Spirits* critiques on a structural level the ideal of progress embedded in Esteban's (mostly linear) narrative sections. For in the end we find that the progress the Spanish patron, Trueba, has brought to the "uncivilized" countryside is just another euphemism for safety, the safety of the privileged few inscribed in the progress narrative itself. Despite the rhetoric of "civilization" and "progress" that justifies his consolidation of power, the treachery of Esteban's narrative of progress is exposed as his conservative politics morph into the authoritarianism of the new regime, leaving him vulnerable, unsafe, hurt. Linking the myths of progress as articulated in the public narratives circulated by the regime to the identity politics that govern imperialism, Allende closes the novel (with the exception of an epilogue narrated in Alba's voice) with a hysterical diatribe from a frightened, disillusioned Esteban. As in the counterhistorical dramatic film, wherein the wounding of native bodies accrues meaning only inasmuch as it signifies the potential threat to the western protagonist, Esteban's disillusion with the regime comes only when his own safety is jeopardized, that is, when his granddaughter is disappeared. Abandoning the measured, disciplined, unforgiving prose characteristic of the sections of the text written from his point of view, Esteban nearly shrieks in these ending pages, his breathless sentences divided not by periods but by commas in an unbroken confessional howl: "She's my granddaughter, the granddaughter of a senator of the Republic, a distinguished member of the Conservative Party, they can't do that to someone from my own family, in my own house, because then what the hell is left for everybody else, if people like us can be arrested then nobody is safe . . . it's not that I'm against repression, I understand that in the beginning you have to be firm if you want a return to order, but things have gotten out of hand . . . and no one can go along with the story about internal security and how you have to eliminate your ideological enemies, they're finishing off everyone" (419).

The safety to which Trueba refers is no small thing: silent partner of all discourses and demonstrations of power, he has spent a lifetime accumulating it, a lifetime forged along the traditional plotline of the patriarchal narrative of progress—work, accumulation of capital and land, maintenance of order and tradition—by which a Euro-American patriarch and patron, and those under his protection, are meant to be kept safe. Significantly, however, the body of the patriarch/patron is not made vulnerable; instead, it is the body of the daughter, or in this case the granddaughter, upon which the vengeance and hatred of years of repression are brutally vented. In a method similar to Kureishi's in *Sammy and Rosie Get Laid*, Allende exhibits the impossibility of the woman's place in this repressive narrative of patriarchal progress, going so far as to expose the foundation for the safety of the ruling patriarchy as the body of the woman, specifically the indigenous woman, at the bottom of the heap of history.

The convergence of gender and ethnicity that structures the novel's politics of identity—evident in the description of the indigenous woman, Pancha Garcia's, "Indian face, . . . broad features, [and] dark skin" at the moment she is raped by Esteban Trueba—links gender and ethnicity as identity positions simultaneously subject to oppression and objectified as pedagogical constructions of a nation's identity. Importantly, however, this foundational act of violence is not a beginning, but one gyration of a cycle spinning out beyond the borders of the novel itself. For we learn, in a particularly devastating translation of what Hortense Spillers has called the "*stillness* of ethnic time" into corporeal experience, that this rape has also been the fate of Pancha's mother and grandmother—and, we can only assume, their mothers and grandmothers. Readers encounter this synchronicity among past, present, and future as nightmarish, traumatic time, contemplating Pancha's literal stillness, history pooling around her as she is raped: "She lay on her back, staring at the sky with terror, until she felt the man drop to the ground beside her with a moan. She began to whimper softly. Before her, her mother—and before her, her grandmother—had suffered the same animal fate" (Allende 57). While critics such as Myriam-Yvonne Jehenson have read this passage as evidence of the novel's fatalistic resignation to an essentialized notion of destiny based upon fixed identity structures, which precludes agency and resistance, this fatalism is part of the novel's interrogation of the efficacy of a temporal simultaneity which may as easily be the time of vengeance as it is the time of understanding, connection, and witness. Indeed, the principle of temporal simultaneity structures the female narrators' contributions and is evidenced in the original source for the novel written by Alba: Clara's notebooks, which "bore witness to life." Upon her deathbed, putting her affairs in order, Clara arranges them "according to events and not in chronological order, for the one thing she had forgotten to record was the dates" (288). Again, we find traces of Ignatieff's troubled nonserial time, in which dates are rendered indistinct. But we also hear the power of the Mora sisters' conception of simultaneous time, in which past, present, and future happen all at once, providing time for a narrator such as Alba to reconstruct events, to understand causes and consequences.

For Jehenson, however, the disturbingly fatalistic representation of Pancha Garcia, a woman fated for rape, exploitation, and grief, prefigures Alba's final "acceptance of rape as a given, a mere link in an essential and natural 'chain of events'" (106). It is this perception that informs Alba's reconciliatory gesture toward her torturer and rapist, Esteban Garcia, whom she can now see as just "part of the design" (Allende 431)—a gesture Jehenson reads as particularly dangerous: "Allende falls at the end into the masculine *topos* of 'rape for a good cause'" (106). Jehenson's argument cannot be taken lightly, as I have articulated in my reading of J. M. Coetzee's rendering of precisely that topos in *Disgrace*. Certainly advancing a view of rape as a price to be paid for a greater good only fortifies the technology of gender by which the characterization of the female as subversive is used to justify her oppression and, in some cases, rape and torture.

Locating her claim historically, "from Verginia and Lucretia in Roman antiquity to the Virgin Mary in Christian tradition," Jehenson argues that "the violation of a woman's will has often been justified by its transcendental consequences. Whether these be the founding of new governments, the birth of a divine being, or, as in Allende's case, the cosmic and circular vindication of past rapes or the anticipation of future peace, woman's body has been made systematically subservient to the body politic. It is with this dangerously contrived resolution that Allende attempts to build a new world at the conclusion of *The House of the Spirits*" (107). Having spent a good part of this book asserting the terrifying extent to which "woman's body has been made systematically subservient to the body politic," operating as both symbol and prop for the display of authoritarian and patriarchal power, I am in agreement with Jehenson that, in refusing to seek retribution from her rapist, Alba risks offering herself in precisely this way. However, I do not find textual evidence that Alba's reconciliatory gesture seeks to "vindicate past rapes," and, while it clearly does attempt to effect future peace, it does so in the hope that by refusing to seek vengeance, by gesturing out of the cosmic and circular time of simultaneity—which, in its raging conflation of dates and events, can do nothing more than forecast rape as a predictable act of vengeance—it will effect an end to rape and torture. Her gesture also, crucially, is not the banal, implausible gesture of simple forgiveness, or of forgetting. Indeed, Alba is at pains to remember and testify to her pain, as demonstrated in her production of the text that becomes the novel itself.

I read Alba's use of the word "fate" as a signifier of a destiny born from the consequences of our own and others' actions, rather than as a divine—and therefore unalterable—plan. These are the consequences to which Alba refers when she argues that writing history as both linear and simultaneous allows one to grasp those connections between events that in the chronological space of a single lifetime are obscured. Rather than vindicating Pancha's rape, Alba's methodology of time and narrative seeks to apportion responsibility for it, to reveal its structural supports and demonstrate its devastating effects:

> I am beginning to suspect that nothing that happens is fortuitous, that it all corresponds to a fate laid down before my birth, and that Esteban Garcia is part of the design. . . . The day my grandfather tumbled his grandmother, Pancha Garcia, among the rushes of the riverbank, he added another link to the chain of events that had to complete itself. Afterward the grandson of the woman who was raped repeats the gesture with the granddaughter of the rapist, and perhaps forty years from now my grandson will knock Garcia's granddaughter down among the rushes, and so on down through the centuries in an unending tale of sorrow, blood, and love. (Allende 431–432).

Identifying the rape as a "gesture"—of hatred, violence, vengeance—Alba's decision to offer a different gesture, to replace hatred, violence, and vengeance with a measure of comprehension and an attempt at reconciliation, is not a vindication of rape and torture but its most profound repudiation: an unwillingness to participate in its cyclical reproduction. This unwillingness is, at least in representational terms, a *matter of time*. It is the novel's temporality, its proleptic structure, that allows the retrospective knowledge necessary for understanding and disengagement. We must remember that Alba does not make her reconciliatory gesture directly after being released from her ordeal. Or perhaps she makes it both then and much later, after having reassembled and pieced together the events of four generations from her grandmother's notebooks and her own experiences. Neither is this reconciliation the product of an easy acceptance of fate, for Alba is initially consumed by hatred. It is only in the long process of writing that she finds the power to gesture out of it: "And now I seek my hatred and cannot seem to find it. I feel its flame going out as I come to understand the existence of Colonel Garcia and the others like him, as I understand my grandfather and piece things together from Clara's notebooks, my mother's letters, the ledgers of Tres Marias, and the many other documents spread before me on the table. It would be very difficult for me to avenge all those who should be avenged, because my revenge would be just another part of the same inexorable rite. I have to break that terrible chain" (Allende 432).

Jehenson's critique, then, does not account for the process that leads Alba to a place of reconciliation. In fact, reading her gesture as a cosmic vindication of rape or torture is misleading, as her gesture consists more precisely of a simple refusal to engage in hatred, violence, or retribution than it does in any positive act of forgiveness or vindication. This refusal to engage may be an act of self-empowerment, indeed of survival. As Desmond Tutu has argued with regard to the South African Truth and Reconciliation Commission: "If the victim could forgive only when the culprit confessed, then the victim would be locked into the culprit's whim, locked into victimhood, whatever her own attitude or intention" (272). For all its potential flaws and difficulties, Tutu's controversial theory of forgiveness renders unnecessary the gesture of self-sacrifice represented in the rape of Lucy in *Disgrace*—the logic of which irrevocably writes retribution into the as-yet-unrealized future.

Jehenson's reading also does not account for Alba's process of reconciliatory thinking as a labor occurring over time, represented in the image of a woman taking the time to process documents, letters, notebooks, and other records. This is the process of testimonial, of bearing witness, which is successfully completed in the writing of the novel. Alba's work sounds something like an individual enactment of the goals of truth and reconciliation commissions, for Alba takes it upon herself to consider testimony from "all sides": her grandmother's as well as her grandfather's, her own as well as her torturer's, as well as "many other documents." However, she does not end with this airing of the reconstructed truth of events, which might feel unsatisfying for the same reasons that hearing the truth in truth and reconciliation commissions does not automatically lead to peace and reconciliation. Instead, Alba concludes her testimony with the public gesture of reconciliation theorized by Ignatieff as necessary supplement to the testimonial discourse of truth commissions and human rights tribunals.

Considering "all sides" of the manifestation of hatred, violence, and vengeance in the act of torture, it is perhaps time to face the torturer himself.

In this case, he is Esteban Garcia, illegitimate and disavowed grandson of Esteban Trueba, who enacts his vengeance against Trueba upon the body of Trueba's legitimate granddaughter, Alba. This is the man whom Alba works to "understand" by piecing together the parallel histories of family and nation, ultimately abandoning her hatred for him. In so doing, Alba uncovers his humanity, buried beneath the hardened layers of his own violent hatred, in the form of the wounds sustained during a lifetime of racial and class oppression, and violent exclusion from the legitimacy of the patriarchal contract: "[Esteban] Trueba had forgotten all about Pancha Garcia and the fact that he had had a child with her, much less the sullen little grandson who despised him but watched him from afar to imitate his gestures and his speech. . . . [Esteban Garcia] always reproached Trueba for the dark existence he had forged for him, and he felt constantly punished, even in the days when he had reached the height of his power and had them all in his fist" (Allende 189). Allende demonstrates the source of Garcia's tortured mix of hatred, fear, and desire in the paternal rejection—racist and capitalist exploitative in origin—which ensured his exclusion from the life of safety, comfort, and wealth that would have been his had he been acknowledged as Trueba's legitimate heir, rather than the product of a long-forgotten rape. Readers may discern this same hatred—witnessing it as a profound grief—as it manifests in Esteban Garcia's first encounter with Alba, when he molests her in an act foreshadowing his later rape and torture of her after her arrest as a subversive: "The boy put his nose against her neck and inhaled that unknown perfume of cleanliness and well-being; without knowing why, his eyes filled with tears. He felt that he hated this little girl almost as much as he did old Trueba. She embodied everything he would never have, never be" (286).

Constructing one of literature's most complex, nonjudgmental, unsentimental portraits of a torturer, Allende mitigates the danger of positing a society's reconciliation upon a woman's reconciliation with her torturer/rapist by examining the familial and political structures that supported, even directed, his "career." That is, by revealing the novel's wounding as reciprocal, as distributed in complex ways according to existing social structures rather than according to the simple binaries victim/executioner, slave/master, good/evil, *The House of the Spirits* demonstrates that in order to eradicate torture, it is necessary first to dismantle those social structures, rather than attempt simply to rid ourselves of evil elements (perpetrators, executioners) capable of carrying out such acts. A system of such deep and abiding social and class inequity, characterized by such profound racism, the text seems to argue, can do nothing but inscribe those conditions upon the bodies of the individuals operating within them. Alba's realization that Garcia's torture of her has nothing to do with the interrogation to find the whereabouts of other subversives, but is a simple act of vengeance, leads her to reject such vengeance at the novel's end, thinking instead that "my task is life and . . . my mission is not to prolong hatred but simply to fill these pages" (432).

In considering the problem of representing such a reconciliatory gesture as the responsibility of the victim rather than of the perpetrator as an act of atonement, we might do well to remember that the patriarch Esteban Trueba, arguably the novel's most brutal character (more even than the torturer Garcia, given his role in building the repressive social structures which created the conditions for Garcia's actions), offers his own gesture of reconciliation. Confronted with the danger Trueba's son-in-law and political enemy Pedro Tercero Garcia faces as a subversive under the postcoup military regime, Trueba's daughter begs him to help Garcia flee the country. In the past, Trueba's hatred for Pedro Tercero Garcia was so great that, during a failed murder attempt, he mutilated Garcia by cutting off three of his fingers. For years Trueba obsessively sought to destroy Garcia in vengeance for the twin crimes of loving his daughter, a woman beyond Garcia's social class, and organizing the peasants at Tres Marias in socialist reform against the patron. And yet, with Pedro Tercero Garcia's fate finally in his hands, Trueba tries "to summon up his fury and hatred and was unable to find them. He thought of the peasant who had shared his daughter's love for half a century and was unable to find a single reason for detesting him." The evaporation of hatred is represented as occurring almost against the will and consciousness of Trueba and Alba—both of whom search strenuously for it. Significantly, it is only after Trueba's gesture of reconciliation with his enemy, if not of forgiveness, that his daughter, Blanca, is able to reach out to him: "Blanca threw her arms around his neck and covered him with kisses, weeping like a child. It was the first spontaneous hug she had given her father since her most remote childhood" (Allende 392).

Finally, in the novel's most important, and most overlooked, manifestation of the radical potential of conscious gestures out of the nonserial temporality of hatred and vengeance, Alba regards the child she carries at the novel's conclusion in a frame beyond the limits of fixed identity. It is unknown whether she is a child of love, the product of the union of Alba and her lover, Miguel (importantly this union itself crosses the lines of class, race, and cultural identity), or a child of hate, "daughter of so many rapes" (Allende 432). Indeed, given this undefined patrilineage, the child is perhaps the perfect symbol for a performance of identity that acknowledges both victim and perpetrator as constitutive of all identity. She is also removed from the patriarchal contract of legitimacy that has been the source of the novel's deepest wounding. Not knowing the child's paternity, Alba decides that the child is, "above all, my own daughter" (432).

Here, Alba refuses to participate in the structures of hatred and vengeance that have caused the death or rejection of millions of children of rape used as a means of mass terror or control. In her analysis of rape and forced pregnancy, Rhonda Copelon identifies the use of forced pregnancy not only for the purpose of "ethnic cleansing," but also as "part of a calculated effort to terrorize and shame women into fleeing their homes, and often their families and communities," by producing a "class of outcast mothers and children" (204–205). In the Chilean and Argentine contexts in particular, children of the disappeared were illegally adopted into military families as a means of cleansing the body politic of its subversive elements.[19] Copelon identifies the "unacceptability of a raped woman to the patriarchal community and, as a result, to herself," a condition which ensures the rejection of children born from rape.

Alba's decision to identify with and love her child regardless of whether she is a product of rape constitutes an act of transcendence not of the act of rape itself, but of the binding identity positions informing its perpetration. It is an act of transcendence that resonates in Archbishop Tutu's theology of Ubuntu, a philosophy of unification that informed his tenure as chair of South Africa's Truth and Reconciliation Commission, and that helped him withstand the critiques of the amnesty offered in exchange for truth which, without hope of justice or retribution, some said, could never lead to reconciliation. One such critique came from Ntsiki Biko, widow of slain Black Consciousness movement leader Steven Biko, who expressed serious reservations as to the commission's efficacy: "Nobody has ever been to me to explain what this Commission is all about, and all that I know is that at the end of it we will have to forgive those people. But how can you forgive without proper justice having been done? It's very difficult for me to go again and listen to the lies that I listened to in 1978 during the inquest. I really wouldn't like to listen to such lies" (67). In light of the commission's ambitious goal of reuniting a deeply wounded, divided nation in the postapartheid era, Biko's statement raises the central issue of the relationship between justice and truth in the context of reconciliation. Is it enough for survivors to hear the truth of their loved ones' fates: tortured and murdered in detention in South Africa; raped and massacred in Rwanda; disappeared in Argentina and Chile; or buried in mass graves in Croatia, Bosnia-Herzegovina, and Kosovo? Or does knowledge of such truth carry with it a demand for justice, even retribution? In the context of truth and reconciliation commissions around the world (in Chile, Argentina, and South Africa, for instance), the truth has been shaped—some would say compromised—by the promise of amnesty for those who willingly offer full disclosure of atrocities committed by themselves and others. Such amnesty, without benefit of judiciary mechanism, disallows imposition of traditional penalties accompanying the act of perjury, a condition which may cultivate lies in the very forum created to produce the truth. Similarly, the collective shame accompanying a shift in national political tide, such as the rise to power of the multiparty coalition led by the African National Congress in South Africa's postapartheid era, is equally likely to produce untruths in the testimonial forum. As journalist Pieter-Dirk Uys points out: "I haven't met anyone in South Africa lately who had anything to do with those years of oppression. . . . So how can a Truth Commission find any truth, when we have no-one who admits to the lies?" (47).

When asked to respond to Ntsiki Biko's anger and upset at the amnesty granted her husband's murderers, Tutu acknowledges its righteousness, adding: "I say to those who say we want justice, that if there were no amnesty, then we would have had justice and ashes" (qtd. in Brittain 41). South Africa's Truth and Reconciliation Commission took years to piece together some connections between and consequences of events, and of course that work continues today. It may have failed because its forum for testimonial discourse could not generate the moral narratives of responsibility required by those who suffered under the regime; however, it did provide a forum for hearing testimony from all parties of the old South Africa, in itself a gesture toward the promise of reconciliation in the new South Africa. In Allende, we see a similar piecing together, with the result that Alba, in loving her child without knowing its paternity (a lineage of love or of hate?), can gesture out of the recursive time of hatred by gesturing toward the exorbitant temporality of love and identification, even if that gesture involves the compromise of abandoning the desire for formal justice—or vengeance.

5

Genocide

Witness

The past two decades have seen a redesignation of many Holocaust studies programs to Holocaust and genocide studies, the emergence of the first doctoral program in genocide studies, and the publication of major studies of genocide that employ comparative analytical tools.[1] This phenomenon may be attributed to a methodological shift from the singular focus upon the Nazi Holocaust that has dominated genocide discourse since the 1960s to the comparative perspective demanded by genocides in Cambodia in the 1970s, Kurdistan in the 1980s (and, arguably, ongoing), and Bosnia and Rwanda in the 1990s, as well as to the slow acknowledgment that the concentration and eradication of Native American people constitutes genocide and the more recent naming in some quarters of the enslavement of Africans as a genocidal event.[2] Or the trend may be perceived as a result of the stark fact that, inasmuch as genocide signifies the ultimate violation of rights enacted upon a collective, rather than individual, body, it warrants the disciplinary energies of its own program of study and preparation for a life's work.[3] Contentious, painful, marked by agonized and agonizing debates, this broadening of perspective has been compelled by the paradoxical proliferation of genocides in the age of never again. With each "It is happening, now," and "There, it happened—once more," the need for comparative study and policy making intensifies.

Definitions and functions of "witness" have expanded during the same period. Some trace the source of this expansion to the 1991 Gulf War, with its blunted production of spectators through new means of television dissemination, others to the advent of the Internet and the proliferation of so-called democratizing media that render the barrage of globally violent imagery not only accessible but also largely unavoidable. Some locate the dawning of what we might call the globalization of the witness with precision at the temporal-spatial junctions of early 11 September 2001 in lower Manhattan and Washington, D.C.[4]

These two expansive trends converge on historical and intellectual ground that had already yoked them by defining and analyzing genocide precisely through the relative efficacy or lack of witness to the substance of its crimes. As many scholars of the Shoah have argued, genocide begs the question of not only the readily theorized survivor witness, but also the prickly position of the bystander witness, or the distanced-observer witness, whether individual, group, or nation, perhaps more urgently than do other rights violations, however extreme, because historically genocide has been marked by a lead time of signs and warnings that the ultimate atrocity is imminent.[5] To make sense of this precarious comparative claim, consider the role of witness in other classes of human rights violations:

- The clandestine prison, built upon impenetrable secrecy and denial, is by definition witnessed only by survivors or perpetrator/participants. The function of the bystander witness is obscured; indeed, a major function of such clandestine sites is to produce a population terrorized and made docile precisely by the ignorance around the fates of the disappeared. Cultural response to the disclosure of these converted spaces as sites of disappearance, torture, and often execution—in Latin America and Asia, for instance—has often simply made visible the space that was once the prison, attempting to force a broader public acknowledgment of that space in existential terms that can be achieved only well after the fact.[6]

- Violations occurring in time of war are widely viewed through the exceptional lens of wartime status quo, and therefore can be said to be both witnessed (known, seen, registered) and not witnessed (not acknowledged as rights violations but rationalized as exigencies of war).

- The routine degradations that fall within the categories of social and economic rights—even when accompanied by violence that may be classified under civil and political rights conventions protecting persons from physical and psychic harm—often so comprise the very foundation of societies that there is a willed or unconscious blindness on both national and international levels to their status as violations. The proliferation of global poverty with its inherent abuses; the massive, mostly unremarked, often tacitly approved violations of the rights of immigrants and refugees; the global trafficking of human beings as sex or labor slaves—these human costs of globalization are both visible and invisible, ruefully acknowledged and willfully disavowed, necessitating a highly nuanced analysis of the role of witnessing on local, national, and global levels.

Genocide diverges in form from these cases inasmuch as historically it has been marked by a lead time of signs and warnings that the ultimate atrocity, proscribed at virtually every level of the law, is imminent. For genocide to proceed, these rumblings must be willfully disregarded after a process of diplomatic scrutiny that dissolves into the collective looking away of rationalized nonintervention. In this case, the atrocity proceeds on such a scale as to make denial of knowledge on both local and international levels impossible.

As I write, genocide is being perpetrated in Darfur, Sudan; Côte d'Ivoire has risen to the preparation stage of genocide, as defined by Genocide Watch.[7] This statement evokes the existential aporia that marks the incommensurable coexistence in time of home and torture chamber, however removed in geographic space; the untenable paradox of simultaneous safety for some and irrevocable harm for others that fuels the global human rights movement. In the case of Sudan, the requisite conversations have been held among diplomats and UN representatives as to whether the crimes against humanity documented in this place "rise" to the definition of genocide.[8] While these conversations were being held, two major feature films were released among other commemorations of the tenth year after the 1994 Rwandan genocide— Terry George's *Hotel Rwanda* and Raoul Peck's *Sometimes in April*. Both critique the semantic dithering that allowed genocide to proceed without international intervention. But what is to be made of these critiques—part of the discourse of never again—by audiences who, bringing news of the current genocide in Darfur to their viewing, may feel a sinking familiarity, even simultaneity, a historical nausea that pervades the dark of the theater? How do we evaluate the motivations for and effects of such narratives of genocide purposefully released as commemorative, retrospective protests, documents that must acknowledge the futility implied by their own belatedness? Is the goal that we—the international community that didn't know or refused to act—simply know about or remember those lost to this genocide in a kind of post hoc memoriam?[9]

The answer, I think, is a tentative no. The films, like most narratives of human rights violation, operate upon the hopeful premise that awareness and an opportunity to reflect commemoratively upon the colossal failure of inaction in Rwanda may produce different action on the part of diplomatic participants and bystander witnesses in the future, and that such action will in the end produce the material condition of "never again" so passionately—if ineffectively—evoked by government officials, human rights activists, and citizens.[10] Both films mislead, however, in implying that nobody knew about Rwanda, and that this not knowing on the part of average citizens of the global community helped produce the conditions that allowed the atrocity to occur (although their comments in this regard do register the obscenity of such not knowing as an existential condition). Peck's *Sometimes in April* disapprovingly suggests that citizens of the United States and Europe may have been more interested in the death of singer Kurt Cobain than in the massacre of Tutsi and moderate Hutu people in Rwanda gathering force on the same day. There may be a gross truth in this critique of focus and attention; however, those in power in the United States, at the United Nations, and in the broader international community undeniably possessed knowledge of the situation and yet chose not to act, or to act only belatedly. The theory implied in the films hypothesizes that if more average citizens had been made aware of these events they would have asserted pressure on their representative governments, and that pressure would have translated into humanitarian intervention. Even if the case could be made for a general lack of knowledge on the part of concerned world citizens as an underlying reason that the genocide in Rwanda proceeded unhindered, certainly the expansion of media via Internet and cable networks in the intervening ten years invalidates the argument that no one knows about genocide in Sudan.[11] A vast number of ordinary people do know about the genocide in Darfur, are currently witnessing, albeit at some remove, its perpetration, and will likely consume—with authentic sorrow and empathic response—the narrative accounts on film and in books in a few years' time. How then might literary and film critics, as well as scholars concerned with human rights, address this gap between the goal of the art of human rights and its effect? How might theories of witness expand to legitimate the experience and voice of the distanced-observer witness—one who accesses atrocity through media and cultural image—so as to prevent the much-maligned devolution from witness to tourist voyeur?

Taking the agonizing belatedness of the cycle of human rights violations in general, and of genocide in particular, as a motivating foundation, we can reflect upon narrative strategies for representing genocide that model a range of witness perspectives at escalating removes from the survivor witness who occupies the space of experience, or authenticity. Two novels, Edwidge Danticat's *Farming of Bones* (1999) and Pat Barker's *Double Vision* (2004), and two films, Edoardo Ponti's *Between Strangers* (2002) and Atom Egoyan's *Ararat* (2002), represent useful examples, although the disparate nature of their subjects, origins, and means of production make them an unwieldy group to gather under a single critical umbrella. Yet the following productive similarities support a reading of the texts as evidence of the expanding generic category of witness literature:

- textual inscription of border economies that offer provocative spins on the dichotomous positions inside/outside, along with their shared threshold, to illuminate the discourses of safety and vulnerability central to the problem of genocide and its aftermath;
- juxtaposition of characters who occupy a variety of witness positions;
- metanarrative reflections upon the act of representing atrocity, particularly through characters who themselves engage in a variety of artistic and representational acts; and
- a turn to the maternal as figure for and alternative to the repetitive genocidal impulse.

Reading these texts comparatively illuminates an emerging, self-reflexive genre of witness literature with shared thematic and generic characteristics, nuanced in its apprehension of the gendered nature of violence, survivorship, and witness.

Pain as Engine: Survivor Witnessing and Emplotment

The genre of witness literature is closely linked to that of testimonial, although the two comprise distinct literary modes. Testimonial, formally emerging from the Latin American genre *testimonio*, is the narrated testimony of a survivor or survivors with close links to the testimonial paradigm in legal and psychoanalytic contexts, and is often characterized as a crucial step in the process of survival. While aestheticizing or narrativizing gestures may be made in this genre, the veracity of the testimony is not generally in question; in other words, the generic forms of story or poetry are not reducible in this instance to fiction or even to imagination. To make this point in teaching the testimonial in a course on literature and human rights, I often pair texts from the period of Argentina's "dirty war." Reading Jacobo Timerman's *Prisoner without a Name, Cell without a Number*, a classic of the testimonial form, with Alicia Partnoy's *Little School: Tales of Disappearance and Survival*, a collection of testimonial stories, poems, and drawings, provides an opportunity to discuss how narratives that depend upon being received as the truth of an author's experience may be delivered in a variety of aesthetic forms, not restricted to the chronicle deriving from legal or psychoanalytic contexts.[12] While the terms "aesthetic forms" and "author" in the previous sentence are critically complicated in the context of *testimonio*, students understand that the basic contract between writer and reader in this genre implies factual truth to the best of one's memory and integrity on the part of the writer, and acknowledgment of that truth as truth to the best of one's experience and subject position on the part of the reader. Of course this contract is broken all the time: one has only to think of Benjamin Wilkormirski's "testimonial" of childhood experiences in Nazi death camps, on the author side, or, on the part of readers, the refusal by Holocaust or other "deniers" to accept as evidentiary truth the testimonials of survivors or witnesses.[13] And still this hopeful compact, linked to individual and collective human desires for survival first, consciousness next, and prevention ultimately, hovers in the aura of the testimonial.

Problems of aesthetics in survivor testimonials are theoretically connected to the critical assessment of testimonial literature as a genre defined precisely by the internal paradox related to its formal qualities. Horace Engdahl describes the "clear objection to coupling testimony with literature" as follows: "What we normally require of true evidence is the opposite at every point of what we usually allow in a literary work, since literature enjoys the privilege of talking about reality as it is not, without being accused of lying" (6).[14] The question of truth and, by extension, of authenticity is productively complicated by the aestheticization of the testimonial narrative and by the emergence of witness literature; that is, literature that plumbs the depths of extreme human experience from a location outside that experience. To be sure, in this age of media spectacle, exposure to and concern about extreme human experiences often take place on the edge of or completely outside the experiential in a strictly corporeal sense. What is to be done with the energy generated by and for these witnesses twice removed? One task for critics is to scrutinize the highly nuanced perspectives offered in this body of literature on the nature of witnessing and the forms and perspectives it might take.

Such nuance, as Nadine Gordimer points out in her important essay "Witness: The Inward Testimony," has never been more necessary than in the aftermath of "the enormity of what happened on a sunny day in September" as people all over the earth are living it, with its attendant crises of faith, governance, and meaning (87). I hasten to assert that this claim is not meant as an assertion of the hegemony of 11 September 2001 as a traumatic event that trumps other traumatic historical events, so many of which were enabled by U.S. military, economic, and political intervention (including the "first" 11 September, in Santiago, Chile, 1973), and that thereby reorients the paradigm for all experiences of trauma and witness. Rather, I mean to register the newness of 11 September 2001 in the extent to which its events were witnessed in real time by masses of viewers who then felt a claim to a form of connection with and survivorship of the event previously unknown, even in our hypermediated world. Also, the chain of events linked to that day—most conspicuously the wars in Afghanistan and Iraq, but also the mandate assumed posthaste by the U.S. government to use any means necessary to export democracy abroad, particularly in Western Asia/the Middle East, while severely constricting the democratic function domestically—have radically shifted the trajectories of lives all across the globe. How, then, do we approach this expanding genre, witness literature, comprised either of dramatized true stories or fictionalized composites imagined by novelists and filmmakers based upon historical research and/or personal, national/ethnic, or cosmopolitan connection and commitment?[15] Witness literature comprises a form different from that of the historical novel because of its dedication to an ethic of telling atrocity for the same reasons associated with testimonial: not simply a dramatization of history, but rather an honoring of those lost to the atrocity; an aiding of survivors by legitimating their experiences; a restoration of accounts denied by hegemonic or official narratives of events; a gesture toward prevention of such events in future. While witness literature does not gesture toward the truth in an experientially authentic or evidentiary mode, it does share many of the representational ethics that characterize the testimonial form.

One notable connection among narratives that dramatize the figure who has suffered severe rights violations, regardless of the relative truth-value of the scene of that violation (Did that exact event take place in that exact time involving those exact persons?), concerns the violation of rights as the well-spring of narrative action. In such narratives the collective or individual experience of torture or terror functions quite literally as the engine that drives the exposition, the rising action, the climactic center of the piece—even the denouement, if such resolution is forthcoming. This is not to say that all such stories are plotted in the classic linear format, but rather that regardless of temporal scheme, one may locate the scene of torture as the motivating mechanism for action, however it is narrated. In the classic case of *The Battle of Algiers* (1966), the film opens with the scene of torture by electric shock of an Algerian man. In the next sequence, we see that this man has taken French police to the flat where Algerian resistance leader Ali La Pointe hides with comrades and family behind a wall. The film then flashes back to narrate the story of the Algerian resistance to French occupation, specifically in the Battle at the Casbah, circling round again to this dramatic final showdown with La Pointe and the French police. Narratively speaking, then, we understand not only that this is a story about torture, but also that torture quite literally is the story. The force that informs and drives the action—including the confession or naming of La Pointe by the tortured man—remains in viewers' minds, as flash-forwards do, while they watch for the narrative return to that point of origin. So too for survivors of torture. In testimony after testimony, one hears that once one has been tortured, time gyrates relentlessly upon that point, which sharpens to the state of determinant of action to come and even intervenes in the past, rebuilding memory itself to its specifications. It is with great will and perseverance on individual and collective levels that the stranglehold upon agency, and therefore upon temporal movement, occasioned by the experience of torture is eased. Crucially, however, we must remember that this is not the cause and effect of classic rhetoric and reason, the tidy explanatory paradigm that brings order to a chaos of plot points; rather, this is causal reason's monstrous other, the overweening abyss of power that folds over those who fall into the gorge of safety's outside and restructures time, space, and event according to its specifications.

Edwidge Danticat's *Farming of Bones*, which recounts the massacre of Haitian people in the Dominican Republic in 1937, is an interesting case in terms of this relation between the scene of torture and emplotment.[16] Danticat's novel is divided into forty-one chapters. The first twenty-five alternate between the present-tense experience of genocide brewing in the Dominican Republic, where protagonist Amabelle and her lover Sebastien live and work, and reflections identified by bold type as internal, indirect discourse about the past, particularly the deaths of Amabelle's parents and Sebastien's father in Haiti. From the twenty-sixth chapter until the book's conclusion, the novel focuses solely upon the events of the genocide and its aftermath, with only one return to the past-tense reflective mode. This structural shift may be read as a function of the urgent need to testify, which becomes the driving concern of the rest of the narrative. In a makeshift camp on the Haitian side of the border, we listen in on a group of survivors as they share their stories, "the haste in their voices sometimes blurring the words, for greater than their desire to be heard was the hunger to tell" (209). The living rhythm of the novel's first section is paralyzed by the experience of torture and terror that overtakes the narrative, freezing it in the perpetual present tense of the traumatic need to testify.

The rhythm established in the first section of the book is one of balance and connection between the private loss of family members to natural forces, such as the rise of the river's current that caused the drowning of Amabelle's parents or the hurricane that took Sebastien's father, and the public devastation of well-planned and -executed genocide. These private and public losses converge at the site of the River Massacre that marks the border between the two countries: claimant of Amabelle's parents' lives, the river is also the dumping ground for bodies struck down in the massacre, and the crossing point that demarcates the vulnerability of Haitians in the Dominican Republic and their safety from the immediate threat of bodily harm as they cross back to the Haitian side. Indeed, the journey to the Dominican Republic in the novel is termed a traverse to "the other side," a double entendre indicating the extent to which the river cartographically and symbolically figures the blurred, flowing border between nations that also signifies life and death in the novel's symbolic scheme. This conjoining of violent/public with natural/private death foregrounds the structural connection between the acute violence of genocide and the sustained violence of poverty, oppression, and the colonial legacy. Danticat complicates the common perception of genocide as whirlwind elemental force, like the hurricane that took the life of Sebastien's father, rising as a primal, chaotic violence that soon settles back to everyday calm. Acknowledging through this parallel that the moment of genocide's perpetration may be experienced as that kind of primal eruption, Danticat also figures genocide as the logical result of the sustained violation of human rights in the social and economic order that originated in slavery and is traumatically repeated in contemporary neocolonial global systems.

This representation coincides with recent sociological studies of genocide that historicize genocidal violence in its specific contexts, exposing its vast bureaucratic efforts and efficiencies.[17]

The climate that emerges through the novel's early rhythm is that of a living death, relieved for Amabelle only by the love and witness she shares with Sebastien. Indeed, the novel's protagonists are acutely conscious of living in an aura of anticipated death: "In the awakened dark, Sebastien says, if we are not touching, then we must be talking. We must talk to remind each other that we are not yet in the slumbering dark, which is an endless death, like a darkened cave" (Danticat 13). Crucially, human connection through touch and speech mitigates possession by a death construed as "endless" and therefore without spirit, without possibility of return. Or, read another way, as ultimately meaningless, without an end or purpose—as in genocide, characterized by its obscene enunciation of a reason for the genocidal program, which is always in the end revealed to be an irrational deduction from hatred, violence, and the will to power. The construction "awakened dark," or night, is repeated in these intermittent chapters, barely distinguishable from the "slumbering" dark that is physical death, always both lived and expected in this border space. Still, even the darkness of death holds the potential for renewal, for the darkened cave is refigured in the novel's complex symbolic scheme as the site of Amabelle's and Sebastien's first lovemaking, a space of natural beauty and supernatural life-force to which Sebastien's spirit ultimately returns: "When the night comes, you don't know it inside the cramped slippery cave because the waterfall, Sebastien says, holds on to some memory of the sun that it will not surrender. On the inside of the cave, there is always light, day and night" (100). Further, the modifier "slumbering" implies a light sleep, a dozing or drowsing as opposed to a leaden sleep from which one may not wake. This subtle etymological distinction holds the premise of geographer Ruth Gilmore's important (re)definition of racism, specifically formulated in terms of the occupation of different geographic spaces. Following Orlando Patterson's earlier work on race and civil death, Gilmore posits that "racism is the state-sanctioned and/or legal production and exploitation of group-differentiated vulnerabilities to premature death, in distinct yet densely interconnected political geographies."[18] Haitian migrants to the Dominican Republic in the mid–twentieth century, as Danticat's narrative dramatizes, were always suspended in this anticipatory space, living within easy reach of death from the elements, from poverty and hard labor, or from violence.

This project of revealing the extent to which certain populations are always already exposed to death's visage, unable to hold the distancing silence around death and dying common to western culture after modernity, is increasingly relevant to an ethical articulation of human rights in the twenty-first century. Specifically, Danticat's *Farming of Bones* dramatizes the way in which the systematic withholding of social and economic rights from a majority of citizens of the so-called third world underpins the distribution of civil and political violence, up to and including genocide. This splitting of "soft" social and economic rights from civil and political rights derives from the early cold war politics that informed the drafting of the UN Universal Declaration of Human Rights, including the hard fact that sub-Saharan Africa, still bound under colonial dominion, was excluded from participation in that drafting. Indeed, the United States continues to aver that the rights enshrined in the Covenant on Social and Economic Rights are not, in fact, rights, but rather "interests" or "aspirations."[19] The refusal of western governments and international human rights actors to attend to social and economic rights as indivisible from civil and political rights is a source of global suspicion of human rights efforts as a masquerade for yet another manifestation of western imperialism. More significantly, it is a root cause of the intractable cycle of human rights violations in both acute (war, genocide, violence) and chronic (hunger, disease, violence) forms. It remains to be seen whether the most influential international human rights organizations will widen their agendas in this direction, thereby relegitimating the promise of universal human rights discourses.

Of Riverbanks and Thresholds: Safety and Vulnerability

In *The Farming of Bones*, the border economy common to much witness literature takes form in the River Massacre that separates Haiti from the Dominican Republic. Specifically, the river figures the vulnerability of Haitian people to the systemic economic and political exploitation that informs migration across its border, and that is analogous to the grand violence of genocide which propels those same people back across the river to momentary safety from the acute threat of massacre (although such safety does not provide sustained relief from the exploitative conditions informing the initial migration). As a margin between life and death, the river figures death as both natural, grief-provoking loss and as return, the site of ancestral vitality common to African diasporic spiritual traditions and the escape from harm that can be had only through the cessation of corporeal sense that is death. It is not, as in the River Styx of the Western tradition, a space of forgetting between two worlds. It is a world unto itself, and the forgetting to be had in it is only that of the pain of the living world, smoothed away in its currents like water over stones.

The river, then, is the massacre, the genocide, but it is also paradoxically a marginal space into which Amabelle slips to escape the new manner of living death she experiences as survivor witness of the genocide. The river is the grave of Amabelle's parents and of many of those lost to the genocide, thereby holding in its current the parallel between the diffuse vulnerability of racism—with its handmaidens, poverty and exploitation—and the acute exposure of genocide. Amabelle crossed the river on market day with her parents to buy cooking pots: the rise of the river's current with an anticipated but not adequately acknowledged force as they attempt to cross back symbolizes the vulnerability of people who, the novel's image system seems to say, must regularly pass close to or even through the space of death as part of daily living. The force of the current parallels the brewing of genocide: denied until too late in the dance of survival that, given the regular encounter with the specter of death, can no longer distinguish between death's rehearsal and the live performance. The river, in the end, holds both kinds of bodies: the one endangered by exposure to poverty, racism, and exploitation, and the other destroyed by genocide. Still, the River Massacre is uncannily both death (slaughter) and life (generative potential), as well as the wide margin of escape between. Read through the lens of Haitian vodou, this multiple sense of the river is not a product of symbolic overdetermination but a representation of the ordinary coexistence of life with death. The novel is dedicated by Amabelle herself: "In confidence to you, Metres Dlo, Mother of the Rivers." Metres Dlo is a form of the vodou spirit, or *loa*, Erzulie, who inhabits the waters and consorts with Legba, guardian of the crossroads between worlds.[20] In this context, Amabelle's entry into the river is not a suicide in the clinical sense but an embrace of a liminal space that holds the spirit of the mother's generative potential and the spiritual promise of the Afro-Caribbean tradition. It also quite simply relieves the pain of the survivor's living death; note that the story is dedicated "in confidence," as a secret—or a testimony. The contract between Amabelle and the mother/deity, Metres Dlo, diffuses as an aura that includes the reader in the bond of trust upon which the testimonial form depends. Whether entering the river's embrace implies crossing into the "slumbering darkness" of death is unimportant in the narrative trajectory, partly because this death would not signify the definitive crossing, and therefore narrative closure, of the modern western tradition. It is also significant that Amabelle chooses to "lie down" in the river because her generative potential, the legacy she might leave her children, has been reduced to the compulsion to repeat the story of the traumatic event of genocide.

In its focus upon the figure of the survivor witness, Danticat's novel provides a point of contrast for a reading of texts that dramatize the function of the distanced-observer witness. In her work on Albert Camus' novel *The Plague*, which she considers exemplary of the possibilities and challenges of the genre of testimonial literature, Shoshana Felman delineates some valences of the distinction between victim-survivor and observer witnesses in the genocidal context. Interpreting the plague at the novel's center as an allegory for the Holocaust, Felman reads the "town under quarantine, which, in its isolation from the outside world, is enclosed within its own contagious, deadly space and abandoned to its fear and desperation, [as] reminiscent of the situation of a concentration camp" (98). This interpretation recognizes the spatial dichotomy inside/outside, which is dramatized in the figure of the journalist Rambert, who is on assignment in the town at the time the plague emerges. As an outside observer, Rambert desires to leave that place unscathed by its trouble, and in making his case to the doctor argues: "I'm not from here." The doctor, of course, turns down his request to leave. Felman reads Rambert as a figure for the distanced-observer witness who must accept "what it means to be 'from here' (from quarantine), wherever one is from," which also means accepting "knowledge of the way in which 'this history concerns us all'" (111). The deictic "here" in Felman's reading is a paradox, figuring the ability to imagine the place of vulnerability as immediate and proximate even though that place is literally "there," somewhere else. In Camus' parable, the journalist has traveled to that place as a formal observer, rendering it literally "here" for him. Reading allegorically in the post-9/11 context, however, we can intuit that the journalist is us, inasmuch as we have found ourselves effectively quarantined within a world's worth of disaster made accessible ("here," often in real time) through the media of television and Internet, even as that disaster remains, for the most part, materially and spatially "there" (Iraq, Palestine, Afghanistan, Sudan, Chad, Cote d'Ivoire . . .). Felman understands that Camus' parable demands acceptance that "this business . . . is everybody's business" and, further, that this acceptance defines the function of contemporary witness literature.

Such acceptance of shared vulnerability to the harm disavowed as naturally meant to occur in the elsewhere that anchors capitalist-democratic safety is echoed in a broad range of contemporary theoretical attempts to grapple with the way in which we are all constituted as witnesses in the post-Holocaust, and now post-9/11, moments. We hear it Jonathan Raban's contention that "although only some three thousand people actually died out of a population of nearly three hundred million, everyone living in American on that morning could feel that we were, in some more-than-merely-metaphoric sense, survivors" (4). We find it in Judith Butler's first-person acknowledgment in *Precarious Life* of the "enigmatic traces of others" whose "nameless and faceless deaths form the melancholic background for my social world, if not my First Worldism" (46); in Dominic LaCapra's validation of the "empathic unsettlement" experienced by the distanced witness, typified by the historian, exposed to testimonies of atrocity; in the notion of "haunting" that in Susan Sontag's estimation justifies producing and circulating images of atrocity in spite of the enormous risks of appropriation and exploitation. Such acceptance is raison d'être of the internationalist who rejects nationalisms that foreclose upon empathic connection between "there" and "here."[21] The emergence of these notions of haunting and witness contemporaneously across disciplines opens space for a timely decentering of the discourse of authenticity attached to experience. As LaCapra asserts: "There is an important sense in which the after-effects—the hauntingly possessive ghosts—of traumatic events are not fully owned by anyone and, in various ways, affect everyone" (ix).

Without diminishing the singularity of traumatic experience, it is instructive to consider the production of energy implied in LaCapra's formulation, its lessons and especially its role in producing an internationalist consciousness with implications for human connection on a wider global scale. Returning to narrative structure, one may observe that while in survivor testimonial the experience of violation is often structurally inscribed as a kind of textual engine, in distanced-observer witness literature it surfaces instead as a grammar of transition. That is, rather than functioning as exposition, drive, and motive for emplotment, traces of the traumatic event observed from a distance emerge narratively as subtle juxtapositions of characters or events, often inscribed in transitional moments between scenes and chapters. Like the experience of the traumatic event by observers at some physical and emotional remove from its perpetration, these narrative components are studies in indirection, reinforcing in formal terms the mediated quality of the traumatic event experienced through representation rather than upon the body. Of course, this observation is entirely predictable, based upon the relative pain experienced by the survivor witness and distanced-observer witness, respectively. As we will see, this structural emphasis upon mediation also informs the turn of contemporary novels and films of witness to meta-textual commentary upon their own representational acts. The value of studying this grammar of transition is in its revelation of the ways in which the collective wounding of atrocity can connect us rather than impel us further into the siege mentalities that produce endless cycles of violence. It also instructs us as to the gendered nature of such connections or divisions.

Emphasis upon the transitional moment between scenes and chapters, and among historical moments and characters, is a central feature of contemporary witness literature that thematizes the energy produced in the distanced-observer witness of the mediated traumatic event. While Danticat's River Massacre represents the richly layered border that quite literally denotes life, death, and a blurring of the two for victims and survivors of genocide, Pat Barker's *Double Vision* sets up border economies in suggestive spatial terms that figure safety and vulnerability within the broader frame of the potential for human connection in relation to the traumatic event. In *Double Vision*, that border is figured by the hearth or the threshold, and the transitional grammar employed in the text can be discerned in the leave-takings that accumulate at the end of nearly every one of the novel's twenty-seven chapters.

Barker's novel is a self-conscious reflection upon the exigencies of representation in the post-9/11 context. The novel portrays characters at varying degrees of separation from historic atrocity engaged in a variety of modes of reflection upon the ethics of representing such atrocity and the human energy produced by witnessing it. Set in the aftermath of 9/11 during the outbreak of hoof-and-mouth disease that prompted the slaughter of thousands of animals in the English countryside, the novel has two protagonists, in keeping with its titular suggestion of double vision. Kate Frobisher is a sculptor working on a larger-than-life Christ figure commissioned for the town square and mourning the death of her photojournalist husband, Ben, killed on the roadside in post-9/11 Afghanistan. Ben's colleague, Stephen Sharkey, is newly divorced and has moved from London to the village near Newcastle where Kate lives and works to write a book about the ethics of representing atrocity. The novel whirls with peripheral characters who refract one another, shedding brief light or energy in their encounters before spinning back to the contours of their own subplots. Barker sets these multiple per-spectives at divergent angles from which to reflect upon immediate human responses to danger or harm, the long-term divisions or connections made possible by those responses, and the exigencies of representing both vulner-ability and the response to it.

Whereas in *The Farming of Bones* vulnerability to exploitation and violence is inscribed upon the bodies of characters accustomed to living in the aura of death, *Double Vision* plots the more nebulous sources of vulnerability in the first world to criminal violence, accidental death, or illness—although these kinds of vulnerability are juxtaposed to the political violence of Rwanda, Bosnia, and Afghanistan witnessed by the journalists Ben and Stephen. The fear of danger finds its symbols in the mythical forest that surrounds the medieval village near Newcastle where the novel is set, and in the white van driven by Kate's assistant, Peter Wingrave, and spotted at the scenes of more than one crime. Indeed, Wingrave's mysterious criminal tendencies lurk menacingly over the mise en scène of the novel as another figure of unnam-able threat, the kind that plagues the sureties of the privileged parts of the first world in its capacity—shared with illness or accident—to materialize at any moment and quite literally wreck everything.

In a sense, however, the authentic setting for the novel is not Newcastle or London, Bosnia or Afghanistan, but an iconic threshold, the space between inside and outside, warmth and cold, safety and vulnerability, connection and division. This threshold is first evoked in the novel's opening scene, when Kate stares back from her yard at "the lighted windows and reflected fire-light" of her home: "All around her the forest waited, humped in silence" (Barker 3). The archetypal rendering of the forest as threatening force per-vades the novel, setting up a dichotomy between culture—figured by the well-lighted home—and nature. In this formulation, nature doubles as the outdoors, doppelganger of the safety that humans desperately seek in their architec-tures and technologies, and as human nature—the dark aspect of human being that resists thousands of years of acculturation and civilization in its relentless raw attraction to power, violence, death.

The border between inside/outside is reinforced in the image of Kate's car traveling through the dark forest: "She kept the windows closed, a fug of warmth and music sealing her off from the outside world" (Barker 4). This wonderfully evocative noun, "fug," is repeated throughout the text and signi-fies the warm safety of the inside. At the end of the novel, Stephen Sharkey and his young lover, Justine, refuse shelter from a storm in the covered cabin of a boat "with its fug of human bodies and damp wool" (229). Inasmuch as inside gathers meaning in its relation to outside, then, this fug can be both the safety and warmth of protection from natural elements and the claustrophobic, funky danger of human contact that exceeds comfortable distance (culturally determined, of course) and that, in its extreme form, moves from distaste to the kind of hatred that can breed genocide.[22]

The novel's play with the archetypal division of space reinscribes the domestic as site of safety. The ambivalence of the word "fug," however, indicates the extent to which this domestic inside holds its own dangers and uncertainties, a hint that is confirmed after the threat of criminal violence materializes at the end of the novel. In this event—a domestic break-in at Stephen Sharkey's brother's home involving a brutal assault against Justine—the family can identify for the police report that the DVD, TV, and "music centre" have been taken; however, while they can see that "the mantelpiece had been swept clean," no one can remember what had been on it (Barker 207). The mantel, signifying the display of meaning in the domestic space, reveals the deficiency of human connection that plagues the novel. Even as the novel sets the domestic as site of human aspirations for warmth, closeness, and safety, it reveals the degradation of this aspiration specifically as a function of modernity, inasmuch as the high-tech equipment in the home appears to hold unnaturally deep meaning, named and remembered in the aftermath of a violence that is also implicated as part of the cold disconnect of modernity.

My location of this aspect of the novel's critique in the modern has also to do with the mise en scène affected by the backdrop of hoof-and-mouth disease in the novel, which deliberately evokes the Nazi Holocaust, and which is also introduced to readers through a scene of witness: "Kate had stood with Angela, whose precious boys had been destroyed in the same cull, on a hill not far away from the farm and watched the fire burn. Clouds of foul-smelling black smoke had obscured the setting sun. The pitiful legs of cows and sheep stuck up from the mound of corpses and rubber tyres. A stench of rotting flesh drifted toward them over the valley, scraps of burnt hair and skin whirled into the air. Kate put her arm around Angela's shoulders and was trying to persuade her to leave, when a flake of singed cowhide landed on her lower lip, and she spat and clawed at her mouth to get the taste away" (Barker 28). The passage evokes the Holocaust through sensory remains: the odor; the smoke; the ash that falls like snow (see the paradigmatic misperception of ash as snow that opens Elie Weisel's *Night*); and the way in which the witness—willing or unwilling—is corporeally implicated in the violation simply by occupying the same space. This latter point, concretized in the singed cowhide that falls on Kate's lip, resonates with testimonies from New Yorkers regarding the horror of breathing the air in lower Manhattan for weeks after 9/11, the way in which they experienced the ingestion of death and violation with every breath. In a vein similar to J. M. Coetzee's recent attention to the treatment of animals as a lens through which to view the endemic cruelty of human nature, the efficient certitude and unfeeling acceptance of the massacre of these animals are part of the aura of everyday life in *Double Vision*.[23] The character Angela, whose four sheep—her "boys"—are unceremoniously slaughtered, legitimates the love of the one both as one and as differentiated member of its group. It is this singular love that is sacrificed in the genocidal impulse.

The symbolic scheme of the sun obscured by the black smoke of the cull in the passage further connects this event to the Nazi Holocaust. Reflecting upon his position as voluntary witness to human atrocity via his journalism, Stephen Sharkey remarks: "There was a guy once—a Holocaust survivor—who said something about seeing the sun rise in Auschwitz and it was black. But you see he chose that experience" (Barker 72). Following the thread of smoke from the pyre in Newcastle through its reference to Auschwitz, we pick it up again after Kate views a Goya painting depicting "the interior of a prison. Seven men in shackles, every tone, every line expressing despair" (127). Leaving the exhibition, Kate "squint[s] up into a pale sun that was rapidly being obscured by trails of black cloud" (128). The image recurs briefly again in an exchange between the two brothers, Stephen and Robert Sharkey, in which Stephen betrays the intimacy of his physician brother's confidence by making a cruel joke comparing him to Josef Mengele. At this moment, "a wisp of cloud drifted across the sun" (176). Bits of the übercruelty that was the Holocaust accumulate through these references. The symbolic system asks us to acknowledge the connection between the everyday cruelties of men—"wisps of cloud"—and the wholesale abandonment of the human that pulls the switch on the force of life, producing the Holocaust's black sun.

The final link in this symbolic chain occurs after Robert Sharkey's home has been broken into and Justine viciously beaten. Robert's son, Adam, has drawn a picture to take to Justine, who is his nanny, in hospital: "It was the scene every child paints: a house with a smoking chimney, curtains at the windows, a tree in the garden, Mum, Dad, child, dog standing on the lawn, and behind them all, filling the whole sky, an enormous, round, golden sun" (Barker 218). Given that Adam's parents are in the process of divorcing, and he is lonely and miserable both at home and in school, the picture serves as a reminder of the way in which images have become available for circulation regardless of the authentic truth-value they may contain. The mythic quality of the novel in its foregrounding of the home versus the forest is repeated here in the archetypal form of the "scene every child paints." This image engenders the most banal qualities necessary to the production of maximum sun-ness: hugeness, roundness, goldenness. Readers know, however, that it is a false, brooding sun, hanging with a malevolent irony over the illusory image of home and family. Most significantly, the image has been drawn by a child afflicted with Asperger's syndrome, a psychological condition that limits the potential for human connection.

And here is one of the great payoffs of Barker's novel, and one of the ways it mirrors other witness literature that employs narrative structure to model something about human connection, which is in its severance foundational to the problem of genocide, and in its potential fulfillment foundational to the vision of a more even distribution of safety across the globe. Virtually every one of the novel's twenty-seven chapters closes with an instance of physical or emotional separation. What to make of such structural emphasis upon leave-takings in a novel about witnessing pain and violence? One way to get at this question is to connect this structural point with the symbolic function of the sun in the novel, for often the departure that closes a chapter is from an inside space of light and warmth to an outside that is cold and dark. These last lines accumulate:

> Chapter 6: "Dragging herself reluctantly away from the warm fug of the studio, [she] let herself out into the icy winter air" (60).
>
> Chapter 7: "He set off down the frosty path, raising his hand to wave to her as he reached the gate, feeling the withdrawal of warmth and light as a minor but real abandonment" (67).
>
> Chapter 9: "The front door released a sliver of golden light onto the trampled snow, and then she was gone" (79).

And so on. Meaning gathers in the transitional space of the threshold between scenes, until the novel's emphasis upon the mythic qualities of home merges finally with its structural emphasis upon connection and separation in the romance of middle-aged Stephen with nubile young Justine. The romance allows another opportunity for Barker to invoke a form, a genre available to be filled with content that may not correspond to the form's signification: the child's picture of family; the mythic tropes of forest and home; and in this case, the love affair by which aging man regains vitality and a sense of youth in erotic coupling with far younger woman. As Adam's enormous golden sun, brooding over the traditional nuclear family in their traditional home, masked the truth of brokenness and disconnection that was Adam's truth; as the warm fug of the home is easily penetrated by the threatening element of the outside, thereby revealing the emptiness at its hearth; so the banal love affair Barker sets up between Stephen and Justine could simply be an empty form, an open genre for the two of them to fall into, seemingly full of meaning yet empty at its core. However, the novel's surprise is the significance at the heart of this relationship. It fulfills all the novel's hints that human desire, nurture, love, and care can override the empty violence lurking at every turn and can also transcend the empty signifiers of generically gendered heteroerotics.

Barker uses form, then, to invite readers to look anew at images, ideas, even relationships that may feel so worn, so clichéd as to be emptied of meaning. In this re-visioning through the denouement of this old, old love story that, in our cynicism, we thought we knew so well, we find a kind of resolution for questions related to atrocity and witnessing posed in the novel's multiple strands. This resolution conveys a position on the important question of the role of rape in genocide, and its treatment in international law (this plot point informs my reasoning for including the novel in a chapter on representations of genocide, although like much literature of witness, the novel's approach to the genocide is diffused by its structure as an ensemble piece of multiple characters and subplots occurring in diverse geopolitical spaces). Many of the novel's metatextual reflections upon the ethics of representing historical atrocity focus upon the body of a girl found by Stephen and his partner, Ben, in Sarajevo during the Bosnian crisis.[24] The body is marked by the signs of rape: skirt pulled up to her waist, "her splayed thighs enclosing a blackness of blood and pain" (45). Note the blackness that links this image to that of the black sun rising over Auschwitz; its relation to that mass atrocity is a matter of scale. So too, as Stephen asserts, is the relationship between the rape of individual women by criminals and the rape of many women as part of war, ethnic cleansing, or genocide: "No way of telling whether this was a casual crime—a punter wanting his money back, a drug deal gone wrong—or a sectarian killing linked to the civil war. Increasingly crime and war shade into each other, Stephen thought. No difference to their victims, certainly, and not much either in the minds of the perpetrators. Patriot, soldier, revolutionary, freedom fighter, terrorist, murderer—cross-section their brains at the moment of killing and the differences might prove rather hard to find" (45). The image haunts Stephen throughout the novel in the traumatic repetition of nightmare and flashback, literalized when from a distance he sees men breaking into his brother's home, with Justine inside. As he runs to her rescue, his mind reverts to the available narrative for what would be happening just then to Justine: "Locked in his brain . . . was the truth. All the way down the hillside he'd had flashbulbs exploding in his head. So many raped and tortured girls— he needed no imagination to picture what might be happening to Justine. It would not have surprised him to find her lying like a broken doll at the foot of the stairs, her skirt bunched up around her waist, her eyes staring" (210). This last image is the picture of the girl in Sarajevo—both her real body witnessed by Stephen and Ben, and the photo taken by Ben the next day. It is also, however, the prosaic, ever-ready image into which rape narratives— ranging from TV crime drama to formal testimonies at the Hague—pour themselves. Transcending the fatigue of the image, the *truth*(s) to which Stephen refers are the broad truth of intolerable pain, the particular truths of violence against women the world over, and the contingent truth that human rights theory and law are finally settling upon: that the rape of a woman constitutes torture whether it is perpetrated in collective, genocidal, or individual criminal contexts.

Of Tears and Clichés: Sentimental Recuperations

The novel's denouement in the unlikely realization of true love—and I mean that literally, as well as in the sense of the cliché—resolves the system of signs and symbols that has structured the novel by moving the narrative off the threshold between the archaic place markers "home" and "forest." We turn, then, to a space bequeathed to the lovers by Kate, whose connection with Ben was most fully realized there, and who advises the lovers to "possess, as I possessed a season, the countries I resign" (Barker 238). Traveling to the space that marked an authentic love whose season ended violently and too soon, Stephen and Justine's relationship is finally legitimized as real in a way that transcends the ruinous risk of cliché that haunts its being—as the pain of the

raped and murdered woman has been understood to transcend the unthinkable cliché of its overcirculated image. Claiming the words "I love you" mitigates, if only momentarily, Stephen's haunting by the image: "For a moment
he saw the girl in the stairwell in Sarajevo, but she'd lost her power. This
moment in this bed banished her, not forever, perhaps, but for long enough.
He rolled over and took Justine in his arms" (253). For the first time in the
novel, a chapter ends upon a note of connection, its power multiplied in contrast to the twenty-five endings/separations that preceded it. The scene
reminds us of the extent to which our ability to connect in ways that exceed—
even as they may remain trapped within—available roles, clichés, stereotypes,
and images depends upon our ability to mitigate the petty cruelties that start
as wisps of cloud and end with a sun blackened to our view.

The closing image of the novel seals the force of this idea, gently invoking
the full weight of the novel's deep symbolic structure: "Then he put his arm
around her shoulders and they walked on . . . while behind them the sun rose
above the dunes, casting fine blue shadows of marram grass onto the white
sand" (Barker 259). Lovers strolling arm and arm on the beach. An image
thoroughly hackneyed in its repetition in classified ads nauseum surfacing
with substance; the powerful incredulity that readers share with the characters themselves in finding that meaning has been made from insubstantial
form. The iconography of the ocean and its dunes evokes an entirely different
mytheme than the home/forest of the novel's frame, resisting the inside/
outside dichotomy and even the figure of the threshold or border between. It
is, instead, an ideal space, simultaneously vast (the ocean) and protected (the
dunes), the satisfaction of our deepest desires for the world itself: that humans
could experience its incalculable potential, its fierce beauty, while at the same
time mitigating the dreadful vulnerability that naturally accrues to such exposure. It is a space of completion, consummation, connection, and the sun is
simply on the rise—neither Holocaust black nor fairytale golden—the shadows
around the lovers visible as what they are and not what is feared. The blue of
ranging natural affect rather than the black of cruelty and dehumanization.

This symbolic space counters the cynicism through which the old
"solidarity-based internationalisms of Socialism and Feminism" have given
way to an internationalism "which has perversely created a political environment where cosmopolitan and translocal affiliations become suspect and are
now virtually unthinkable outside of the limited codes of human-rights talk,
medical emergency, and environmental catastrophe" (Gilroy 5). Paul Gilroy's

analysis of the ways in which "cosmopolitical responses" have been co-opted from above in a "revival of imperialism . . . revised and rendered newly benign, progressive, and liberal" exposes hegemonic forces quite willing to adapt multicultural tools in service of their Forever War, which may be characterized as a war on dissent against the teleological narrative of global capitalist empire (92). Acknowledging the cruel cynicism of cosmopolitan sensitivities deployed as cover for the extralegal brutalities that mark our new international engagement—the "culturally appropriate meals which we are told have been served to U.S. prisoners at Camp Delta" are a case in point—Gilroy argues that progressive forms of cosmopolitan solidarity must be rescued from their current dismissal by agents across the political spectrum as naïve, idealistic, sentimental, impractical (92). He considers Rachel Corrie, U.S. activist with the International Solidarity Movement killed by Israeli forces in Rafah, Gaza, in the Palestinian Occupied Terroritories, as a paradigmatic example of such activism wrongly dismissed as "trivial"; activists who served as human shields in Iraq have been considered in the same light.[25] I perceive a productive thread connecting Gilroy's retrieval of such actions in the global sphere and the generic turn to the sentimental specifically focused upon challenges to and possibilities for human connection in the body of texts I study here. Such retrieval in the cultural sphere is of a piece with the power of the sentimental defended by Jane Tompkins in her study of the cultural work of sentimental fiction in the fraught historical contexts of the eighteenth and nineteenth centuries.

Tompkins's recuperation of women's domestic fiction from this period identifies the characteristics that I observe emerging in contemporary witness literature and film: the stereotyped character, the clichéd or improbable plot point, and the sentimental as, precisely, women's fiction or fiction that addresses "trivial" women's concerns (xiv). In the contemporary moment, the context is global human rights rather than, say, abolitionism or temperance. Importantly, benefiting from decades of literary criticism of the exclusions of race, class, and sexuality as critical terms informing the production and reception of domestic or sentimental narratives, current work in this vein is more deeply reflexive about the complex interplay among and exclusions based upon these identity categories.[26] Indeed, its power in the postmodern moment is not in the reproduction of "the formulaic and derivative . . . in a typical and familiar form," as Tompkins identifies in the texts she studies, but in the strategic scrutiny of such generic conventions via complex metanarrative reflections. The function of the metanarrative to reflect upon the ethics and politics of representing human rights violations and their causes and effects in the texts under consideration here also marks a stark contrast with the unthinking formulae of the counterhistorical dramatic film discussed in chapters 1 and 2.

Another text of witness—Edoardo Ponti's *Between Strangers*—uses gendered narrative conventions in the context of witnessing atrocity to comment upon human connections too easily dismissed as banal, sentimental, or naively idealistic. Using a transitional grammar that juxtaposes signs and symbols of loss and its representation to build the stories of three women, the film employs the sentimental to evoke the possibility of a radical—and radically gendered—connection. The three women are Natalia (Mira Sorvino), a photojournalist who has just scored the cover of *Time* magazine with an image of a small Angolan girl snapped at the moment her home and village are being decimated in that country's longstanding civil war; Olivia (Sophia Loren), an artist married to a disabled man who is abusive and cruel; and Katherine, a cellist whose father murdered her mother after years of abusing her. Each woman feels responsible for the loss of a child—specifically, a girl child—and each tries to mitigate the harmful effects of guilt and pain by engaging in a representational act. Natalia has lost the child in her award-winning photo, who died in the second after the last frame of film, and her representational medium is photography. Olivia's lost child is the daughter whom she was forced as a teenager to give up for adoption; her furious charcoal sketches are iconic in their representation of women being consumed by flames. Katherine's child is both her child self, devastated by her father's abuse of her mother, and now her own daughter, whom she is unable to mother as a result of her trauma. Her music bears the same mark of intensity as the other women's representational acts both in the sound and in the desperate force with which she draws her bow across the strings. As in *Double Vision*, the film shows how the women are connected through their loss and their attempts to represent it using a grammar of transition in which scenes shift, for example, through the livid movement of Olivia's charcoal across the page as it dissolves into the thrust of Katherine's bow across the strings.

These transitional mechanisms accumulate in the film, instructing us that what lies between these strangers is what connects us all, and what I return to as sites for connective ties that can be made productive with careful attention to their complexities: vulnerability to violence and loss; the desire for safety and, even, joy; and an embrace of the creative, connective impulse. Its pedagogy, introduced in the film's epigraph—"Be kind and be kind, for everyone you meet is engaged in a great struggle"—surfaces in transitions between scenes, revealing the kind of connections that in real life prompt incredulous responses at seemingly impossible coincidences: What a small world! That these coincidences are unknown to the characters themselves suggests the melancholy of missed opportunity—not only the blindness to everyday miracles that is part of the techne of modernity, but also our larger failed visions of solidarity in, say, feminism, or the political Left, or antiracist, -classist, or-homophobic activism.

Significantly, these coincidences that connect characters stand for the perpetration of violence and the desire to protect. The specter of violence materializes early in a gang of volatile teenage boys who vandalize the store at which Olivia works, nearly knocking her down as they run out. They jostle Natalia as they emerge onto the sidewalk, screaming, "Fuck you!" at her when she protests. Later they will kill Katherine's father in a brutal street crime. The representation of this gang asserts something about the characteristics of violence: its gendered nature, including the threat of sexual violence made explicit in the epithet "Fuck you," and its utter lack of sense, a category of thought and action lacking meaning, achieving nothing. These characteristics are confirmed in the broader cases of violence in the film, which are also explicitly gendered male: the civil war in Angola witnessed by Natalia, waged by men and suffered by women and children; the global plague of domestic violence witnessed by Katherine; the violent separation of Olivia from her daughter by paternal force and then her subjugation by a brutalizing husband.[27] As do other examples of contemporary witness literature, the film juxtaposes different strains, scales, and sites of violence in order to make meaningful connections and distinctions among their effects and the variety of responses to them from survivors and witnesses.

The obverse of the youthful gang as a kind of metaviolence connecting the particular brutalities experienced by the women in the film takes shape in a little girl who is, like the paradoxical blend of loss and joy she emblematizes, both real and unreal—ghostly. This ethereal child figures both the loss caused by pervasive masculinist violence and the desire to protect oneself and others from harm. In a powerful scene filmed in one long handheld shot, the little girl materializes on a busy street, walks smiling toward Olivia, and then vanishes, only to emerge with the same serene smile in Natalia's vision. As

Natalia walks toward her, she vanishes again; running to find her, Natalia passes Katherine walking toward the perpendicular street corner. In the same scene, Katherine passes Olivia, who sits on a park bench, sketching. It is precisely the unrealism of the scene—emphasized by its framing in one extended, unbroken shot—and its unapologetic appeal to the sentimental in both the figure of the little girl and the near-miss connections of these female strangers that sends a message validating the kinds of solidarity currently dismissed as utopian, impractical, banal. This point is crystallized in the shot of one street on which three women's lives cross, ghostlike, inscribed as the gendered inflections of shared experiences of loss, violence, and witness on the one hand, and the drive to creativity, nurture, and potentiality on the other.

In the metanarrative common in witness literature, each woman experiments with responses to violence, manifesting guilt and trauma at being unable to intervene in the violence through compulsive repetitions of the pain she feels she has caused, which doubles as the pain she has suffered. Natalia scalds her arm in an echo of the burning death of the child she photographed in Angola; Olivia submits to a brutalized existence at the hands of her disabled husband to atone for letting her daughter go all those years ago; Katherine ponders suicide as a result of her inability to connect with her daughter through her pain at her own mother's brutal death. These internalizations of pain register an essentially gendered notion of women's tendency to take on the pain of others. They also constitute the fusing against which Dominic LaCapra repeatedly warns in his discussion of the difference between identification and empathy in the process of witnessing: "By identification I mean the unmediated fusion of self and other in which the otherness or alterity of the other is not recognized and respected. . . . Empathy may be contrasted with identification . . . insofar as empathy marks the point at which the other is indeed recognized and respected as other, and one does not feel compelled or authorized to speak in the other's voice or take the other's place, for example, as surrogate victim or perpetrator" (27). In the film, the inward-turning mimetic reconstruction of the victim's pain through identification is in each case countered by an act of representation or expression through the media of art, photography, or music, directing the pain outward until finally the women abandon both internal and external representations of their pain in order to work it through. Katherine cancels a concert to return to her daughter; Olivia puts down her sketchpad to consummate a lifelong dream of visiting Florence to view the work of Michelangelo; Natalia leaves her camera and heads to Angola as a UN volunteer.

The film closes with the chance meeting of these women in the airport. Like their earlier ephemeral passings by, this stylized scene foregrounds its own unlikeliness as antidote to the horror of (witnessing) violence. The camera follows the women in slow motion as they move through the airport, the sound muted to a ghostly echo, and take seats together at the only available table in the busy café. The three look on as the little girl who has haunted each of them materializes once more, laughing, running past them into her father's arms. Her father carries the child to her mother, and the camera holds the shot of the exultant nuclear family. Like Barker's reworking of clichéd romantic form at the end of *Double Vision*, this closing scene holds up in a moment of excessive closure the image of the nuclear family that has been so troubling and troubled in the lives of the three protagonists. In its self-conscious emphasis upon a clearly contrived closure, however, the image does not renew the hegemony of the nuclear family structure so much as it restores the function of the maternal—supported by the paternal, rather than destroyed as it had been in the lives of the three women. Significantly, the hyperclosure of the scene is signified as simultaneously empowering and destabilizing, as the three women erupt into the laughter begun by the little girl, who is now not ghostly, but real. As Regina Barreca has noted in her work on women and comedy, women's comedy and laughter are "subversive and gleefully threatening to the dominant order" (15). This subversion is linked to a gendered sense of closure, indeed to a lack of closure; in *Between Strangers*, Ponti draws on this subversive sense of a seemingly full-circle (en)closure of the film's "strange" women, leaving viewers with an uncanny sense of what their shared laughter might signify. The film ends with the image of triumphantly subversive women, delighted with their collective refusal of patriarchal control and violence and roaring into the subversive tradition of women's laughter delineated by Barreca: "In exploring laughter, women are exploring their own powers; they are refusing to accept social and cultural boundaries that make the need or desire for closure a 'universal'; . . . laughter is refusal and triumph" (30).

Genocide and the Maternal Function

The image of these mothers and surrogate mothers sharing a moment's laughter brings me to a final observation about the gendered nature of strategies employed in witness literature: the maternal as figure for both the consequences of and alternatives to genocide and the class of violence of which it is the nadir: those "wisps of cloud" that gather to the eclipse of Holocaust in Barker's novel.

Consider again the trauma of survival: "For consciousness, then, the act of survival, as the experience of trauma, is the repeated confrontation with the necessity and impossibility of grasping the threat to one's own life. It is because the mind cannot confront the possibility of its death directly that survival becomes for the human being, paradoxically, an endless testimony to the impossibility of living" (Caruth, "Traumatic," 62). Not surprisingly in light of this definition of survival, the traumatic need to repeat, often thematized in witness literature that features survivor witnesses, sometimes ends in suicide, ironically chosen after the threat of genocidal death has passed. This is the case for Amabelle, survivor of the massacre of Haitians in the Dominican Republic dramatized in *The Farming of Bones*, and for the Armenian artist Arshile Gorky, whose story comprises one thread of Atom Egoyan's exploration of the denial of the Armenian genocide and its cinematic reconstruction in *Ararat* (1999).[28] In *Farming of Bones*, Amabelle's decision not to have children and to end her life in the waters where her mother died, watched over by the maternal *loa*, Metres Dlo, results from her feeling that she has nothing to pass on to her heirs except her testimony. *Ararat* similarly probes the loss of the maternal in both its everyday and its regenerative functions as symbol for the devastation of genocide. The film's metanarrative technique enables the viewer to witness both the substance of this loss and the consequences of its (re)construction in the representational act, whether art, narrative, or film—which is also the act of interpreting the genocide in personal, historical, and artistic accounts. Everywhere, there is violence—of the genocide, and of its remembrance by survivors, of its legacy for descendants, and of its interpretation (including on the most basic level of public acknowledgment or denial) by witnesses through representations distanced in time and place from the original event. These fluid levels of violence crystallize in two stark questions of truth whose resolutions form an argument about the ethical contours of witness to genocide.

These two questions of truth-value involve members of a triangulated family structure that holds space for two absent fathers, therefore prompting primal Oedipal familial subtexts as part of any analytical reading. The film revolves around an Armenian art historian, Ani; her son, Raffi, whose father was killed in the process of attempting to assassinate a Turkish diplomat and is read alternatively as a heroic Armenian freedom fighter or as a terrorist;

and her stepdaughter, Celia, whose father, Ani's second husband, fell from a cliff and died in what Celia considers a suicide and Ani calls an accident. Raffi and Celia are involved in a high-strung love affair that is deeply imbricated in both the quest for truth about the Armenian genocide and about the differential values placed upon their fathers' deaths. Despite Celia's frantic attempts, Ani refuses to acknowledge her role in Celia's father's death, setting up an early parallel between an individual and her denial, and those who would deny the event of the Armenian genocide that Ani, herself of Armenian descent, devotes her personal and scholarly life to legitimating. The interpretative question that preoccupies readers of Gorky's art as a rare piece of testimony representative of the Armenian genocide has to do with the hands of his mother, which are missing in the portrait he painted from the image of a photo taken just before the genocidal event. Ani, an art historian who frequently lectures from her recently published book on Gorky's life and work, insists that "Gorky leaves his mother's hand unfinished, as if the history of its composition, like that of his people, had been violently interrupted. The earthly sensuality of the mother's touch is no more; only pure burning spiritual light remains." Celia argues that he painted the hands but later erased them, destroying what he had created from the ashes of history. In the film's circuitous manner of re-creation, we later discover that Celia is correct.

I read Celia's character allegorically, as a figure for the collective trauma of genocide and its survivors: hysterical, intrusive, ceaselessly repeating her claims, enacting her pain in increasingly public and corporeal ways, seeking validation from her interlocutors. Embodying trauma's unbidden return, she repeatedly disrupts the ordered historical narrative represented by Ani's attempt to establish her book as authoritative account in the public sphere. When Ani refuses to acknowledge Celia's father's death as suicide, Celia renders her pain visible by slashing the canvas of Gorky's painting, the iconic embodiment of a collective pain that Ani *will* acknowledge. The film valorizes the intuitive understanding of shared pain and delegitimation of the hegemonic, official narrative, which also stands for a kind of denial, when viewers later learn that Celia's interpretation of the painting was the correct one. This complex metanarrative composes a plea for public affirmation of events denied in official history—and surely there has rarely been such a virulent national denial as that of the Turkish government regarding the Armenian genocide.

The message is reinforced in the film's other major problem of truth-value, this one the literal truth of whether the canisters Raffi claims hold footage of the site of the Armenian genocide actually hold drugs to be smuggled into Canada.

Raffi's interrogation at the Toronto airport is intercut across the length of the film, at the end of which the border guard tells him: "The truth finally comes down to shit. By the time I get them to this room it's just a matter of time before it all comes out . . . the shit . . . I sit where you are and watch them on this toilet, waiting for the truth. The compressed tablets of heroin." Contrary to the subtleties of interpretation required to address competing truth claims in other arenas of the film, here the truth is constructed in its base, evidentiary form; however, this too is complicated by the fact that the guard lets Raffi go, even after asserting that "there's no way of confirming that a single word of what you've told me tonight is true." When Raffi replies, "Everything I've told you is exactly what happened," he refers both to the events of the genocide, which he has narrated to the guard, and the event of his carrying drugs unknowingly over the border in his film canisters. His unknowing about the drugs is the same willful unknowing of many about the Armenian genocide, a refusal to acknowledge a deeper, undeniable truth; paradoxically, however, his assertion of the truth of his narrative is accurate. He both knew and did not know about the drugs in his canister, as citizens fed an official history based upon denial both know and do not know about the genocide. The film, then, probes the role of cultural texts and images— Gorky's painting, U.S. missionary Clarence Usher's journal, the filmmaker Saroyan's (likely a figure for Egoyan himself) feature film, the images on Raffi's video camera—in sorting through the competing claims of veracity and varying levels of acknowledgment and denial that structure intergenerational survivor and witness responses to the legacy of genocide. In its affirmation of both Celia's and Raffi's claims, *Ararat* counters the official denial of the genocide.

The image that plays repeatedly on the video screen during Raffi's interrogation is a long shot of a barren landscape. Mt. Ararat, site of the genocide, rises in the background, while the foreground harbors a phallic concrete monument, symbolic testament to the masculinist ruin of war and genocide. The recurring image that fills the void in this landscape left barren by genocide is a woman who carries an infant across its screen, icon of the regenerative potential purposely destroyed in the genocidal act, but also of a destruction that is more immediate—the loss of the everyday function of maternal nurture, of cultural life. This image recalls the signs and symbols that accumulate in the interpretation of Gorky's painting, culminating in the devastating proof delivered to viewers of the legitimacy of Celia's claim.

The painting is a representation of a photo of Gorky and his mother taken on the eve of genocide, after Gorky's father had already escaped. The chain of signs leading to an accurate interpretation of the painting originates in a missing button on Gorky's coat. His mother, noticing, positions his hands in front of his coat to hide the missing button. The very pose of the photo, then, inscribes this sense of maternal attention, which recalls the sense of safety evoked by the inside in Barker's *Double Vision*. As if to confirm the importance of the everyday function of the maternal, its attention and care juxtaposed with the nihilism of ethnic hatred and genocide, the film's final image, set outside the narrative to the rolling of credits, is of Gorky's mother sewing this button, her hands restored to motion and function. The argument about whether the painting was left unfinished or the hands painted in and then erased is essentially an argument about assigning or refusing meaning: Ani, of Armenian descent and clearly invested in legitimating the genocide and its effects, is made complicit in complex ways with its denial. Even as she struggles as advisor to Saroyan's film for geographic and historical accuracy in narrating the genocide, her denial of Celia's claim to meaning for her father's death—suicide, not accident—evokes the historic denial of the genocide. So too with the interpretation of the (un)painting of the hands: an accident, or a deliberate, significant event?

The event that clarifies this mystery also joins the two questions of truth—Raffi's truth at the border and the truth of Gorky's mother's hands. As part of Raffi's doubled testimony to the border guard, he reads the statement of a German woman who witnessed the murder of a group of Armenian women and who testifies "so that people will remember what man does to man." The various metanarrative reflections upon representing atrocity—Ani's academic narrative, Gorky's painting, and Saroyan's film—also converge in the reenactment of this story in Saroyan's film. The woman tells of the massacre of a group of Armenian women, brides, forced to strip and to dance naked for the soldiers, and then set alight. The camera holds a shot of the hand of one of the brides, and we see that our perspective is mediated by the child Gorky, hiding from soldiers, his gaze fixated on the burning hand.

And so we learn that the symbolism of hands in the film signifies the annihilation of the romantic and erotic, and of the maternal, all at once in the figures of the brides, and it is this total annihilation that informs

Gorky's weeping erasure of the hands, as we witness in a scene set in his studio just before he hangs himself. At the end of her testimony, we learn that the German woman asked: "How shall I dig out these eyes of mine? Tell me, how?" The woman's inability to erase her eyes and what they have seen is mirrored in Gorky's tragic erasure of his mother's hands from the painting, which prefigures the erasure that is suicide. The film poses, then, the essential question of witnessing from a variety of removes—the survivor (Gorky); the firsthand witness (the German woman); intergenerational survivors (Ani, Raffi); and the distanced-observer witness (Celia): what to do with the energy generated in the event of witness so that it does not curdle into the mimetic reproduction of trauma and pain in the form of personal and global violence?

Another image of the maternal has haunted me since I first encountered it in Michael Ondaatje's novel of witnessing in the context of Sri Lanka's civil war, *Anil's Ghost* (2000). The novel joins those I have examined here in juxtaposing a variety of figures of witness, each representing a unique approach to coping with the strenuous demands of their particular relation to atrocity. One strategy is modeled by a doctor, Gamini, whose tours of duty in the emergency room treating the wounded from all sides of Sri Lanka's triangulated internal war sometimes run longer than three days at a time. Staying upright with the help of a range of barbiturates, Gamini cannot find the shelter of sleep even when his body demands rest. In these moments of restless exhaustion, Gamini retreats to the pediatric ward to observe mothers watching over their children through the night, finding solace in "the great sexuality of motherhood" as an alternative to the endless destruction of war (119). This image solves in some fundamental way the most persistent binds of gender(ed) history and violence, the virgin/whore dichotomy dissolved in the flick of a phrase. Not sexuality for (pro)creative purposes only, but rather the idea of conjoining, the very erotic gesture of nurturance that extends back from the prepositional object—motherhood—to greet the subject—sexuality—on its own term: *desire*, the program of desire embedded at the original coordinates marking the physiological, biological, psychological, emotional, intellectual, and spiritual aspects of human being. This great sexuality holds the point at which these gargantuan life forces can achieve a kind of harmonic resolution from the cacophony of their push and pull by dominant cultural forces that want to reduce woman to the one or the other and to base their political programs—including war and genocide—in their definitions.

On this note, there is a body of work expansive in its exploration of a variety of witness positions and reflexive in its formal address. This growing body of work approximates a representational ethic of witness by weaving an assertion of the inherent dangers of its own attempt to narrate atrocity into its metanarrative form. Refusing simply to tell the story in readily available narrative forms, these texts reflect upon the exhaustion of available forms while strategically arguing in their imagery for the recuperation of substance. Employing a subtle grammar of transition to dramatize witnesses at increasing removes from atrocity, the narratives show how the banal breakdowns of human connection are spun into violence that reaches its apex in the genocidal event. They also unabashedly engage the sentimental to retrieve the naively optimistic, idealistic impossibility of connection from the wastebin of realpolitik, cynicism, or simply the self-defeat of the political Left. It is no accident that the texts under examination here turn to the maternal as icon for both loss and renewal in these fearsome times. Inscribed in the interrogation of witnessing and representing atrocity, this is not the reproduction of the maternal as icon of nature or culture, mobilized in a specious argument for making war, but a revelation of the pain and care of individual mothers as humans who most often do not make but rather suffer the effects of torture, war, genocide.

EPILOGUE

In a review of Susan Sontag's *Regarding the Pain of Others*, Charles Simic with characteristic eloquence asserts: "Sontag is a moralist, as anyone who thinks about violence against the innocent is liable to become. The time she spent in Sarajevo under fire gives her the authority. Most of us don't understand what people go through, she writes" (10). It is difficult to discern in this construction whether the attribution of authority to moralize on this topic to the choice of living for a time under fire is Simic's or Sontag's. However, the claim cordons off for prospective readers of Sontag's work a narrow swath of conditions by which writing about atrocity may be legitimated, delegitimating by contrast those who would comment upon the exigencies of "regarding the pain of others" but who have not been exposed or exposed themselves firsthand to one or another of the world's hot zones. This endorsement moves beyond the promissory structure of witnessing in juridical and—more complexly—psychoanalytic contexts that presumes the delivery of the truthful account from the participant or the firsthand observer. Readers understand through Simic's comment that the reflections upon mediated looking delivered by Sontag bear an intrinsic ethical value because of her putatively unmediated looking in another time and place, or because she exposed her body to a vulnerability to bullets and shells that she need not have endured. (Interestingly, the remark does not seem to assert that her authority is a technical one, based upon firsthand experience of framing and circulating images taken under fire.)

The statement contains rich complexities: most notably, the paradox that a book about witnessing pain through images or the written word can rise to the ethical only if written by someone who has observed a certain kind of pain with his or her own eyes. I find it noteworthy that Simic chooses the term "moralist" to describe Sontag, with its "depreciative" sense, per the online *Oxford English Dictionary*, of "a person given to moralizing or making moral

judgments; a person who seeks to dictate or prescribe the morals of others."
Rather than informing readers that Sontag's project explores the ethics of
making, circulating, and receiving images of suffering at a desperate time in
world history—a descriptive rather than evaluative statement—Simic evokes
a discourse that depreciates critical consideration of the good and the right,
the bad and the wrong, and the differences between them as so much self-
righteous judgment. While I believe that Simic uses this language in his very
positive review of Sontag's book to invite people to consider her work without fear that she will prove a morally "smug" (the term is also Simic's) interlocutor, the effect, especially as it is reproduced as a fragment from the
review on the book jacket, is to reify the narrow conditions by which one may
make ethical judgments about images and texts, the events and persons they
purport to represent, and the effects they have on those who receive them.

If I understand Simic's premise, there is something repellant about the
moralist that can easily turn to smug righteousness and an ill-gotten superiority, but this repellant quality can be mitigated if the one who makes moral
judgments has put her own body on the line, as it were. The warrant of this
assertion is worth noting: that Sontag's observation of human pain in wartime
Bosnia-Herzegovina, 1991, enables her moral(izing) commentary upon the
representational ethics of news images of the U.S. Civil War or of artwork by
Francisco Goya. Here the others whose imagined and represented pain is the
subject of her book are evacuated of unique meaning and value. This warrant
contradicts the discourse of authenticity Simic's comment evokes.

While I appreciate Simic's attention to the space held by the ethical in
criticism of representation, the division between authorized and unauthorized
voices staked by his claim is part of a line of thinking that can have a chilling
effect upon public discourse about the proliferation of human rights violations and the role of representation in aiding their perpetration or eradication. In yet another spin on the ideal of authenticity, this assessment assigns
the authentic to the position held by the observer witness who signifies experience (despite the widespread critique of this position from survivor witnesses, among others, including observer witnesses themselves). Yet surely we
must reconceive the notion of the experiential observer in the post-9/11 age of
real-time news coverage, the twenty-four-hour news broadcast, the embedded
journalist, and the dedicated list-serv. How to theorize the experience of
observing mediated images that have varying degrees of immediate connection
in time, space, and being to the viewer's identity position or life story? How to

capture the energy generated by and for these distanced observers so that it does not shrivel on the vine, falling into the barren plot of undirected outrage and grief lived by many in the twenty-first century?

As I noted in chapter 5, a strain in contemporary theory and criticism of witnessing seeks to expand upon this notion of authenticity connected with the experiential, and a body of film and literature is also emerging that provides ideas about how to acknowledge the energy of the distanced observer witness in service of a sophisticated, well theorized, humane cosmopolitanism.[1] In closing this project, I question the extent to which we are endangered and diminished by the muffling of outrage, sorrow, or other affective charge that may be felt by the person who is relatively privileged in her witnessing of certain experiences of suffering from afar, through images upon the canvas, page, or screen (although this does not imply a lack of suffering in her own experience that may provide ground for an identification that may contribute to the global struggle against war and the violation of human rights). My critique of the discourse of authenticity does not, however, extend to the position of the survivor witness, in whose name much of the work toward a representational ethic in this book has been done.

Physical experience, as articulated in Simic's assertion, lends one an aura of truth and a purity of motive that is often under suspicion for the distanced observer witness and may limit the extent to which one feels authorized to speak or to act in public contexts. The guilt-producing image of the armchair radical (or worse, armchair liberal) justifiably hovers in the aura of those who from a distance speak sorrow or outrage about the proliferation of war, atrocity, and economic imbalance globally; however, I worry about how this image—and the anxiety it produces—forecloses potential energies that may be harnessed for change. This change may not be the radical one of leaving one's home to witness the pain of others firsthand as a journalist or aid worker. Rather, it may be a change of consciousness, begun in outrage or an activated sense of pathos, that results in a vote for a candidate representing a platform critical of contemporary corporate or governmental or military policies, for instance, or a new consideration of how to utilize one's purchasing power to achieve political, social, or economic goals. To be expressed as consciousness or action in the world, these energies must first find space in which to be acknowledged, without the premature foreclosure brought about by discourses of authenticity. This is not to say that all distanced observers are interested in speaking or acting as a result of their observations, or that the contributions

they might make based upon those observations will automatically be legitimate in ethical or political senses, avoiding the pitfalls of identification theorized by Dominic LaCapra, Saidiya Hartman, and others who consider the
power dynamics of the empathic response. However, I am concerned with the
loss signified by unrecognized affective, intellectual, or activist energy generated in increasing numbers of mediated witnesses (including students) globally, and the resulting devolution to a status quo in which the proliferation of
war and human rights violations is grudgingly accepted as an unavoidable
product of human nature or an unassailable production of contemporary
corporate/military/political theaters. Just as the loss and pain experienced by
those whose human rights are violated leave their marks in a variety of sites,
so the energy generated in mediated witnesses leaves a trace in the public
sphere that may or may not be recognizable as such. Further, devaluing or
silencing this energy bears negative consequences, and developing modes of
authorizing and receiving these latter traces is a vital work that our art, literature, and theory can help us to conceive.

As I noted earlier, Pat Barker's *Double Vision* reflects upon the challenges
of representation in the post-9/11 context. The mythical ethos of the novel
divides the space of home from nature to demarcate vulnerability to and
safety from harm; it also attributes an agency to the natural world that helps
to theorize traces left in the wake of violence done and witnessed. When
Kate's car veers off the road in the novel's first traumatic event, we learn that
"trees loomed up, leapt towards her, branches shattered the windscreen,
clawed at her eyes and throat" (4). While the sharp agency embedded in the
verbs signifies the projection of human fear in the context of the paradigmatic trauma, the accident, we may also note that the construction of nature
as willful gathers meaning within the context of a philosophical consideration of the nature of the witness, and nature (the natural world) *as* witness.

The novel's first scene, which introduces us to the trope of space divided
between home and nature and culminates in Kate's car crash, constructs the
landscape as both threatening and willful—in the sense of having an uncanny
agency—in relation to the particular question of witnessing. As Kate satisfies
her needs for nourishment ("heated a bowl of soup") and warmth ("built up
the fire and huddled over it"), the temperature drops outside "until a solitary
brown oak leaf detaching itself from the tree fell onto the frost-hard ground
with a crackle that echoed through the whole forest" (Barker 3–4). Here we
have the fundamental existential conundrum of the relationship between

event and witness: if a tree falls in the wood and no one is there to hear it, did it make a sound? If 200,000 Burmese protestors and students are massacred and the international community does not witness it, did the massacre have an effect?[2] Barker's formulation transforms the question to a declarative and implicates the natural world in the question of hearing that has exclusively been conceived as the capacity of the human. The diminution of tree in the original formulation to leaf here amplifies its echo through the "whole forest" to an almost supernatural impact, translating what must have been the crash of the original tree to a paradoxically more consequential "crackle." We also see that there is some agency in the leaf's fall: it "detaches itself" as a result of the drop in temperature that must signify its death. The leaf, elevated from its ordinary state of powerlessness and insignificance, takes the leap, as it were, at the moment of its death, and the impact of its loss is magnified in its natural setting, as it "echoes through the *whole* forest" (emphasis mine). In the context of the metaphorical structure of Barker's novel, highlighting the significance of the death of one leaf in autumn parallels the insistence upon the value of individuals dissolved in the mass remains of collective atrocities, such as genocides in Rwanda and Bosnia-Herzegovina witnessed by characters Ben and Stephen, hot-zone photojournalists.

The failure of the western world to represent its others as individuated humans rather than undifferentiated masses has a long history, infamously expressed in Marlow's explanation of his grief at the death of his helmsman during the journey into the interior in Conrad's *Heart of Darkness*: "Perhaps you will think it passing strange this regret for a savage who was no more account than a grain of sand in a black Sahara" (93). This same failure plagues the construction of—and thereby the response to—human rights crises in Africa in the contemporary moment, as Sontag notes: "The more remote or exotic the place, the more likely we are to have full frontal views of the dead and dying. Thus postcolonial Africa exists in the consciousness of the general public in the rich world . . . mainly as a succession of unforgettable photographs of large-eyed victims, starting with figures in the famine lands of Biafra in the late 1960s. . . . These sights carry a double message. They show a suffering that is outrageous, unjust, and should be repaired. They confirm that this is the sort of thing which happens in that place" (*Regarding the Pain of Others* 71). Surely the first casualty of this confirmation is the conception of individuated, consequential human lives with inherent dignity and attainable aspirations, and along with it, the mobilization of technologies and actors cranked up by the global human rights movement and (inter)national security machines when such individuated human lives are under collective threat.[3]

This early gesture in the novel toward the problem of witness does not resolve the question of whether events actually happen without witnesses to observe and, in the act of observing, to ascribe value to them. However, it does emphatically avow the distinct value of each person lost to violence that comes to be known as historical and collective, and that in its representation as such serves the dehumanizing function of blurring the reception of individuals as individuals. Returning to the role of nature, Barker's formulation reverses the negation of the original question—if a tree falls in the wood and there is no one there to hear it—which probes the possibility of event without witness. Instead, the statement that the leaf's fall "echoed through the whole forest" leaves the question of hearers open, but with a subtle implication that the occupants of the forest, or, preternaturally, the forest itself, felt or heard the echo. It follows then that pain, loss, death—the violent events traced so meticulously in their various forms throughout the novel—have an effect upon the natural world, the state of things, even if they are not seen or heard by particular human witnesses, and that this effect upon the natural world reflects back upon human experience and event. As if to confirm this revision of the notion of witness, in the next paragraph we learn that Kate's car crash is observed, as "somewhere in the heart of the wood an antlered head turned to watch her pass" (4). Here again an unusual agency is implied in this animal's observation, as it "turn[s] its head" for the specific purpose of watching Kate's movement. Witnessing, the text implies early on, occurs in an expansive context that is not limited to the human witness, but that includes the natural world and its inhabitants. Perhaps, then, the answer the text offers to the proverbial question of whether the tree makes a sound—has effects—without a witness who can report back is yes. Energy is formed, circulated, and leaves its trace. It matters.

The notion of the traces left upon the natural world by the violent follies of man, the idea that the natural world serves as a kind of witness reflecting the consequences of those follies in its landscape, is particularly powerful in the context of the human failure to engage in the processes activated by witnessing. In this case, crucially, another witness to Kate's car crash materializes as she lies bleeding, trapped in the vehicle: "A headless figure was all she could see, since he didn't bend to look in. . . . He didn't move, didn't open the door, didn't check to see how she was, didn't ring or go for help. Just stood there, breathing" (Barker 5). This complex refusal on the part of the witness to engage is the source of the nebulous threat that haunts the novel in the figure of Peter Wingrave and that morphs from the distinct menace of this passive disengagement to active criminal violence over the course of the novel. In this case, the failure to witness is particularly egregious—its moral reprehensibility particularly unambiguous—because the witness is physically present. Interestingly, however, the witness in this case both refuses to look (that is, he rejects the up-close rubbernecking opportunity that is the deep desire at the heart of accident-scene traffic bottlenecks everywhere) and to engage by helping or calling others. The only activity that the victim can discern in her would-be witness is that he breathes. He lives, while she is in danger of dying, as distanced-observer witnesses live while looking at images or reading stories of others in the process of being harmed, dying, or already dead (and perhaps in structural economic terms, the standards of living of some distanced-observer witnesses depends upon the conditions that produce the well-represented dying of those others).

In contrast to this figure of disengagement, Barker offers a complex figure for the potential of the witness capable of and willing to receive the sensory impressions of the event, but unable to release them or to reply, as it were, to the stimulation. Justine, a young woman taking a year off from university to recover from an illness, becomes the novel's object lesson in receiving and managing pain, first in the abstract sense of the distanced-observer witness, and second in the physical sense of the survivor witness as she is brutally beaten during a robbery. Significantly, the mutual attraction she shares with Stephen Sharkey, the photojournalist back from tours in the world's most infamous war zones, is based upon her capacity to receive and experience a variety of modes of pain—her own and others'. As I noted in chapter 5, it would be easy to dismiss the relationship as the facile attempt of a middle-aged man in the midst of a divorce to regain life force and vitality through an affair with a woman half his age; however, Barker employs a complex metaphorical structure throughout the text to give substance to this otherwise exhausted form (as the position of the distanced-observer witness can seem at times an exhausted, banal form—it is precisely because of its exhaustion that its recuperation in the text becomes so meaningful). One aspect of this substance is the basis of Stephen's attraction to Justine in an intangible sense of her capacity to feel pain. Observing her as she reads, "he watched her brow furrow in that elusive expression of pain that was, he realized suddenly, the thing he found most erotic about her. She was so strong, so full of energy and hope. What did it say about him that it was her capacity to feel pain that aroused him?" (138). In this construction, the visible signs of her reception of pain (the "elusive expression" indicated by her "furrowed brow") unexpectedly signifies her strength, energy, and hope—indeed, the very qualities most desired in an ethical witness. Not a witness defeated or overcome by—or worse, numb to—the pain witnessed, but one in whom there is strength to help carry the burden of represented and experienced pain and in whom the specific energy of hope is activated in the process. Indeed, what Stephen discerns in Justine could describe the human rights movement, made up largely of people who may not have experienced the kinds of pains they have devoted their lives to trying to end for others, and who manage to find and retain hope in the process of witnessing (and protesting against) the conditions that produce such pain. In Stephen's case, Justine's pain and the abstract air she carries that indicates a broad ability to feel pain unattached to any particular event or identification is the source of his desire for her. If we consider that Stephen occupies the position of firsthand observer witness (photojournalist), and Justine the potential distanced-observer witness (receiver of his work), then his attraction to her as a woman with a particular capacity to receive and manage pain is logical and substantive in a way that further gives the lie to the banal frame of their affair.

In constructing Stephen's early sensory perception of Justine as a woman with a particular relation to pain, Barker offers an image of the distanced-observer witness that I find profoundly instructive in theorizing the flow of energy generated in the circulation of text and image of atrocity: "[Stephen] pictured her [at university], jogging along the Backs, . . . one of the hundreds who pass through and make no impression, but years later can recall the precise sound of oars in rowlocks, hear the voices of the coaches yelling encouragement from the banks, smell woodsmoke, see misty light around a street lamp and feel an obscure pain, a longing, thinking of a key that never turned properly in a lock, a door that might have opened but didn't" (51). The image captures the state of the distanced-observer witness who takes in sensory cues in extreme, vivid detail but who leaves no trace, no impression in return. Can the pain generated in the distanced-observer witness change anything? Can it matter?

Considering Barker's setup early in the book of the foundational question of the relationship between event and witness, we might well assert here that yes, the pain of the distanced-observer witness leaves a trace; however, it may also be our task to magnify that trace, to help it be heard, felt, and perhaps transformed into various kinds of action. In an expression of the desire for such an exchange of energy, filmmaker Idrissa Ouedraogo from Burkina-Faso articulates, with regard to his contribution to the film collection 11.09.01: "While I sympathise with the pain of the families and of the American people, I expect in return the same wave of solidarity with Africa for malaria, Aids, famine, thirst" (qtd. in Henley). Can art and literature help us acknowledge and shift the global balance of reception, of the flow of energies and engagements, the distribution of human suffering and its naming as internationally legitimated human rights violation?

My book has traced the contours of an ethic of fictionalizing historical experiences of torture, rape, and genocide. The focus upon the relationship between event and text of course implies something about the producers of representations. I end, however, with this consideration of audiences, whom I call distanced-observer witnesses—although, as with texts, not all audiences will rise to the level of witness. The question of what audiences will do with information gathered and emotion generated by these narratives haunts the work of literary or cinematic artist and of scholar/critic. The answer to that question is, of course, that no one can know; however, I argue here for authorization for a healthy public discourse that acknowledges the identifications and empathic responses that are generated by media, artistic, and other representational forms and that does not muffle those responses on the basis that they are generated in persons who are relatively privileged in witnessing certain experiences of suffering from afar. One danger in artistically representing historical atrocity is that the energy of the narrative and images that flow from author through text to reader/viewer will fail to find release from the reader-reception triangle to engage with the world. The stories will have been told and received, but the energy generated in the audience witness will not leave a visible trace in return. The risk is that some of the energy generated may be unwelcome and may produce abhorrent or unethical responses. In spite of this risk, however, as Barker's character Stephen Sharkey reminds us, there is pain in this deadened flow of energy, and the deep consequence of failed opportunity, of "a door that might have opened, but didn't."

NOTES

INTRODUCTION

1 I emphasize the word "global" here in order to assert the centrality of basic discourses of human rights in a variety of philosophies and movements to which
they are at times not attributed, for instance, in the massive decolonization
movements and accompanying philosophies in Asia and Africa from roughly the
last century until the present, and even—paradoxically, given the turn of Stalinist
Soviet history—in the articulation of human rights via economic critique by
Marxism/socialism in some of its theoretical forms.

2 See Morsink for a historical overview of the drafting of the declaration and the
process by which civil and political rights were separated from social and
economic rights. See also Mutua for a discussion of this separation and its
consequences as signs of the imperialist nature of human rights discourse and
practice.

3 In addition to the more visible challenges to the Geneva Conventions and the UN
Universal Declaration of Human Rights, this deconstruction has taken such
Orwellian forms as the "unsigning" of the mandate of the International Criminal
Court by the Bush administration; changing ten-year-old language negotiated at
the 1995 UN World Conference on Women, Beijing; suspending the right of
habeas corpus; and writing a new definition of acts which constitute torture.

4 In her analysis of the function of Amnesty International, Elaine Scarry has read
the Amnesty letters as "not only a denunciation of the pain but almost a diminution of the pain, a partial reversal of the process of torture itself," inasmuch as
they "restore to each person tortured his or her voice . . . us[ing] language to let
pain give an accurate account of itself, to present regimes that torture with a deluge of letters and telegrams, a deluge of voices speaking on behalf of, voices
speaking in the voice of, the person silenced" (50).

5 See Rieff for an assessment of humanitarian intervention in the contemporary
moment.

6 J. M. Coetzee's "Into the Dark Chamber: The Novelist and South Africa" is an
important exploration of the ethics of representing the torture room; he suggests,
for example, that its status as a "site of extreme human experience, accessible to
no one save the participants, is a second reason why the novelist in particular
should be fascinated by it" (363).

7 The neutral pronoun here indicates the extent to which the body in the image is
not only purposely ungendered, but also rendered nonhuman by the act of torture depicted.

8 The "whole" to which this image may be metonymically related may also be the whole of inexplicably brutal popular culture, surely as surreal in its excess as the "real" violence depicted in the Abu Ghraib photos.

9 The testimony of Haj Ali, the former prisoner at Abu Ghraib believed to be depicted in the photo, is given in Webster. Evidence that Haj Ali may not be the man in the iconic image is presented in Zernike.

10 The School of the Americas was operated by the United States in Panama between 1946 and 1989, when it was relocated to Ft. Benning, Georgia. After the release by the Pentagon in 1996 of manuals that included materials on torture and other illegal methods of "counterinsurgency" training, the school officially closed in 2001, reopening almost immediately as the Western Hemisphere Institute for Security Cooperation (WHINSEC). Arguing that the change of name does not denote major changes of policy or pedagogy, the activist group School of the Americas Watch has continued its efforts to have the school closed. In June 2006, Representative Jim McGovern (D-Mass.) garnered unprecedented congressional support for HR 1217, his amendment to the Foreign Operations Appropriations Bill that would suspend funding for WHINSEC and call for investigation of its pedagogies and practices. See the School of the Americas Watch official Web site, <http://www.soaw.org/new/>.

11 "*Washington Post:* ABC News Poll December 2005." <www.washingtonpost.com/wp-srv/politics/polls/121905_monthly_ trendfinal.pdf>.

12 See M. Goldberg for analysis of the Bush administration's decision to "unsign" the Rome statute; see Greenberg and Dratel, *The Torture Papers*, for Gonzalez's memorandum reinterpreting customary international law regarding torture; see Jehl and Johnston and "Renditions Save Lives" on the practice of extraordinary rendition.

13 While the outcome of the 2004 presidential election can be read as a statement of implicit consent to the policy of torture by a majority of U.S. citizens, the dissent of a large percentage of Americans remains unaccounted for in terms of the election's official results, and the many factors that informed the outcome of that election cannot be reduced to the public's response to the issue of torture by U.S. military and civilian personnel around the world. Also, it is crucial to note that the legitimacy of the 2000 and 2004 presidential elections in the United States was compromised by serious procedural problems, which complicates further the matter of implied consent to the policies of the executive branch.

14 Timerman 33.

15 See Sanders for the special issue of *Diacritics* devoted to "the ethical turn in literary studies."

16 On behalf of the United Nations, Secretary General Kofi Annan has acknowledged such widespread abuses of women with the status of refugee and IDP by peacekeeping forces in Burundi, Cambodia, Democratic Republic of Congo, Guinea, Kosovo, Liberia, and Sierra Leone. As Gita Sahgal of Amnesty International articulates: "The issue with the U.N. is that peacekeeping operations unfortunately seem to be doing the same thing that other militaries do. . . . Even the guardians have to be guarded" (qtd. in Loconte).

17 See Butler, *Undoing Gender*, for the author's "most recent work on gender and sexuality focusing on the question of what it might mean to undo restrictively normative conceptions of sexual and gendered life" (1).

18 The very posing of such questions presumes a mode of narrative or artistic creation that is invested in such an ethic; such investment is obviously at high risk when positioned within the circulation of cultural artifacts in the consumerist context of the profit motive. This problem will be addressed more fully in chapters 1 and 2.

19 Michael Hoffman of the International Committee of the Red Cross used the term "toxins" at the 2000 Amnesty International Annual General Meeting as part of an argument for cultural approaches to ending cyclical patterns of human rights violations.

CHAPTER ONE — TORTURE I

1 *Schindler's List* has been the subject of a long, much-publicized debate about its narrative strategies in relation to the Shoah in general and Claude Lanzmann's film *Shoah* in particular (see Loshitzky). For a critical response to this debate, see Hansen. For a study of reader reception across cultures, see Arva. See E. Goldberg, "Splitting Difference," for an account of the counterhistorical dramatic film and its development as a genre.

2 *Schindler's List* is an exception in the sense that its other is located within national borders. However, Nazi revocation of the citizenship of European Jews neutralizes the traditional significance of national borders in identity formation in this context.

3 Counterhistorical drama commonly uses images of children to generate maximum pathos in the dramatic rendering of atrocity; however, the pervasive use of these images belies the relative invisibility of human rights violations against children in the general human rights discourse, at least until quite recently. For more information regarding children's rights, see United Nations, *Convention on the Rights of the Child* and its two "Optional Protocol" additions, as well as UNICEF, *State of the World's Children*. Michael Winterbottom's *Welcome to Sarajevo* (1997), which tells the story of children in an orphanage during the siege of Sarajevo, borrows some techniques from the counterhistorical dramatic film but ultimately utilizes more effective postmodern narrative strategies and cinematography to represent the suffering of children under siege.

4 I do not purport to undertake statistical analysis of audience response to individual films, but rather to study the interpretive signals or cues embedded in films' generic imperatives, plotlines, and cinematic structure, along with broad-based audience effects. As David Bordwell asserts, "Every film trains its spectator" (45); films adhering closely to classic generic formulae are particularly overbearing in terms of the expectations and responses they conjure.

5 MacCannell's discussion of the routinization of violence is part of his critique of postmodern theorists' deconstruction of "the subject," which he asserts is, at worst, tantamount to a recuperation of fascism and, at best, an apolitical looking away from the material conditions of violence.

6 Most human rights sources do not rank countries or regions in terms of severity or frequency of rights violations. However, a database compiled by the Danish Institute for Human Rights identified West Africa, the Mediterranean, Russia and the Western Commonwealth of Independent States, the Caucuses, and Central, East, and Southeastern Asia as the regions with the lowest overall commitment to human rights, based on information contained in the annual country reports of Human Rights Watch, Amnesty International, and the U.S. Department of

State. See Kobila for an analysis of the causes of this North-South human rights disparity.

7   While *Hotel Rwanda* is progressive in its focus upon a black Rwandan protagonist and its critique of the racial politics of genocide, it still relies upon a formulaic salvation narrative of an exceptional hero figure; in this sense, it stands in contrast to Raoul Peck's *Sometimes in April*, a narratively sophisticated HBO film about the Rwandan genocide. As Joshua Land asserted in a review of the 2005 documentary about UN commander General Romeo Dallaire, *Shake Hands with the Devil*: "[Rwanda's] 1994 genocide . . . got the full-on *Schindler's List* treatment in Terry George's . . . *Hotel Rwanda*. Raoul Peck's recent made-for-HBO *Sometimes in April* was a more diffuse, if less involving, take on the crisis." See chapter 5 for a discussion of the release of these films on the tenth anniversary of the genocide in relation to the genocide in Darfur, Sudan.

8   Burma, a Southeast Asian country whose total population of 52 million people includes 18 million ethnic minorities (constituting 35 percent of the total), gained its independence in 1948. In 1962, General Ne Win seized control of the country and by the 1980s the military Tatadaw controlled most of the country. In 1988, the ruling State Law and Order Restoration Council (SLORC, which changed its name to the State Peace and Development Council in 1997) put down a pro-democracy protest by students and others, resulting in what is estimated to be thousands of deaths (given the lack of access of independent observers, no reliable figures are available). The popular opposition movement, the National League for Democracy (NLD) won 82 percent of the seats in the 1990 elections. The military junta ignored these results and refused to concede defeat. For a discussion of the lasting impact of the events of 1988–1990, as well as other social and political issues in modern Burma, see Carey.

9   Aung San Suu Kyi was the leader of the NLD during the 1990 elections and, as such, should have assumed leadership of the country following those elections. A well-known democracy activist and 1991 Nobel peace laureate, she was under house arrest from 1989 until 1995. She was again placed under house arrest in 2000, released again in 2002, but returned to house arrest, where she remains, in 2003. Her house arrest was extended indefinitely in 2006. For more about Aung San Suu Kyi, see her own writings in *Freedom from Fear and Other Writings* (1991) and *Letters from Burma* (1997).

10 See Shelley for an examination of the role of the media in response to the 1989 massacre in Tiananmen Square.

11 Part of the problem relates to selectivity and specificity of historic representation, that is, how much detailed information it is possible to include in a fictionalized film history. In this case, as in many counterhistorical dramatic films, the conflict appears to be between the Burmese military and Burmese people. Beyond indications that the military was particularly repressive of students, professors, and suspected Communists, the characteristics of specific targets of repression are not fleshed out. The film provides no historical context for this clash and elides the ethnic distinctions among particular groups targeted by the military. See Steinberg for a sociopolitical analysis of the 1988 protests in the context of Burmese history, and for data and analysis of ethnicity and social issues. For documentation of human rights abuses in Burma, including survivor testimony, see Human Rights Watch, "'They came and destroyed our village again.'"

12 My use of the distinctions "first" and "third" worlds here does not imply an assertion of the primacy of a world-systems theory (first, second, and third worlds). In
general, I situate my discussion of cultural representations of torture within the
discourse of political theory as it navigates the terrain between world-systems
theory and theories of cultural and economic globalization. Plot and characterization in counterhistorical dramatic films, however, often reinforce political,
economic, and cultural divisions traditionally attributed to the first and third
worlds; hence my use of that terminology here. See Buell for a detailed examination of the relationship between world-systems and global political theories.

13 Domestic violence is widely considered one of the most significant threats facing
women worldwide; 40–70 percent of female murder victims die at the hands of
an intimate partner, according to a 2002 World Health Organization survey conducted in forty-eight countries. Global data regarding the prevalence of domestic violence are limited both by the underreporting of such private violence, the
difficulties of collecting statistics in many countries that suffer from either
extreme poverty or widespread violence, and differing definitions of what constitutes domestic abuse. The WHO survey showed prevalence rates of domestic
violence ranging from 10–69 percent in the countries surveyed; for more data
and interpretations thereof see WHO, "Violence by Intimate Partners." Human
rights discourse in the late 1990s began incorporating considerations of domestic violence as a basic human rights violation and, in some cases, as torture.
For an example of this argument, see Thomas and Beasley; see also Peters and
Wolper.

14 Prashad 15.

15 In contrast to Bowman's peaceful closure in refugee camps along the Thai-Burmese
border, most of the approximately 145,000 Burmese in Thai refugee camps (of an
estimated 2 million Burmese in Thailand) experience no such relief. Considered
unwanted guests by the Thai government, Burmese refugees who seek safety across
the Thai border have been subject to periods of suspended registry of asylum
seekers, as well as to efforts to return refugees to Burma (Human Rights Watch,
"Out of Sight"). In addition, refugees in camps along the border are subject to the
conditions of poverty and crowded living typical of refugee camps globally, as
well as to efforts by the Thai government to target Burmese democracy activists
within their borders.

16 Human rights reports from an array of sources contend that the Burmese military junta's human rights record had not improved as of 2004. According to the
U.S. Department of State's 2004 report on Burma's human rights practices, the
government's "extremely poor human rights record worsened." Aung San Suu
Kyi turned sixty under house arrest, where she remains as this book goes to
press. In July 2005, 200 political prisoners were released but, according to
Amnesty International, at least 1,100 political prisoners remain in Burma, many
of them nonviolent prisoners of conscience. For more information, see Amnesty
International, "Myanmar (Burma)."

17 The political and ideological lines dividing these separate plots correspond to a
traditional vision of history as a totalizing linear system, on the one hand, and
the sense of evolving, fragmented, chaotic history (or historical dispossession)
that characterizes the (neo)colonial world, on the other. See Glissant for a
discussion of such views of history and narrative in the context of Caribbean
writing and identity.

18 Members of the military in the countries in which counterhistorical dramatic films are set are often portrayed as one-dimensional, dehumanized brutes, incapable of empathic response and consumed by western audiences as other to the dominant representation of the U.S. military as rational, law-abiding helpmate rather than death machine. The irony of such representations is all the more pointed after the revelations of torture by U.S. military in the Iraq War, which, as Naomi Klein has argued, only brought to light the long history of institutionalized extralegal practices, not least of which is the training at the School of the Americas in Fort Benning, Georgia, of torturers now operating throughout Latin America. (Closed in December 2000, after manuals detailing torture techniques were discovered to be part of its curricula, the school reopened in January 2001, renamed the Western Hemisphere Institute for Security Co-operation, WHINSEC.) See also McLeod.

19 Rankin writes: "We are naturally too callous to the sufferings of others, and consequently prone to look upon them with cold indifference, until, in imagination we identify ourselves with the sufferers, and make their sufferings our own" (qtd. in Hartman 18). Joel Schumacher's *A Time to Kill* (1996; based upon the 1992 novel by John Grisham) uses this strategy to aid white viewers' identification with a black father who kills his daughter's white rapists. The protagonist of the film is the lawyer who represents the father, who convinces the all-white jury to acquit by asking them to imagine in painful detail the bodily experience of rape and beating endured by this child, ending his closing statement by demanding that they "now imagine that she is white." When the all-white jury returns with a verdict of innocent, we understand that they have been able to imagine the pain and experience of this child only by replacing her body with one like their own, confirming Hartman's argument that such empathic response obliterates the other even in its intervention on her behalf.

20 Of course, such uses of images of atrocity are complex and easily manipulated, as Susan Sontag describes in *Regarding the Pain of Others*: "All photographs wait to be explained or falsified by their captions. During the fighting between Serbs and Croats at the beginning of the recent Balkan wars, the same photographs of children killed in the shelling of a village were passed around at both Serb and Croat propaganda briefings. Alter the caption, and the children's deaths could be used and reused" (10). As Sontag concludes, however, the possibility for such manipulation should not foreclose the circulation of such images. For instance, documentation of the condition of Stephen Biko's body is precisely what gave the lie to the account of his death as resulting from "renal failure" offered by apartheid minister of police James Kruger.

21 Stephen (Steve) Biko was born in 1946 in South Africa and went on to found the Black People's Convention and the Black Consciousness Movement. He attracted the attention of the South African apartheid government for his anti-apartheid activities and was banned (constrained to his hometown with limits on movement and gathering with others) in 1973. Between 1975 and 1977 he was arrested and interrogated four times. His final arrest led to his death in custody in September 1977. The police initially claimed that he died of health complications resulting from a hunger strike but withdrew that claim following pressure from the international media, especially Donald Woods. An inquest into Biko's death later found that he died as a result of head injuries sustained in custody. Ntsiki Biko, Steve Biko's widow, protested the Truth and Reconciliation Commission's

offer of amnesty in exchange for criminals' "full disclosure of the truth." After listening to Commission chair Archbishop Desmond Tutu's remarks in 1996 she responded: "There is a lot of talk about reconciliation . . . but I don't know who is supposed to be reconciled with whom. What I want is the proper course of justice" (qtd. in Block). The five men who claimed responsibility for Biko's death testified before the Truth and Reconciliation Commission in 1997. The leader among them, Gideon Nieuwoudt, was denied amnesty due to his refusal to fully disclose the truth by admitting to the crime of murder. He claimed that he killed Biko in an act of self-defense and that he was unaware of Biko's political significance. The commission turned down Nieuwoudt's repeated pleas for amnesty, which were opposed by Biko's surviving family, in 1999. Nieuwoudt was in jail at the time for other crimes, and his prosecution in the Biko case was considered unlikely due to the difficulty of proving murder and intent and the expiration of the statute of limitations for all other possible charges related to the Biko case. See Daley.

22 For instance, traditional African music rises to mark moments of particular defiance or triumph as Woods moves toward his final border crossing.

23 See Scarry, *The Body in Pain*, for an analysis of the parallel between torture and war, inasmuch as "war [and torture] entail a similar structure of physical and perceptual events: requir[ing] both the reciprocal infliction of massive injury and the eventual disowning of the injury so that its attributes can be transferred elsewhere, as they cannot if they are permitted to cling to the original site of the wound, the human body" (64).

24 See White for an analysis of the new era of war coverage focused on the role of reporters themselves, ushered in with the 1991 Gulf War. For an analysis of the dehumanization of Iraqi victims through western media coverage, see Kendrick. See McAlister, especially chap. 6, for a review of dominant critical reception of televised coverage of the 1991 Gulf War.

25 See Nussbaum, *Poetic Justice*, for explication of the concept "ethical imagination" in terms of literary study; see also E. Goldberg, "Who Was Afraid of Patrice Lumumba?"

26 Maslin, "Fighting the Battle." Given the frenetic nature of camera work marking the action-adventure genre more broadly, one wonders whether the description of Russell's camerawork in the film as "music-video" style has its source in a confusion of Russell with his friend the acclaimed music-video director Spike Jonze (who went on to direct the similarly edgy *Being John Malkovich*), who plays Conrad Vig in *Three Kings*.

27 See Arendt, *Eichmann in Jerusalem* and "On the Nature of Totalitarianism."

CHAPTER TWO — TORTURE II

1 This is not to say that all patriotisms preclude identification across national borders. My concern here is the way in which the counterhistorical dramatic film uses global others to consolidate a noncosmopolitan patriotism that contributes to the violent bodily consequences of exclusionary identity politics. See Nussbaum for an extensive debate on patriotism as compared to cosmopolitanism.

2 In analyzing national limitations of universal human rights conventions, it is instructive to consider the case of the United States, which has signed but not ratified the Convention on the Elimination of All Forms of Discrimination against Women (CEDAW) as well as the Convention on the Rights of the Child. In the latter

case, the United States is in the company of only Somalia in declining to ratify. In addition, the United States has refused to become signatory to the International Criminal Court. The formal U.S. position on these decisions is an expression of its unwillingness to be bound by international human rights treaties that embody principles of universal application—in other words, to which U.S. agents might be legally and ethically bound. Its position against the ICC represents an unabashed embrace of the kind of national sovereignty approaching impunity that the human rights community has struggled to eradicate through such cases as the Pinochet extradition. See Ignatieff, *American Exceptionalism and Human Rights,* for a collection of essays examining issues related to U.S. exceptionalism, including what Ignatieff terms "exemptionism"—U.S. support for treaties only when U.S. citizens remain outside the treaties' reach.

3 In common parlance, this understanding of U.S. identity as organically safe is pervasive. At the 2000 Amnesty International Annual General Meeting (Providence, Rhode Island, March 10–12, 2000) it was repeated in testimony from many survivors of human rights violations. Carla Bernardes, a survivor of domestic violence in Portugal, claims that she emigrated to the United States because of her belief that "I would be safe here. I thought that the U.S. has the best laws." Testimony from Sita Balthazar-Thomas, an aid worker with survivors of sexual torture during the 1994 Rwandan genocide revealed that Tutsi women "refused to believe that women in the U.S. experienced rape, thinking U.S. women were safe from such atrocities."

4 Victoria L. Smith, letter to the author, 28 July 1999.

5 Michael Fay, a U.S. teenager, was sentenced to six strokes with a bamboo cane as punishment for vandalism in Singapore in 1994. The sentence was reduced to four strokes (in addition to four months in prison and a $2,250 fine) following a plea for clemency by President Bill Clinton, inspired largely by domestic outrage at what was seen by many as a cruel and unusual punishment. However, the media coverage of the sentence and its accompanying political activism (especially by Fay's family) included debates about the virtues and appeals of corporal punishment, as well as the tensions between societal and individual rights. For one such discussion, see Matthews.

6 Distinctions between natural and legal rights date to classical Greece, with certain rights said to extend even to those who were not citizens of the empire. For a discussion of Aristotle's writings on both natural and legal rights, see Miller. For an examination of the early writings on natural rights, see Mitsis.

7 This invisibility of nonwestern (non)citizens also exemplifies the importance of citizenship in a shared, democratic political community. In the case of human rights protections both within an individual's home country and while abroad, such membership in a shared democratic world citizenship may in fact be more important than which country issues the passport that ultimately leads to escape and salvation. For a discussion of national and so-called democratic citizenship, see Stewart.

8 The "Human Rights" section of the *Red Corner* Web site posted cases of violations of the rights of travelers abroad, for instance, the case of two British nurses arrested, tortured, and sentenced to death in Saudi Arabia. It also questioned visitors to the site: "Have you been jailed abroad? Please email us and tell us about it. We will post the most interesting stories on this page." These features and the external links to human rights organizations no longer appear on the MGM page for *Red Corner.*

9 During the late 1980s and throughout the 1990s, China replaced Japan as the Asian nation that Americans most feared as a rising political and, especially, economic power. These fears played out during annual debates about China's Most Favored Nation status in Congress as well as during China's application for WTO membership during the last years of the Clinton administration. Largely based on China's strength in the manufacturing sector and on its trade surplus, which corresponded to U.S. weaknesses in manufacturing and its trade deficit, these fears were widespread among both the conservative and liberal wings of U.S. politics. For an excellent examination of these aspects of the Sino-U.S. relationship in historical context, see Gurbaxani and Opper. For a summary of the political dynamics of U.S. fear of Chinese power, see "America's Dose of Sinophobia." For an example of academic justifications for these fears, see Bernstein and Munro.

10 The war in El Salvador originated in protest against oligarchic-military control of the country, along with civil strife in the 1970s that included the fracturing of the Communist Party of El Salvador into multiple splinter leftist groups. In 1980, five of these groups officially united to form the Farabundo Marti Liberation Front (FMLN), a loose alliance of revolutionary groups with disparate ideologies. The FMLN allied with the Democratic Revolutionary Front (FDR) to link revolutionary and popular (sometimes called left and center) elements of the movement. The war reached a violent peak during its first years (1980–1981), fueled by large-scale security assistance from the U.S. government to the Salvadoran military and especially to units that became known as death squads. The war escalated after an attack by the FMLN on military installations across the country in January 1981. Regarding the years 1980–1981 (the setting of *Salvador*), the UN Truth Commission received direct complaints or testimonies related to 4,230 victims of serious acts of violence. Disappearances were at their wartime high during the first years of the war, and individual assassinations (including that of Archbishop Oscar Romero) and mass executions were also frequent. For the total period of the war (1980–1992), 85 percent of the complaints registered with the commission related to violence committed by state agents, particularly paramilitaries and death squads. Half the complaints the commission analyzed occurred during 1980–1981 (see the U.S. Institute of Peace online library for the complete report of the commission). The war continued until a negotiated cease-fire in 1992, which implemented broad-based reform, elections, and a coalition government that included the FMLN and FDR. The San Jose Agreement, a component of the final peace agreement, emphasized human rights and obligated the government to investigate human rights violations committed during the war and to punish those responsible, an obligation that many, including Amnesty International, argue the government has not fulfilled. The Inter-American Court and the Truth Commission have recommended that the Salvadoran government form a committee to investigate the fate of the disappeared and to include civil society actors in this effort. The Salvadoran government established an "Inter-institutional Commission for the Search of Children who disappeared as a result of the armed conflict in El Salvador" in October 2005. Many have argued, however, that this body does not sufficiently promote the involvement of nongovernmental actors in the search process. For more on the continued search for the many thousands of children who disappeared during the conflict, see Amnesty International, *El Salvador*.

11 My reading of populism to signify an early stage of constitutional democracy in *Salvador* is indebted to John F. Stone, who attributes this cultural differentiation to a "rational racism" consistent with imperialist ethnocentrism: "Collectively, these cultural personifications are the by-products of a century-old social Darwinism that has undergirded Euro-American justifications of foreign expansion and intervention" (182).

12   FMLN commander Joaquin Villalobos described the FMLN-FDR coalition alternatively as a "social democratic" movement and a "Latin Americanist" one. Acknowledging the popular, pluralist base of revolutionary supporters (including Social Christians, Social Democrats, and Marxists), Villalobos argued for popular democratic reform in El Salvador that would include elections, demilitarization, and massive agrarian reform. While the FMLN clearly had a populist base, it also was deeply rooted in the socialist guerrilla movements of the 1970s. For an examination of the FMLN, see C. McClintock 48–63.

13   *A Sunday at the Pool in Kigali* was made into a film by Equinoxe Films of Quebec (dir. Robert Favreau) in 2005 (see M. Robinson). According to Aubin, the book, published in French in 2000, was translated into English in 2003; as of December 2003, rights to the book had been sold in thirteen countries and it had been translated into fourteen languages, with royalties and advances in excess of $400,000. It is also a required text in many undergraduate courses in the humanities and social sciences.

14   *Toni Morrison Uncensored.*

15   See Collins for a definition of pornography in terms of historical intersections of race, gender, and class in the United States.

16   Rwanda's primary inhabitants are the Hutu and the Tutsi, terms that referred to agriculturalists and cattle owners, respectively, prior to colonization. Once a German colony, Rwanda became a Belgian colony after World War I. The Belgians emphasized—in fact, arguably created—a racial distinction between Hutus and Tutsis, deeming the Tutsi minority the superior "ethnic group." Tutsi elite began struggling for independence after World War II, at which point the Belgians shifted their support to the majority Hutus, who overthrew the Tutsi monarchy in 1961. In 1962, the Hutu-ruled Rwanda was granted independence. The second Rwandan president, Juvenil Habyarimana, seized power in a coup d'état in 1973 and proceeded to cultivate close ties with the French government, especially with respect to military assistance. This period of time was marked by mistreatment of Tutsis, and many fled the country. In 1990, the Rwandan Patriotic Front (RPF), a Tutsi militia, invaded Rwanda from the refugee camps in Uganda where it was formed. The French military supported Habyarimana's regime and the conflict resulted in a stalemate, with RPF forces controlling much of Northern Rwanda and the government controlling Kigali (the capital) and other areas. In 1992, negotiations began between the government and the RPF, leading to the signing of the Arusha Accords in August 1993. A UN peacekeeping force, UNAMIR, mandated to oversee the implementation of the accords, arrived in November 1993, and the French troops departed. The government stalled rather than implement the power-sharing aspects of the accords, and members of the government and Hutu extremists began planning the genocide of Tutsis. On 6 April 1994, Habyarimana was assassinated and genocide of Tutsis and moderate Hutus commenced, fueled by local "hate radio" broadcasts while the world political community refused to act decisively. UNAMIR forces pulled out of Rwanda, as did most foreigners, and the genocide ended in July 1994 when the RPF gained control of the country. It is estimated that more than 800,000 people died in the hundred-day genocide.

For an excellent summary of Rwandan history and examination of the genocide and its aftermath, see Neuffer. See also Mamdani.

17 See Prunier for a critique of the sexual mores in the book as historically and culturally inaccurate within the Rwandan context.

18 "Interahamwe," which literally means "those who fight together" in Kinyarwanda, refers to the government-backed Hutu extremist militias that implemented the 1994 Rwandan genocide. Interahamwe used rape and the transmission of HIV/AIDS as tools of the genocide. As reported in IRIN Plus/News: "A study by the Rwandan Association of Genocide Widows, Avega Agahozo, conducted in three of Rwanda's 12 provinces shows that 66 percent out of the 1,200 widows sampled tested HIV positive. The same statistics—limited because the study could not cover all the provinces due to the lack of money—revealed that the experience of 100 days of killing and raping left 80 percent of the widows traumatized" (Integrated Regional Information Networks). Visit <http://www.avega.org.rw/english.html> for more.

19 Women's rights have long been included, albeit in varied and often weak formulations, in the twentieth-century human rights movement. The UN Commission on the Status of Women was formed in 1946 and put forth conventions specifically related to women's rights in marriage and the familial sphere but trusted general human rights instruments, such as the Universal Declaration of Human Rights, to secure women's rights as part of the movement for human rights. In 1963, the UN General Assembly asked the commission to develop a declaration regarding the elimination of discrimination against women, which had no legal impact but was adopted by the General Assembly in 1967. In 1975, the World Conference on the International Women's Year was held in Mexico City to "remind the international community that discrimination of women continued to be a persistent problem in much of the world." (See UN General Assembly Resolution 3379, "Elimination of All Forms of Racial Discrimination.") The plan for action that emerged from the conference led to the drafting of the Convention on the Elimination of All Forms of Discrimination against Women (CEDAW), entered into force in 1981. In the 1990s, the global women's movement increased its activity, with Human Rights Watch establishing the Women's Rights Project (now the Women's Rights Division). Women's rights (or lack thereof) were spotlighted with the 1995 Fourth World Conference on Women in Beijing, China. Concurrent with Beijing, Amnesty International launched its global campaign "Women's rights are human rights." For a look at the global women's movement, with a particular focus on the world conferences, see Wetzel.

CHAPTER THREE — TORTURE III

1 For broad address of transcultural repression and exploitation of women, see Kimmel, *The Gendered Society*, especially chap. 3, "Spanning the World," and Meyers, *Gender in the Mirror*, especially chap. 1, "Gender Identity and Woman's Agency: Culture, Norms, and Internalized Oppression Revisited," 3–29. See also Peters and Wolper.

2 In the ticking-bomb scenario, many, including Dershowitz, argue that torture can be both necessary and acceptable. There are two central arguments against the use of this scenario: first, that torture is under any and all circumstances immoral and therefore inherently unacceptable; and second, that torture, once permitted, cannot be—and historically has not been—limited to single cases or isolated scenarios. For the transcript of a debate between Dershowitz and Human Rights Watch executive director Kenneth Roth regarding the use of

torture, see CNN.com's International Law Center page at http://edition.cnn.com/2003/LAW/03/03/cnna.Dershowitz/. For an excellent legal argument in favor of an absolute prohibition on torture, see Waldron.

3 Dershowitz, "Tortured Reasoning." See Dershowitz, *Why Terrorism Works,* for the full elaboration of this argument. One danger inherent in Dershowitz's plan is the bureaucratization of pain and torture; in the wake of the Nazi Holocaust and the Eichmann trial in particular, it is difficult to countenance Dershowitz's choice to enter at any point upon this exceedingly slippery slope.

4 There has been a vibrant academic discourse across cultures surrounding the application of human rights conventions and laws. However, certain rights have frequently been accepted as truly universal, first among them the prohibition of torture. For a discussion of the continuum of cultural relativism and absolutism in international human rights discourse, see section 2, "Cultural Relativism and Human Rights," in Donnelly; also An-Na'im. Dershowitz claims that to acknowledge the use of torture would control its usage in ways that are impossible within the current status quo of nominal prohibition and under-the-radar practice. Yet international human rights instruments, including the multiple legal manifestations of the prohibition against torture, have proven useful in advocating for the improvement of governments' human rights records through diplomatic efforts and have served as tools for those seeking to resolve individual cases of human rights abuses across the globe. While Dershowitz's argument promotes the absence of hypocrisy as the fundamental good necessary for an ethical foreign policy, others have argued that commitment to international treaties is a key diplomatic tool for pursuing an ethical and effective foreign policy. For a collection of essays that explore the place of ethics in foreign policy and the mechanisms for promoting an ethical foreign policy, including human rights principles and treaties, see Smith and Light.

5 See Ortiz' book detailing her ordeal and recovery, *The Blindfold's Eyes.*

6 I use the term "masculinist" as opposed to "masculine" to denote the set of gender norms associated with masculinity in patriarchal cultures. Like "the feminine," which I use in a similar manner in this chapter, this term does not refer to the actions or ideas of individual men or women. For a discussion of gender norms and a critique of gendered perceptions, see S. Smith, *Gender Thinking.*

7 See Dershowitz, "Tortured Reasoning," for Dershowitz's account of this event. Although he locates the conference at John Jay College, his description of events matches those of the CUNY Conference; perhaps the confusion arises from the fact that the CUNY event was hosted and run by Professor Charles Strozier of John Jay College, which is part of the CUNY system. The quotations reproduced here from that day's events are from my notes, and the perspective on these events is also my own as an audience member.

8 See Gugelberger, especially the introduction, for a discussion of the complexities of the narrative "I" in the *testimonio* genre.

9 See Arias for a critical examination of the debates surrounding the publication, reception, and veracity of *I, Rigoberta Menchú.* See Bernard-Donals for a sophisticated reading of veracity and the narrative "I" in the case of Benjamin Wilkomerski's *Fragments.*

10 The crime of forced disappearance has been particularly widespread in Latin America, especially during the 1970s and 1980s, although it continues to be a tool of terror and repression globally. Usually a crime committed by government

forces, the term *desaparecidos* (literally: the disappeared) refers to those taken and held in secret detention, many of whom are never found. In the cases of Chile and Argentina, such bodies were often disposed of by airdrop into the ocean; in most other sites the bodies are dumped in mass graves. Disappearances were especially high in Guatemala; according to the REMHI report *Guatemala: Never Again*, more than thirty thousand individuals were disappeared during the country's thirty-six-year civil war (Archdiocese of Guatemala). According to the Commission for Historical Clarification (CEH), state agents applied torture systematically throughout the war, usually coordinated with arbitrary executions and detentions. While executions in Guatemala were often arbitrary (including brutal targeting of women and children), disappearances were anything but arbitrary. Common targets included individuals affiliated with unions, social organizations, and political parties, as well as students and church workers, such as Sister Dianna Ortiz. (For more information about human rights abuses in Guatemala, see Commission for Historical Clarification). Throughout Latin America, many torture survivors refer to their time in clandestine detention as the time that they were "disappeared," because their family members could not locate them or gain information about their detention.

11 In fact, Dershowitz claims to support lifting the prohibition precisely to lessen the incidence of torture, although scholars such as Elaine Scarry have identified the faulty logic informing such a view (see Scarry, "Five Errors"). See Greenberg and Dratel for primary source documents on the military, judicial, legislative, and executive processes that would lead to lifting the prohibition.

12 Dershowitz's terminology is telling. Referring to Sister Dianna Ortiz as a "victim" is another veiled dismissal. The acknowledged term in survivor, activist, and academic human rights communities for someone who did not die as a result of her torture is "survivor," not "victim." Victims did not survive. The term "survivor" carries an ethical charge in terms of the reclamation of one's life and self after the traumatic ordeal of torture. Dershowitz's pointed refusal to employ it reveals the limits of his perspective upon the torture debate he has initiated. Specifically, the origin of Dershowitz's interest in the practice of torture in the Israeli/ Palestinian context bears upon his current position. Dershowitz's book *Why Terrorism Works* analyzes the use of torture as a tool in Israel's security arsenal. His investment in the issue of state security informs his extrapolation from the Israeli case to the post-9/11 context in the United States. It also prompts his persistent evocation of the statistically irrelevant ticking-bomb scenario as frame for arguments that address far broader implications and applications of torture, revealing his prioritization of security over human rights. The frame of his arguments also sets security and human rights in an extreme, and thereby misleading, opposition. For a well-articulated argument that "security" and "human rights" are not oppositional terms, see Pearlstein. For a critique of Dershowitz's arguments about human rights in the Israeli context, see Finkelstein, especially his chapter "Israel's Abu Ghraib," 142–167. Finkelstein's text counters Dershowitz's *Why Terrorism Works* with data from Amnesty International, Human Rights Watch, and B'tselem on Israel's terror practices against Palestinians.

13 This subject is famously raised in "The Grand Inquisitor" section of Dostoevsky's *Brothers Karamazov*, when the rationalist Ivan poses this question to his naïve brother, Alyosha: "Imagine that you are creating a fabric of human destiny with the object of making men happy in the end, giving them peace and rest at last, but

that it was essential and inevitable to torture to death only one tiny creature . . . and to found that edifice on its unavenged tears, would you consent to be the architect on this condition?" (16); for a reading of the problem staged by Dostoevsky in context of post-9/11 torture debates, see Dorfman, "Are There Times."

14 The irony of Dershowitz's refusal to name Sister Dianna Ortiz in this paragraph is heavy: the collection of essays in which Dershowitz's contribution appears contains a foreword by Chilean writer Ariel Dorfman that Dorfman identifies as "a revised version of a keynote speech delivered on June 25, 2002, at a conference in Washington, D.C., organized by Sister Dianna Ortiz and the TASSC," and he specifically cites TASSC as "a splendid example and model" in his characterization of the organization of torture survivors themselves as a "paramount" part of the "resilient army of citizens, victims, and lawyers" working on the problem of human rights. The irony of this highly visible reference to Sister Dianna Ortiz in her professional aspect is further compounded by editor Sanford Levinson's revelation: "I am . . . pleased to say that every contributor concurred in a suggestion that all of the royalties attached to this book will go not to the authors but rather to the Torture Abolition and Survivors Support Coalition"—the NGO that Sister Dianna Ortiz founded, TASSC International. In a parallel with geopolitical and economic relationships between first and third worlds, TASSC, an easy object of the charitable impulse, can legitimately receive the largesse of intellectuals like Dershowitz; however, the resistance typical of a global power broker meets Sister Dianna's entrance into the professional public sphere and her desire to set the agenda.

15 References to women's inability to act or think as rational beings were used as excuses to preclude suffrage and broad entry into the public sphere. See Virginia Woolf, "A Room of One's Own" (627–652), and other documents in Rossi, *The Feminist Papers: From Adams to Beauvoir*, for references to women's absence from "the world of intellect." The Seneca Falls "Declaration of Sentiments and Resolutions" in 1848 also referenced this exclusion of women from the professional fields (specifically law, medicine, and theology). In modern times, feminist interpretations of women's exclusion from the rational sphere have contributed to academic fields such as feminist economics. For a collection of essays exploring the exclusion of "typically feminine" traits and issues from economics, see Ferber and Nelson.

16 Importantly, the category of terrorist includes both those known to be terrorists (e.g., the so-called twentieth hijacker) and those suspected of being terrorists. Due to the secrecy maintained by the U.S. government regarding post-9/11 detainees, calculating the number of suspected terrorists and known terrorists is enormously difficult, if not impossible. However, Human Rights First has documented that, as of February 2005, approximately 65,000 people were "screened for possible detention," of whom 30,000 were "entered into the system" and assigned internment serial numbers. A list released by the U.S. government pursuant to a Freedom of Information Act filing by the Associated Press of detainees at Guantánamo Bay named 558 people from forty-one countries at the prison as of April 2006. Postings by the American Civil Liberties Union estimate that between 3,000 and 5,000 people are being detained by the U.S. Department of Justice as of October 2006 (see <www.aclu.org/safefree/detention/index.html>). Numerous U.S. and world media outlets documented the imprisonment or arrest of innocent people in the wide net cast by U.S. law enforcement and military forces in the war on terror. Human Rights Watch has documented for many prisoners at Guantánamo and in Iraq and Afghanistan detention without charge, refusal to release detainees on posted bond or pursuant to release orders, and misuse of material witness warrants. Finally, President George W. Bush signed the Military Commissions Act into law on 17 October 2006. Under this act, the president is authorized to establish military commissions to try unlawful enemy combatants. Defendants are prevented from invoking the Geneva Conventions, and their right to file writs of habeas corpus is suspended. Under the act, U.S. interrogators are subject to a limited range of "grave breaches" related to Common Article 3 of the Geneva Convention, and their liability for abuses is severely curtailed.

17 See Yuval-Davis for a full explication of these tropes.

18 See Douglas for her full treatment of this subject.

19 For specific discussion of Saartjie Baartman, the "Hottentot Venus," see Pieterse 181–182; Gilman, especially chap. 3, "The Hottentot and the Prostitute: Toward an Iconography of Female Sexuality," 76–108; and A. McClintock 40–42.

20 When Sister Dianna Ortiz pursued her claim that a North American agent had been present in her torture chamber in Guatemala by staging a hunger strike on the steps of the White House to protest the continued classification of documents related to her case, the line used to discredit her claims was that she had been involved in a sado-masochistic lesbian tryst, and that the 111 cigarette-burn marks on her back were a result of that sexual encounter (see Ortiz' memoir).

21 See Freud, "Beyond the Pleasure Principle," especially 607–610, for discussion of the psychic "protective shield" against traumatic occurrence.

22 Griggers's essay, which examines postmodern constructions of the lesbian body, analyzes "phallic body prostheses," the use of which by lesbians, Griggers maintains, amounts to an appropriation of the phallus that works against "the naturalization of masculinist hegemony" (181). In a further contestation of the power and unity of the phallic sign in *Sammy and Rosie*, the camera pans the communal squatter settlement, the site of struggle between London's conservative economic/political forces and its young, anticapitalist anarchist element (as well as of Rafi's ultimate abject encounter with his ghostly torture victim), holding a medium shot of a young woman watering a makeshift garden with a can that sports a dildo for a spout, exposing, as Griggers asserts, "the cultural organ of the phallus as a simulacrum" (181).

23 See Lindroth for a reading of the movie as "a filmed version of the poem, . . . a poetic, symbolic, visionary presentation of Thatcher's England as Eliot's Waste Land" (95).

24 Hooks's argument is undermined by its many inaccuracies; for instance, her claim—advanced as part of an argument about the absence of black women on screen—that Rafi meets Danny with his girlfriend and child and invites him to a party, at which point Danny hands the child to the woman and leaves with Rafi. Actually, Danny kisses the woman goodbye and takes the child with him to the party. Hooks mistakenly attributes to Alice a line spoken by Vivia, a lesbian friend of Rosie's ("the penis was your life-line"—spoken to Rafi's love interest, Alice, during the party scene as a critique of Alice's passiveness in the face of Rafi's sexism), claiming that Alice uses this assertion to "critique [Rafi's] sexism" (160). Most irresponsible of the essay's factual errors is hooks's assertion that "Rosie is visibly sexually turned on when Danny shares with her that the murdered black woman nursed him as a child" (161). The issue of nursing is not mentioned in the film. Danny's line in this scene is: "The woman who brought me up—because my mum was out at work all day—lived right near you" (Kureishi 42). Such inaccuracies do a deep injustice to Kureishi's work and weaken hooks's own argument.

25 Kureishi, however, is aware of the inherent problems of representation in this case, wondering in his diary: "But what are we doing using this material in the film. . . . Aren't we stealing other people's lives, their hard experience, for our own purposes?" (102).

26 See especially Rieff.

27 Shannon Faulkner was admitted to the Citadel, the Military College of South Carolina, in 1995; however, she left after less than one week, citing stress and isolation. The Supreme Court then struck down an all-male admissions policy at the Virginia Military Institute, and the Citadel subsequently admitted three additional women in fall 1996. Two of them later left, citing harassment as the reason for their departure, and the first female graduate of the Citadel was Nancy Mace in May 1999. The masthead image of the Citadel Web site (<http://www.citadel.edu/>) is provocative in terms of the gendered history of the institution, as well as of the military more broadly: on the left, the photo of a single female cadet, positioned so that she is facing, on the right, a line of male cadets in full-dress uniform. The effect is a kind of standoff between the single female and the collectivity of males in the institutional context of the military academy.

28 Sexual and domestic violence have long plagued all branches of the military, with both receiving increased media and public attention in 2002–2003 following the emergence of a series of major cases. Domestic violence in particular has been a longstanding problem in military communities but returned to the spotlight in 2002 following five domestic murders at Fort Bragg in North Carolina and the release of the Department of Defense's Task Force on Domestic Violence's final report in March 2003 (following three years of investigation). The report recommended increases in services to victims, increased efficacy and sensitivity of interventions, and greater training and accountability for officers, as well as increased cooperation with civilian authorities in military communities. For an excellent discussion of the prevalence and causes of domestic violence specifically within the military context, see Lutz. In addition, the Miles Foundation (<http://hometown.aol.com/milesfdn>) tracks domestic and sexual violence in the U.S. military. Sexual violence at all branches of the military academies gained increased attention following the February 2003 allegations of a former Air Force Academy cadet that her allegations of rape while a cadet resulted in her being punished for engaging in a sexual relationship on campus. According to the Department of Defense report, in the ten reporting years prior to its publication, the Air Force Academy received 142 reports of sexual assault while West Point received 36 such accusations. The Naval Academy received 14 allegations of sexual assault from 2001 to 2003. The reports on these allegations, including civilian oversight reports mandated by Congress, uniformly cited inappropriate and inadequate responses of superiors and institutions as primary factors in the pervasive nature of assault on military academy campuses.

29 The military's "Don't ask, don't tell, don't pursue" policy was born in the World War II era with a differentiation between homosexual and "normal" recruits in army mobilization regulations that classified homosexuality as a pathology. In 1981, the Department of Defense stated that homosexuality was incompatible

with military service, and in 1993 this was codified as the "Don't ask, don't tell, don't pursue" policy under the Clinton administration. The policy has been subject to legal challenges, most notably through the Service Members Legal Defense Network (<www.sldn.org>), which also provides a history of the policy. The most recent legal activity surrounding "Don't ask, don't tell" focused not on the policy itself but on the right of universities to refuse military recruiters on antidiscrimination grounds. The U.S. Supreme Court ruled in March 2006 that federal policies stipulating that the universities that refuse recruiters on these grounds may lose their federal funding did not, in fact, violate the universities' free speech rights. The Military Readiness Enhancement Act (H.R. 1059), which would repeal the probation of open service by homosexuals and bisexuals, was introduced in March 2005 and currently has 115 cosponsors. See Halley.

30 For descriptions of such tactics see Human Rights Watch, *The Road to Abu Ghraib*. For a firsthand account of the role of race and religion in treatment of Arab and Muslim men at Guantánamo, see Yee. See Karpinski for an account of torture tactics at Abu Ghraib prison as well as an account of Karpinski's experience as the first woman to command troops in a U.S. combat zone.

31 Considering gender issues at stake in the case of Lynndie England, it is important to note the manipulation of gender norms in the case of Jessica Lynch, whose capture and dramatic liberation borrow from the conventions of the counterhistorical dramatic film in foregrounding the rescue against all odds of one white woman against the backdrop of war. Crucially, her liberation was later discovered to have been staged by the military to boost morale at a time when the news from the war "was not good" (see Richburg). Lynch also plays the heroic antithesis to the figure of England in considerations of the place of women in the theater of war. Finally, it is also relevant that the only officer demoted in relation to the events at Abu Ghraib is a woman, former Brigadier General Janis Karpinski, who has toured the country and testified before a tribunal held by the nonprofit organization Not in Our Name with her claims that responsibility for the crimes at Abu Ghraib lies in orders given by high-ranking government and military officials, including Major General Geoffrey Miller, General Ricardo Sanchez, and Secretary of Defense Donald Rumsfeld.

32 England is in this sense akin to, but cannot be read through the same lens as, the "monstrous mothers" who commit infanticide. In the latter case, the horror stems from the fact that a mother could extinguish the life she has created; in the former, it results from the disjunction between the biological act of creation and nurturance implied by the pregnancy and the performance of obscenity and brutality exhibited in the torture directed at another person, even a person constructed as a mortal enemy. In both cases, the problem goes to the heart of essentialist notions of the maternal body.

33 See Farrell and McDermott for an extensive analysis of the struggle for meaning and agency on the part of Afghani women in the context of the war on terror.

CHAPTER FOUR — RAPE

1 To focus upon these uses of rape is not to assert that their contexts render the act any more consequential or damaging than rape in a private, nonpolitical setting. Rhonda Copelon has convincingly argued that the cost of identifying rape as torture only in the context of armed conflict and direct state action might be the continued acceptance of the distinction between rape as atrocity in war or genocidal contexts, and other rape. She writes: "The recognition of rape as a war crime is thus a critical step toward understanding rape as violence. The next step is to recognize that rape that acquires the imprimatur of the state is not necessarily more brutal, relentless, or dehumanizing than the private rapes of everyday life, nor is violation by a state official or enemy soldier necessarily more devastating than violation by an intimate" (199).

2 See Horeck, especially chap. 2, "Body Politics: Rousseau's *Le Levite D'Ephraim*," for a reading of rape in the context of Pateman's theories of the sexual contract.

3 South Africa was colonized by Jan van Riebeeck and the Dutch East India Company in 1652, was taken over by the British in 1775, and changed hands between the Dutch and the British until finally it became a British colony in 1814. In the 1830s, Afrikaners distanced themselves further from the Cape Colony through the Great Trek to areas outside British control. The discovery of valuable minerals in the late nineteenth century increased conflict between British colonizers and Afrikaners, culminating in the Anglo-Boer South African War (1899–1902), which ended in British victory. From the formation of the Union of South Africa in 1910, whites were granted exclusive franchise in many areas, and privilege in all. In response, black activists began organizing more intensely and formed the African National Congress (ANC) in 1912. In 1948, the Boer National Party won the general election and furthered its apartheid ideology through legislation such as the Prohibition of Mixed Marriages Act (1949), Population Registration Act (1950), and Group Areas Act (1950). The latter removed all persons classified "Black" and "Coloured" to small, impoverished townships. The ANC joined the Congress Alliance in support of the nonviolent Defiance Campaign in 1952. The 1960s brought increased protests and repression, but the first protest of what would become the successful international anti-apartheid movement took place in the Soweto uprising of 1976. Under increasing international and domestic pressure during the 1980s, the apartheid government responded with minor reforms and increased oppression until it finally announced the release of political prisoners, including Nelson Mandela, in 1989. The country's first democratic elections in April 1994 resulted in a 62 percent win for the African National Congress and the presidency of Nelson Mandela, marking the end of apartheid. For more information on the history of South Africa, see Terreblanche.

4 Isidore Diala offers the astute observation that "Lucy's will to sacrifice notwithstanding, in her supposedly objective evaluation of her place and that of other white farmers in her neighborhood is inherent the dread of virtual ethnic cleansing" (66).

5 See Diala for a reading of *Disgrace* that traces its relevance to and commentary upon the South African Truth and Reconciliation Commission.

6 See Graham for a reading of *Disgrace* through the lens of the historical use of the black-peril narrative.

7 The first modern international legal instruments to regulate human rights during times of war (primarily the Geneva Conventions) and peace (the Universal Declaration of Human Rights) do not address crimes against women, including rape, as distinct cases. However, during the 1990s there was increased attention to the specific nature of crimes against women during conflict, especially the Bosnian and Rwanda genocides. In addition to the case law from the International Tribunal for the Former Yugoslavia and the International Tribunal for Rwanda, which recognizes rape as a crime against humanity, the Convention on the Elimination of All Forms of Discrimination against Women (CEDAW) prohibits discrimination and

disparaging treatment on the basis of sex, and the CEDAW Committee has stated that this extends to a prohibition of all forms of violence against women. In addition, the UN Declaration on the Elimination of Violence against Women and the Inter-American Convention on Violence address violence against women during peace and war and in the public and private spheres. In a notable victory for advocates of recognizing crimes against women as war crimes within the mainstream body of international law, the Rome Statutes of the International Criminal Court include rape as both a crime against humanity and a war crime and as a potential element of genocide. For an excellent overview of the evolution of the place of violence against women in international law and its current status, see Askin. There is also a movement to identify rape in the private sphere as torture, led by Amnesty International's Stop Violence against Women campaign (<www.amnestyusa.org/ stopviolence/factsheets/sexualviolence.html>). Finally, under the Convention against Torture and Other Cruel, Inhuman or Degrading Treatment or Punishment (CAT), state acquiescence is a key component of the definition of torture. International law has typically failed to include state failure or refusal to act as a violation of human rights treaties, but under the CAT the absence of legal recourse for women victims of violence does potentially open the door for private rape to be considered torture. To date, this has remained a largely academic discourse, which has not been recognized in the documents of international law or international jurisprudence.

8 Although torture has often been recognized as a tool of degradation rather than of information extraction, especially in the context of Central and South America, torture in the post-9/11 context has once again become a method for information extraction through degradation based specifically upon (religious and ethnic) identity. And while the Convention against Torture and Other Cruel, Inhuman or Degrading Treatment or Punishment, to which the United States is a party, clearly states that "no exceptional circumstances whatsoever . . . may be invoked as a justification of torture," the U.S. government has, since 9/11, repeatedly sought to redefine torture so as to exclude acts once accepted as torture, such as waterboarding (simulated drowning). See United Nations, *Convention against Torture,* art. 2(2), S. Treaty Doc No. 100–20, 1465 U.N.T.S. 85, 114 (entered into force 28 June 28 1984). In an infamous memorandum approved by former White House counsel (and current attorney general) Alberto Gonzalez, the Department of Justice insisted that abusive treatment constitutes torture only when it causes "injury such as death, organ failure, or serious impairment of bodily functions." In the same memo, the Department of Justice sought to separate torture and inhuman treatment, grouped together in the CAT, by asserting that "acts may be cruel, inhuman or degrading but still not produce pain and suffering of the requisite nature" to constitute torture. The memorandum, dated 1 August 2002, is available at <http://www.humanrightsfirst.org/us_law/etn/ index.asp>. There is no internationally accepted distinction of torture as compared to cruel, inhuman, and degrading punishment, in part because of reluctance to establish a limit at which inhuman treatment ends and torture begins, presuming that states would capitalize on that definition for maximum abuse with minimal accountability. However, the Bush administration's arguments for separating the two ignore the United States' signature on a treaty that outlaws both in all circumstances.

9 For analyses of the problem of consent in sexual relationships under slavery, see Clinton, Spillers.

10 Considering the delineations of "home and world" from the perspective of human rights theory, "history's most intricate invasions" might well describe the invasions of both the public (in the form of the regime/torturer) and the domestic (in the form of the ordinary household objects commonly used to inflict torture) into the very body of the torture victim. Hear the resonance with Scarry, who identifies the conversion of everyday domestic objects into weapons, "agents of pain," as one of the principle techniques of the torturer (*The Body in Pain*, 40). This process, which undertakes the "mutilation of the domestic" to maximize human pain, is part of torture's "almost obscene conflation of private and public," which "brings with it all the solitude of absolute privacy with none of its safety, all the self-exposure of the utterly public with none of its possibility for camaraderie or shared experience" (53).

11 For an important intervention in feminist conceptions of the private sphere, see Anannya Bhattacharjee and other essays in the same volume edited by Silliman and Bhattacharjee. Bhattacharjee examines "the supposedly private space of home and family [as] another significant site of [law] enforcement violence against women," showing how "the supposed privacy and sanctity of the home is a relative concept, whose application is heavily conditioned by racial and economic status" (29).

12 For thorough historicization of *Corregidora*'s setting in the Brazilian (as opposed to U.S.) slave system, see Coser and Robinson. As discussed earlier in the notes to this chapter, institutionalized rape (including the strategic use of rape for ethnic cleansing, sexual slavery, and enforced pregnancy) has been interpreted as a crime against humanity in the Rome Statutes of the International Criminal Court and the International Criminal Tribunal for Rwanda. Although rape is absent from the statutes of the International Tribunal for the Former Yugoslavia, several defendants at the Tribunals for the Former Yugoslavia (ICTY) and Rwanda (ICTR) have been prosecuted for committing rape as a crime against humanity. See Gutman and Rieff 323–329. Specifically, Jean-Paul Akayesu, the former mayor of Taba, Rwanda, was found guilty of rape as a crime against humanity in a 1998 ICTR ruling, in addition to being found guilty of genocide. See the judgment and sentencing documents of the Akayesu trial at <http://69.94.11.53/default.htm> (under "Cases"). Perhaps even more notable is Pauline Nyiramasuhoko's indictment by the ICTR for genocide and crimes against humanity by inciting rape.

13 For historicization of the convergence of racial and sexual violence in the acts of rape and lynching, see Hall, Carby, Spillers.

14 Given the historical and racial context of *Corregidora*, it is important to note that Spivak's comments about the denial of what she calls "female subject-function" that accompanies effacement of the clitoris are part of an exploration of the role of first-world academic feminism in an international context; her comments are qualified by warnings against reductive constructions of female subjectivity in terms of reproductive freedom and individualism: "For to see women's liberation as identical with reproductive liberation is to . . . see the establishment of women's subject-status as an unquestioned good and indeed not to heed the best lessons of French anti-humanism, which discloses the historical dangers of a subjectivist normativity" (150–151).

15 See Scarry, *The Body in Pain*, especially chap. 1, "The Structure of Torture: The Conversion of Real Pain into the Fiction of Power." See also E. Goldberg, "Living the Legacy," for a fuller reading of the parallels between the scene of heterosexual sex in the legacy of slavery and the formal scene of torture as delineated by Scarry.

16 While the official reason for the U.S. pullout was its objection to the topic "Zionism as Racism," Bharati Sadasivam reports in the *Village Voice* that "many saw the U.S. focus on Zionism as a diversionary tactic to duck the question of reparations."

17 The Spanish first built settlements in Chile in 1541, on land belonging to Quechua, Inca, and Araucanian Indians; by the mid–nineteenth century there were over one million Spanish settlers. Chile gained its independence in 1810, but its parliamentary system remained controlled by a Spanish-dominated oligarchy until the election of Marxist president Salvador Allende, the uncle of Isabel Allende, in 1970. Allende implemented socialist policies, such as providing free early childhood education and nationalizing industry and social services, that met with great opposition from the right wing in business, politics, and the military. After three years, Allende's presidency was disrupted by covert CIA-backed military intervention ending in the coup led by General Augusto Pinochet on 11 September 1973. Under the dictatorship of Pinochet between 1973 and 1989, over 3,000 Chileans were disappeared, and an estimated 27,000 were imprisoned and tortured as part of Pinochet's "dirty war" against subversion. Chile was returned to democratic rule in 1990, with Pinochet retaining impunity under his designation "president for life." However, in a precedent-setting case, Pinochet was arrested in Great Britain in 1998 on a warrant issued by Spanish judge Balthazar Garzón for nine counts of disappearance and murder. Placed under house arrest in Chile, he was released after one year upon the court's ruling that he was medically unfit to stand trial. In May 2004, Chile's Supreme Court pronounced Pinochet capable of standing trial; court cases related to Pinochet's immunity from prosecution for various crimes are currently in process. On 30 October 2006, Pinochet was placed under house arrest in connection with charges of torture, homicide, and kidnap. See Collier and Sater for broad historical coverage of Chile.

18 Examples of public gestures of atonement Ignatieff offers in his theorization of the reconciliatory potential of the gesture include "Chilean President Patricio Alwyn's appearance on television to apologise to the victims of Pinochet's repression [and] . . . German Chancellor Willy Brandt's gesture of going down on his knees at a death camp" ("Overview" 121–122). As a result of such public expressions of atonement, Ignatieff avers, a public climate was created in which "a thousand acts of private repentance and atonement became possible" (122).

19 See Arditti for an account of these disappeared children, and of the work of the Madres and especially the Abuelas of the Plaza de Mayo on their behalf.

CHAPTER FIVE — GENOCIDE

1 Clark University in Worcester, Massachusetts, inaugurated its PhD program in Holocaust and genocide studies in 1998. While some programs (University of Vermont, University of Maryland) retain a singular focus upon the Nazi Holocaust, programs at the University of Nevada and in the New Jersey state system have expanded as Holocaust and genocide studies. At the same time, centers for Holocaust and genocide studies have emerged in affiliation with Drew University, the University of Montreal, and the University of Minnesota; the Institute of Holocaust and Genocide Studies in Australia is affiliated with three major universities.

2 See Churchill, Charny. See also Laremont.

3 Rafael Lemkin, a Polish lawyer who lost his entire family in the Holocaust, coined the term "genocide," drafted the Convention on the Prevention and Punishment of Genocide, and then made its ratification by individual states his life's work. See Power, especially chap. 1, for an account of Lemkin's struggle and the 1951 ratification of the UN Convention on the Prevention and Punishment of the Crime of Genocide.

4 Chilean writer Ariel Dorfman immediately began publishing articles in mainstream international press organs arguing for the necessity of a comparative perspective in the hours and days following 9/11, reminding U.S. citizens that this was not the first 11 September to have destroyed the illusions of a nation. He urged that the United States remember its own role in the Chilean 9/11 (1973) and take that event's legacy of vengeance and violence as instructive when measuring its response to the attacks on Manhattan and Washington. Many of these writings are collected in Dorfman. See also Kingsolver, Gordimer.

5 See especially Laub.

6 For instance, the series "Urban Intervention in the City of Rosario" by Argentinean artist Fernando Traveres consists of 350 bicycles spray-painted throughout the city of Rosario, Argentina, to mark the spaces where 350 citizens were disappeared during the "dirty war," as well as the sites of the clandestine prisons where they were held. A statement from an exhibit, "The Disappeared," featuring Traveres' work and curated by Laurel Reuter, director of the North Dakota Museum of Art, asserts: "Bicycles were a common form of travel for members of the resistance. An abandoned bicycle was often the first sign that its owner had been kidnapped, or disappeared. . . . [Traveres'] many painted bicycles become shadows, or memories of kidnappings, of disappearances. The silhouette of the bicycle is the metaphor of absence." (The exhibit will travel to museums in North and South America between 2006–2009. See <http://www.ndmoa.com/PastEx/Disappeared/index.html>.) Other such spaces include the Tuol Sleng Museum on the site of the former S-21 Prison in Phnom Penh, Cambodia; and the Museum of Memory being established at the Naval Mechanics School, known as Argentina's Auschwitz (see Goni). Importantly, these memorials bear witness not only to the crimes committed within the sites, but also fundamentally to the existence of the site itself, marking the absences of the humans who disappeared and died there.

7 According to Genocide Watch, coordinating organization for the International Campaign to End Genocide, founded in the Hague, Netherlands, May 1999: "Ethnic conflict develops in eight predictable stages: *Classification* of groups into "us versus them"; *Symbolization* of group identity, as with national ID cards; *Dehumanization* of one group, by equating them with alien or enemy forces; *Organization* of hate groups and militias; *Polarization* of the country; *Preparation* for mass killing through trial massacres, activation of militias and death squads with impunity; *Genocide* or widespread genocidal massacres; and *Denial* of responsibility. The situation in Côte d'Ivoire has reached stage six, Preparation, when a Genocide Watch must be declared." <http://www.genocidewatch.org/CotedIvoire GenocideWatch.htm.>

8 See Weisman.

9 This question is implicit in analyses of all the narratives under study in this book; however, the temporal connection with a genocide in process coupled with the urgency of witnessing specific to the case of genocide render the inquiry more pointed and complex here.

10 See Cohen for the seminal case study of denial on individual and cultural levels.

11 Nicholas Kristof is responsible for a virtual cottage industry of reportage about the genocide in Sudan in the *New York Times*, including extensive video footage available at the *Times* online; reports on Darfur have appeared continuously in news outlets, including popular mainstream television news programs, throughout the United States since 2003.

12 While Timerman's narrative cannot be said to be constructed without aesthetic license—as for instance, a moving poetic rumination upon the eye of another prisoner seen through the peephole of his cell door that opens the book—it is a chronological account of Timerman's experience as a journalist at the time the military dictatorship commenced its covert war against the Argentine people; his subsequent imprisonment and torture by that government as a subversive; and his ultimate release and deportation to Israel as a result of international pressure. The text is marked by journalistic discourse that provides historical, political, and cultural context for the events described. Partnoy's account, in contrast, is highly aestheticized in its use of short story and poetic forms accompanied by artwork to capture the experiences of a variety of prisoners in the first-person voice. In sections in which she relates as a firsthand witness observer the experiences of other prisoners who did not survive, Partnoy fulfills one of the key functions of testimonial: that is, the use of the "I" voice to represent a collective silenced by systematic oppression, by lack of access to witnesses in either legal or media venues, or by death. This adoption of perspectives or voices other than one's own is in accordance with the ethic of truth telling at the heart of the testimonial. See Gugelberger, especially the introduction, for a discussion of the relation between the first-person narrator and the collective she may represent.

13 See Maechler for an account of the investigation of Wilkomirski's claims about spending his childhood in Nazi concentration camps. Whereas Wilkomirski's case raises questions of truth and memory, the case of Rigoberta Menchú raises more clearly the central issue of veracity in the context of *testimonio*; that is, the "I" voice representing a collective unable to speak on its own behalf in the public sphere. See Menchú Tum, Stoll, Arias. More recently, this issue made international news with discrepancies of truth discovered in James Frey's memoir of hard living, *A Million Little Pieces*, after its imprimatur as one of "Oprah's books."

14 See Gilmore for a compelling argument about the consideration of autobiography as part of a "fuller archive" of the testimonial form.

15 Acknowledging theoretical contention around the term "cosmopolitanism," I use it here to mean the kind of internationalist human connection and identification that informs the human rights movement in its global and local manifestations. See Robbins for a nuanced discussion of competing forces laying claim to "global feeling"; see also Robbins and Cheah; Brennan; Appadurai et al.

16 The island of Hispaniola, populated in the pre-Columbian era by Arawak and Carib Indians, was first colonized as Santo Domingo by Christopher Columbus in his 1492 expedition. In the sixteenth century, France began to compete with Spain for dominance in the West Indies, and by 1700 the French occupied the western portion of the island, naming it Haiti. The island was a major producer of sugarcane, dependent upon the labor of African slaves. Haiti has the distinction of being the first black republic in the Western Hemisphere, defeating Napoleon's forces and declaring independence in 1804. The Dominican Republic fell under Haitian control in 1821 and gained independence in 1844. General Rafael Trujillo came to power in 1930, with ambitions to restore the island fully to Dominican control. In October 1937, Trujillo ordered the slaughter by the Dominican military of Haitians living on the border dividing Haiti from the Dominican Republic. In addition to Trujillo's ambition for control of Haitian territory, the massacre has been attributed to tension related to economic decline; struggles over Haitian immigration to the Dominican Republic; and retaliation for the assassination of several of Trujillo's men in Haiti. Estimates of Haitians killed in the massacre range from twelve to eighteen thousand. According to international legal convention, the slaughter of Haitians at the command of General Rafael Trujillo in the Dominican Republic in 1937, is a "genocidal event" or "massacre," as opposed to a genocide; however, I have chosen to include instances of massacre in this chapter on genocide because the difference is one of scale, largely irrelevant to the victims and survivors experiencing the onslaught of violence designed to destroy them as "members of national, ethnic, racial, or religious group" (see United Nations, *Convention on the Prevention and Punishment*). It is also named by historians as genocide (see, for instance, Derby; see also Turits). Genocides and genocidal massacres have most often occurred within the context of a broader civil or cross-border conflict. However, even within such contexts, genocidal intent and incident can be separated from other forms of brutal violence through careful investigation and research. Notable examples are the case of genocide against Mayan people in Guatemala, the Armenian genocide, and genocide in Bosnia-Herzegovina. An excellent summary of scholarship on this issue can be found in Krain.

17 See Mamdani for an analysis of the Rwandan genocide as a political event rooted in the colonial encounter.

18 See also Gilroy for an argument about the urgency of foregrounding racism in human rights discourses and practices in the twenty-first century.

19 See Koshy for an excellent explication of this problem in the contemporary context.

20 See Rigaud for elucidation of the vodou (voodoo) pantheon.

21 See Cheah for an intervention into the construction of cosmopolitanism and nationalism as binary opposites.

22 This doubled meaning of "fug" evokes dual philosophical approaches to human relationships: spiritual and secular traditions of individuation and deep love for the intrinsic dignity and worth of individual human beings on the one hand, and the existentialist nausea induced by reflection upon the qualities of those same human beings on the other.

23 See Coetzee, *Lives of Animals*; also see *Disgrace*. This line of thinking can be traced, among other sources, to Dostoevsky's exploration of human cruelty in chapter 4, "Rebellion," *The Brothers Karamazov*.

24 The Bosnian war (1992–1995) pitted the country's ethnic Serbs, Croats, and Bosniaks (Bosnian Muslims) against one another and took place in the context of the breakup of the former Yugoslavia. The war was genocidal in character for its duration and throughout the country but is most notorious for the genocidal Srebrenica massacres in July 1995, when Serb forces killed at least eight thousand Bosniak men and boys. The massacres that took place following the fall of the UN Safe Area in Srebrenica were deemed a genocide by the International Criminal Tribunal for the Former Yugoslavia (ICTY) in the Krstic case (see <www.un.org/icty/krstic/TrialC1/judgement/index.htm>) and are documented in detail in Rohde. In addition, the tribunal indicted both Bosnian Serb wartime political

leader Radovan Karadzic and Bosnian Serb general Ratko Mladic (both still at large as of November 2006) for genocide and complicity in genocide in Srebrenica and multiple other Bosnian municipalities. In addition to widespread massacres and the burning of villages in a ruthless campaign of ethnic cleansing, rape was used widely as a weapon of war and genocide throughout the country. The ICTY statute included rape as a crime against humanity but not among the "grave breaches or violations of the laws and customs of war." However, in the precedent-setting Celebici case (see <www.un.org/icty/celebici/trialC2/judgement/index. htm>), the tribunal found that "there can be no question that acts of rape may constitute torture under customary international law." Rape was most widely used by Serb forces, though the Celebici case was a finding against Bosnian government soldiers for the rape of Serb women. Throughout the country, rape camps (in addition to labor and concentration camps) were established, especially during the early years of the war. Journalist Roy Gutman documented the camps extensively in his writings at the time and in his book *A Witness to Genocide* (in particular, see 64–73 and 142–163 for a discussion of the issue of rape in the camps). See also Silber and Little for a complete historical background of the war.

25 For selections of Rachel Corrie's writings and critical contextualization of her life and work, see Stohlman and Aladin, Sandercock et al.

26 See Merish for a critical examination of nineteenth-century sentimental fiction.

27 The civil war in Angola (once a colony of Portugal) began before the official departure of the Portuguese in 1975 and did not come to a conclusive end until 2002. During the twenty-seven years of fighting, violence included arbitrary killing of civilians, extensive use of child soldiers and land mines, enslavement of women and children for sexual and other purposes, and widespread violence by both government and National Union for the Total Independence of Angola (UNITA) rebel forces. The civil war was supposed to have concluded with the 1994 Lusaka Peace Process, but violence resumed in December 1998 and did not end until 2002. In addition to the enormous human cost of the civil war in general terms, the conflict is particularly notorious for the widespread, abusive, and illegal use of child soldiers, as well as for the relationships between the diamond and oil industries and the violence. For an excellent overview of the conflict and the extensive human rights abuses that it entailed, see Human Rights Watch's Report, "Angola Unravels." See also V. Brittain.

28 The Armenian genocide took place in the context of fighting between the Ottoman Empire and the Russians in World War I. In 1915, after a winter filled with defeats for the Ottoman forces, the government effectively cast Armenians, whose population was largely concentrated in key border areas where fighting occurred, as traitors for supposed collaboration with Russian forces (which was in fact true of some Armenians). Turkish (Ottoman) government forces began killing Armenian intellectuals, political leaders, artists, and others in April 1915 and continued systematic deportation of Armenian citizens until 1918. The Turkish government has admitted that 800,000 Armenians were killed but vehemently denies that the killings constituted genocide. Others estimate that up to 1.5 million Armenians died during those years and insist that the killings constitute a classic genocide, precisely following the six phases of genocide listed earlier. The Armenian genocide was documented by U.S. ambassador Henry Morgenthau in his cables to the State Department and his later writings (see his recently reprinted book, *Ambassador Morgenthau's Story*. For a summary of the history of the genocide and

the Turkish arguments against its label as such, see Cooper and Akcam. See also Cohan.

EPILOGUE

1 The cosmopolitan is, of course, available for appropriation and exploitation and is not therefore a priori an ethical or humane discourse or mode of being. In its embrace of what James Clifford has called "the messy . . . work of translation" across borders, its centrality to human rights discourse and practice is clear. My usage of the term evokes its ethical foundations in the Kantian idea of "world citizen," one who identifies with others based upon a shared humanity expressed by the dual capacity of experiencing pain and desire.

2 This is the question raised in John Boorman's *Beyond Rangoon*; see chapter 2 for analysis of this representation.

3 The cases of an individuated (usually western) human having the full force of global attention and modes of rescue available to it in the context of mass killing are numerous; recently, the case of Jessica Lynch provides an example of the human individuated from the mass of people being killed in war and rescued as a result of that individuation, which rested upon the conventional myth of the rescue of white womanhood. See chapter 3n31 for a brief discussion of this event.

REFERENCES

Agosin, Marjorie. *A Map of Hope: Women's Writings on Human Rights—An International Anthology*. New Brunswick, N.J.: Rutgers University Press, 1999.

Allende, Isabel. *The House of the Spirits*. Trans. Magda Bogin. New York: Bantam, 1982; 1993.

"America's Dose of Sinophobia." *The Economist* 29 March 1997: 35.

Amnesty International. *Annual Report 1998*. London and New York: Amnesty International Publications, 1998.

———. *Annual Report 1996*. London and New York: Amnesty International Publications, 1996.

———. *El Salvador: Where Are the Disappeared Children?* New York: Amnesty International (July 2003). Accessed 31 March 2006. <http://www.amnestyusa.org/countries/elsalvador/index.do>.

———. "Myanmar (Burma)." Accessed 30 May 2006. <http://www.amnestyusa.org/countries/ myanmar_burma/index.do>.

———. Urgent Action Network. "Urgent Action Saves Lives: Sign Up Today." <http://web.amnesty.org/pages/ua-index-eng>.

Anderson, Benedict. *Imagined Communities: Reflections on the Origin and Spread of Nationalism*. New York and London: Verso, 1983; 1995.

An-Na'im, Abdullahi Ahmed, ed. *Human Rights in Cross-Cultural Perspectives: A Quest for Consensus*. Philadelphia: University of Pennsylvania Press, 1992.

Appadurai, Anthony, Carol Breckenridge, Homi Bhabha, and Dipesh Chakrabarty, eds. *Cosmopolitanisms*. Durham, N.C.: Duke University Press, 2002.

Appiah, Kwame Anthony. "Cosmopolitan Patriots." *For Love of Country: Debating the Limits of Patriotism.*" Eds. Joshua Cohen and Martha C. Nussbaum. Boston: Beacon Press, 1996. 21–29.

Ararat. Dir. Atom Egoyan. Perf. David Alpay, Charles Aznevour, Eric Bogosian. Miramax, 2002.

Archdiocese of Guatemala. *Guatemala: Never Again, The Official Report of the Human Rights Office, Archdiocese of Guatemala (REMHI)*. Forward by Thomas Quigley. Maryknoll, New York: Orbis Books, Catholic Institute for International Relations, and Latin America Bureau, 1999.

Arendt, Hannah. *Eichmann in Jerusalem: A Report on the Banality of Evil*. New York: Penguin Books, 1994.

———. "On the Nature of Totalitarianism: An Essay in Understanding." *Arendt: Essays in Understanding, 1930–1954*. New York: Harcourt Brace, 1993. 328–360.

Arestivo, Carlos. "Testimonial." Torture Abolition and Survivor Support Coalition One-day Forum. Catholic University, Washington, D.C. 24 June 2003.

Arias, Arturo. *The Rigoberta Menchú Controversy.* St. Paul: University of Minnesota Press, 2001.

Askin, Kelly D. "Prosecuting War-Time Rape and Other Gender-Related Crimes under International Law: Extraordinary Advances, Enduring Obstacles." *Berkeley Journal of International Law* 21 (2003): 288–349.

Arva, Eugene. "Working through the Holocaust Blockbuster: *Schindler's List* and *Hitler's Willing Executioners* Locally and Globally." *Film and Philosophy* 8 (2004): 51–62.

Aubin, Benoit. "Voila, a Hit Novel (*A Sunday at the Pool in Kigali*)." *MacLean's* 8 December 2003: 52.

Aung San Suu Kyi. *Freedom from Fear and Other Writings.* Ed. Michael Aris. New York: Viking, 1991.

———. *Letters from Burma.* New York: Penguin Books, 1997.

Ball, John Clement. "The Semi-Detached Metropolis: Hanif Kureishi's London." *ARIEL: A Review of International English Literature* 27 (October 1996): 7–27.

Balthazar-Thomas, Sita. Panelist, "Protecting Women in Time of War." Amnesty International Annual General Meeting. Westin Hotel, Providence, R.I. 11 March 2000.

Barker, Pat. *Double Vision: A Novel.* London and New York: Picador, 2004.

Barreca, Regina. *Untamed and Unabashed: Essays on Women and Humor in British Literature.* Detroit: Wayne State University Press, 1994.

The Battle of Algiers. Dir. Gillo Pontecorvo. Perf. Saadi Yacef, Jean Martin. Casbah Film, 1966.

Bernard-Donals, Michael. "Beyond the Question of Authenticity: Witness and Testimony in the *Fragments* Controversy." *PMLA* 116.5 (October 2001): 1302–1315.

Bernardes, Carla. Panelist, "Cross-Cultural Manifestations of Gender-based Violence against Women." Amnesty International Annual General Meeting. Westin Hotel, Providence, R.I. 11 March 2000.

Bernstein, Richard, and Ross H. Munro. "The Coming Conflict with America." *Foreign Affairs* March/April 1997: 18.

Between Strangers. Dir. Edoardo Ponti. Perf. Sophia Loren, Mira Sorvino, Deborah Kara Unger. Overseas Filmgroup, 2002.

Beyond Borders. Dir. Martin Campbell. Perf. Angelina Jolie, Clive Owen. Paramount, 2003.

Beyond Rangoon. Dir. John Boorman. Perf. Patricia Arquette, Aung Ko. Miramax, 1995.

Bhabha, Homi. *The Location of Culture.* New York: Routledge, 1994.

Bhattacharjee, Annanya. "Private Fists and Public Force: Race Gender, and Surveillance." *Policing the National Body: Race, Gender, and Criminalization in the United States.* Eds. Annanya Bhattacharjee and Jael Silliman. Boston: South End Press, 2002. 1–54.

Bhattacharjee, Annanya, and Jael Silliman, eds. *Policing the National Body: Race, Gender, and Criminalization in the United States.* Boston: South End Press, 2002.

Biko, Ntsiki. "Justice First." *Index on Culture* 5 (1996): 67–68.

Biko, Steven. *I Write What I Like: A Selection of His Writings.* Ed. Alfred Stubbs. London: Harper and Row, 1986.

Block, Robert. "In South Africa, What Price Reconciliation?" *World Press Review* 43.6 (June 1996): 10.

Bordwell, David. *Narrative in the Fiction Film.* Madison: University of Wisconsin Press, 1985.

Bourke, Joanna. "Sexy Snaps." *Index on Censorship* 1 (2005): 39–45.

Brennan, Timothy. *At Home in the World: Cosmopolitanism Now.* Cambridge, Mass.: Harvard University Press, 1997.

Brittain, James. "Healing a Nation: Interview with Desmond Tutu." *Index on Censorship* 5 (1996): 38–43.

Brittain, Victoria. *Death and Dignity: Angola's Civil War.* Trenton, N.J.: Africa World Press, 1998.

Bronfen, Elisabeth. *Over Her Dead Body: Death, Femininity and the Aesthetic.* New York: Routledge, 1992.

Brown, Laura S. "Not Outside the Range: One Feminist Perspective on Psychic Trauma." *Trauma: Explorations in Memory.* Ed. Cathy Caruth. Baltimore: Johns Hopkins University Press, 1995. 100–112.

Brown, Wendy. "Resisting Left Melancholy." *Boundary 2* 26.3 (1999): 19–27.

Buell, Frederic. *National Culture and the New Global System.* Baltimore: Johns Hopkins University Press, 1994.

Bunch, Charlotte. "Transforming Human Rights from a Feminist Perspective." *Women's Rights, Human Rights: International Feminist Perspectives.* Eds. Julie Peters and Andrea Wolper. New York: Routledge, 1995. 11–17.

Bush, George W. "President's Statement on the U.N. International Day in Support of Victims of Torture." Accessed 26 June 2004. <http://www.whitehouse.gov/news/releases/2004/0a6/2004062619.html>.

Butler, Judith. *Precarious Life: The Power of Mourning and Violence.* New York: Verso, 2006.

———. *Undoing Gender.* Abingdon, UK: Taylor and Francis, 2004.

"Can Justice Be Done?" *World Press Review* (June 1996): 6.

Calvino, Italo. *Invisible Cities.* New York: Harvest Books, 1978.

Canby, Vincent. "Film: 'Sammy and Rosie.'" *New York Times* 23 October 1987: C5.

Carby, Hazel. "It Jus Be's Dat Way Sometime: The Sexual Politics of Women's Blues." *Feminisms: An Anthology of Literary Theory and Criticism.* Eds. Robyn R. Warhol and Diana Price Herndl. New Brunswick, N.J.: Rutgers University Press, 1991. 746–758.

Carey, Peter, ed. *Burma: The Challenge of Change in a Divided Society.* New York: St. Martin's Press, 1997.

Caruth, Cathy. Introduction to *Trauma: Explorations in Memory.* Ed. Cathy Caruth. Baltimore and London: Johns Hopkins University Press, 1995. 3–12.

———. "Traumatic Departures: Survival and History in Freud." *Unclaimed Experience: Trauma, Narrative, and History.* Baltimore: Johns Hopkins University Press, 1996. 57–72.

Charney, Israel, ed. *The Encyclopedia of Genocide.* Santa Barbara, Calif.: ABC-Clio, 1990.

Cheah, Pheng. *Spectral Nationality: Passages of Freedom from Kant to Postcolonial Literatures of Liberation.* New York: Columbia University Press, 2003.

Chen, Kevin B. Unpublished biography of Claudia Bernardi for Intersection for the Arts, San Francisco, 2006.

Churchill, Ward. *A Little Matter of Genocide: Holocaust and Denial in the Americas, 1492–the Present*. San Francisco: City Lights Publishers, 1998.

Clinton, Catherine. "'With a Whip in His Hand': Rape, Memory, and African-American Women." *History and Memory in African-American Culture*. Eds. Genevieve Fabre and Robert O'Meally. New York: Oxford University Press, 1994. 205–218.

Coetzee, J. M. *Disgrace*. New York and London: Viking Press, 1999.

———. "Into the Dark Chamber: The Novelist and South Africa." *Doubling the Point: Essays and Interviews*. Ed. David Atwell. Rpt. Cambridge, Mass.: Harvard University Press, 2005. 361–368.

———. *The Lives of Animals*. Princeton: Princeton University Press, 2001.

Cohan, Sarah. "A Brief History of the Armenian Genocide." *Social Education* 69.6 (October 2005): 333–338.

Cohen, Stanley. *States of Denial: Knowing about Atrocities and Suffering*. Cambridge, UK: Polity Press, 2001.

Collier, Simon, and William F. Sater. *A History of Chile, 1808–2002*. Cambridge, UK: Cambridge University Press, 2004.

Collins, Patricia Hill. *Black Feminist Thought: Knowledge, Consciousness, and the Politics of Empowerment*. New York: Routledge, 2000.

Commission for Historical Clarification. *Guatemala: Memory of Silence*. Guatemala City, Guatemala: Commission for Historical Clarification, 1999. Accessed 6 June 2006. <http://shr.aaas.org/guatemala/ceh/report/english/toc.html>.

Commission on the Truth for El Salvador. "From Madness to Hope: The 12-Year War in El Salvador: Report of the Commission on the Truth for El Salvador." Commission on the Truth for El Salvador, Belisario Betancur, Chair. Accessed 15 March 2006. <http://www.usip.org/library/tc/doc/reports/el_salvador/tc_es_03151993_toc.html>.

Conrad, Joseph. *The Heart of Darkness*. New York: Penguin Books, 1999.

Cooper, Belinda, and Taner Akcam. "Turks, Armenians, and the 'G' Word." *World Policy Journal* 22.3 (Fall 2005): 81–94.

Copelon, Rhonda. "Gendered War Crimes: Reconceptualizing Rape in Time of War." *Women's Rights, Human Rights: International Feminist Perspectives*. Eds. Julie Peters and Andrea Wolper. New York: Routledge, 1995. 197–214.

Coser, Stela Maris. "The Dry Wombs of Black Women: Memories of Brazilian Slavery in *Corregidora* and *Song for Anninho*." *Bridging the Americas: The Literature of Paule Marshall, Toni Morrison, and Gayl Jones*. Philadelphia: Temple University Press, 1994. 120–163.

Courtemanche, Gil. *A Sunday at the Pool in Kigali*. New York: Vintage, 2004.

Creative Work Fund. Accessed 19 November 2006. <http://www.creativeworkfund.org/pages/bios/claudia_bernardi.html>.

Cry Freedom. Dir. Richard Attenborough. Perf. Denzel Washington, Kevin Kline. Universal Studios, 1985.

Daley, Suzanne. "A Killer's Ignorance Adds Poignancy to Biko Case." *New York Times* 12 January 1999.

Danish Institute for Human Rights. "Human Rights Indicators, Country and Regional Database." Danish Institute for Human Rights (2000). Accessed 25 March 2005. <http://www.humanrights.dk/upload/application/a4ef919/indicator1.pdf>.

Danticat, Edwidge. *The Farming of Bones.* New York: Penguin, 1999.

de Lauretis, Teresa. *Alice Doesn't: Feminism Semiotics Cinema.* Bloomington: Indiana University Press, 1984.

———. *The Practice of Love: Lesbian Sexuality and Perverse Desire.* Bloomington: Indiana University Press, 1994.

———. *Technologies of Gender: Essays on Theory, Film, and Fiction.* Bloomington: Indiana University Press, 1987.

Denby, David. "Review: *Three Kings.*" *New Yorker* 4 October 1999: 115–118.

Derby, Lauren. "Temwayaj Kout Kouto, 1937: Eyewitnesses to the Genocide." Accessed 14 June 2006. <http://www.webster.edu/~corbetre/haiti-archive/msg00 235.html>.

Derrida, Jacques. "Force of Law: The 'Mystical Foundations of Authority.'" *Deconstruction and the Possibility of Justice.* Eds. David Gray Carlson, Drucilla Cornell, and Michel Rosenfeld. New York: Routledge, 1992. 3–67.

———. "On Forgiveness." *Cosmopolitanism and Forgiveness.* Trans. Mark Dooley and Michael Hughes. New York: Routledge, 2001.

Dershowitz, Alan M. "Tortured Reasoning." *Torture: A Collection.* Ed. Sanford Levinson. New York: Oxford University Press, 2004. 257–280.

———. *Why Terrorism Works: Understanding the Threat, Responding to the Challenge.* New Haven: Yale University Press, 2003.

Diala, Isadore. "Nadine Gordimer, J. M. Coetzee, and Andre Brink: Guilt, Expiation, and the Reconciliation Process in Post-Apartheid South Africa." *Journal of Modern Literature* 25.2 (Winter 2001–2002): 50–68.

Dixon, Melvin. "Singing a Deep Song: Language as Evidence in the Novels of Gayl Jones." *Black Women Writers at Work.* Ed. Claudia Tate. New York: Continuum Press, 1983. 236–257.

Doane, Mary Anne. *The Emergence of Cinematic Time: Modernity, Contingency, the Archive.* Cambridge, Mass.: Harvard University Press, 2002.

Dogville. Dir. Lars von Trier. Perf. Paul Bettany, Nicole Kidman. Lions Gate Films, 2003.

Donnelly, Jack. *Universal Human Rights in Theory and Practice.* 2nd ed. Ithaca, N.Y.: Cornell University Press, 2002.

Dorfman, Ariel. "Are There Times When We Have to Accept Torture?" *Guardian* 8 May 2004.

———. *Other Septembers, Many Americas: Selected Provocations, 1980–2004.* New York: Seven Stories Press, 2004.

Dostoyevsky, Fyodor. The Brothers Karamazov. Trans. Constance Garnett. New York: W. W. Norton, 1976.

Douglas, Mary. *Purity and Danger: An Analysis of the Concepts of Pollution and Taboo.* New York: Routledge, 2002.

Dubey, Madhu. "Gayl Jones and the Matrilineal Metaphor of Tradition." *Signs: Journal of Women in Culture and Society* 20.2 (Winter 1995): 245–267.

Edelman, Lee. "Tearooms and Sympathy, or, The Epistemology of the Water Closet." *Nationalisms and Sexualities.* Eds. Andrew Parker, Mary Russo, Doris Sommer, and Patricia Yaeger. New York: Routledge, 1992. 263–284.

Ehrenreich, Barbara. "Feminism's Assumptions Upended." *Abu Ghraib and the Politics of Torture.* Berkeley, Calif.: North Atlantic Books, 2005. 65–70.

Engdahl, Horace. "Philomela's Tongue: Introductory Remarks on Witness Literature." *Witness Literature: Proceedings of the Nobel Centennial Symposium.* Ed. Horace Engdahl. Singapore: World Scientific Publishing, 2002. 6.

Farrell, Amy, and Patrice McDermott. "Claiming Afghan Women: The Challenge of Human Rights Discourse for Transnational Feminism." *Just Advocacy? Women's Human Rights, Transnational Feminisms, and the Politics of Representation.* Eds. Wendy S. Hesford and Wendy Kozol. New Brunswick, N.J.: Rutgers University Press, 2005. 33–35.

Felman, Shoshana. "*Camus' The Plague,* or a Monument to Witnessing." *Testimony: Crises of Witnessing in Literature, Psychoanalysis, and History.* Shoshana Felman and Dori Laub. New York: Routledge, 1992.

Ferber, Marianne A., and Julie Nelson, eds. *Beyond Economic Man: Feminist Theory and Economics.* Chicago: University of Chicago Press, 1993.

Finkelstein, Norman. *Beyond Chutzpah: On the Misuse of Anti-Semitism and the Abuse of History.* Berkeley: University of California Press, 2005.

Freud, Sigmund. "Beyond the Pleasure Principle." *The Freud Reader.* Ed. Peter Gay. New York: W. W. Norton, 1989. 594–625.

——. "The Dissolution of the Oedipus Complex." *The Freud Reader.* Ed. Peter Gay. New York: W. W. Norton, 1989. 661–665.

Frey, James. *A Million Little Pieces.* New York: Anchor Books, 2004.

Friedlander, Saul. Introduction to *Probing the Limits of Representation: Nazism and the "Final Solution."* Ed. Saul Friedlander. Cambridge, Mass.: Harvard University Press, 1992. 1–21.

Fuss, Diana. "Freud's Fallen Woman: Identification, Desire, and 'A Case of Homosexuality in a Woman.'" *Fear of a Queer Planet: Queer Politics and Social Theory.* Ed Michael Warner. Minneapolis: University of Minnesota Press, 1993. 42–68.

Gilman, Sander L. *Difference and Pathology: Stereotypes of Sexuality, Race, and Madness.* Ithaca, N.Y.: Cornell University Press, 1985.

Gilmore, Leigh. "Autobiography's Wounds." *Just Advocacy? Women's Human Rights, Transnational Feminisms, and the Politics of Representation.* Eds. Wendy S. Hesford and Wendy Kozol. New Brunswick, N.J.: Rutgers University Press, 2005. 99–119.

Gilmore, Ruth. Panelist, "Premature Death: A Roundtable on Racism." American Studies Association Annual Meeting, Hartford, Conn. 17 October 2004.

Gilroy, Paul. *After Empire: Melancholy and Convivial Culture.* New York: Routledge, 2004.

Glissant, Edouard. *Caribbean Discourse: Selected Essays.* Eds. A. J. Arnold and Kandioura Drame. Trans. J. Michael Dash. Charlottesville: University Press of Virginia, 1986.

Goldberg, Elizabeth Swanson. "Living the Legacy: Pain, Desire, and Narrative Time in Gayl Jones's *Corregidora.*" *Callaloo: A Journal of African Diaspora Arts and Letters* 26.2 (Spring 2003): 446–472.

——. "Notes." Mock United Nations Tribunal. Non-Governmental Organization Meetings. United Nations World Conference on Women, Hairou, China. August 1995.

———. "Splitting Difference: Global Identity Politics and the Representation of Torture in the Counter-Historical Dramatic Film." *Violence and American Cinema.* Ed. J. David Slocum. New York: Routledge, 2000. 245–270.

———. "Who Was Afraid of Patrice Lumumba? Terror and the Ethical Imagination in *Lumumba: La Mort du Prophet.*" *Terrorism, Media, Liberation.* Ed. J. David Slocum. New Brunswick, N.J.: Rutgers University Press, 2005.

Goldberg, Mark Leon. "Court Jesters: Remember the International Criminal Court? House Republicans Sure Do." *American Prospect Online* 1 September 2004. Accessed 16 June 2006. <http://www.prospect.org/web/page.ww?section=root& name=ViewWeb&articleID=8443>.

Goni, Uki. "Former Argentinean Death Camp to Become Museum." *Guardian* 24 March 2004.

Gordimer, Nadine. "Witness: The Inward Testimony." *Witness Literature: Proceedings of the Nobel Centennial Symposium.* Ed. Horace Engdahl. Singapore: World Scientific Publishing, 2002.

Gottfried, Amy. "Angry Arts: Silence, Speech, and Song in Gayl Jones's *Corregidora.*" *African American Review* 28.4 (Winter 1994): 559–570.

Gourgouris, Stathis. "Enlightenment and *Paranomia,*" *Violence, Identity, and Self-Determination.* Eds. Hent de Vries and Samuel Weber. Stanford, Calif.: Stanford University Press, 1997. 119–149.

Graham, Lucy Valerie. "Reading the Unspeakable: Rape in J. M. Coetzee's *Disgrace.*" *Journal of Southern African Studies* 29.2 (June 2003): 433–444.

Greenberg, Karen J., and Joshua L. Dratel, eds. *The Torture Papers: The Road to Abu Ghraib.* Cambridge, UK: Cambridge University Press, 2005.

Griggers, Cathy. "Lesbian Bodies in the Age of (Post)mechanical Reproduction." *Fear of a Queer Planet: Queer Politics and Social Theory.* Ed Michael Warner. Minneapolis: University of Minnesota Press, 1993. 178–192.

Grisham, John. *A Time to Kill.* New York: Dell, 1992.

Gugelberger, Georg M., ed. *The Real Thing: Testimonial Discourse and Latin America.* Durham, N.C.: Duke University Press, 1996.

Gurbaxani, Indira, and Sonja Opper. "How Tensions between Specific Chinese and American Interests Affect China's Entry into the WTO." *Intereconomics* 33.5 (September–October 1998): 212–222.

Gutman, Roy. *Witness to Genocide: The First Inside Account of the Horrors of "Ethnic Cleansing" in Bosnia.* New York: Element Books, 1993.

Gutman, Roy, and David Rieff, eds. *Crimes of War: What the Public Should Know.* New York: W. W. Norton, 1999.

Haidu, Peter. "The Dialectics of Unspeakability: Language, Silence, and the Narratives of Desubjectification." *Probing the Limits of Representation: Nazism and the Final Solution.* Ed. Saul Friedlander. Cambridge, Mass.: Harvard University Press, 1992. 277–299.

Hall, Jacquelyn Dowd. "'The Mind That Burns in Each Body': Women, Rape, and Racial Violence." *Powers of Desire.* Eds. Ann Snitow, Christine Stansell, and Sharon Thompson. New York: Monthly Review Press, 1983. 328–349.

Halley, Janet E. *Don't: A Reader's Guide to the Military's Anti-Gay Policy.* Durham, N.C.: Duke University Press, 1999.

Hansen, Miriam. "Schindler's List Is *Not Shoah*: The Second Commandment, Popular Modernism, and Public Memory." *Spielberg's Holocaust: Critical Perspectives*. Ed. Yosefa Loshitzky. Bloomington: Indiana University Press, 1997.

Hartman, Saidiya V. *Scenes of Subjection: Terror, Slavery, and Self-Making in Nineteenth-Century America*. New York: Oxford University Press, 1997.

Henley, John. "A Very Different Take." *Guardian* 5 September 2002.

Hersh, Seymour. "The Gray Zone: How a Secret Pentagon Program Came to Abu Ghraib." *New Yorker* 24 May 2005: 38–44.

Hesford, Wendy S., and Wendy Kozol, eds. Introduction to *Just Advocacy? Women's Human Rights, Transnational Feminisms, and the Politics of Representation*. New Brunswick, N.J.: Rutgers University Press, 2005. 1–29.

Hobbes, Thomas. *Leviathan*. Oxford: Oxford University Press, 1996.

Hoffman, Michael. Panelist, "Protecting Women in Time of War." Amnesty International Annual General Meeting. Westin Hotel, Providence, R.I. 11 March 2000.

Holland, Sharon Patricia. *Raising the Dead: Readings in Death and (Black) Subjectivity*. Durham, N.C.: Duke University Press, 2000.

hooks, bell. "Stylish Nihilism: Race, Sex, and Class at the Movies." *Yearning: Race, Gender, and Cultural Politics*. Boston: South End Press, 1990. 155–164.

Horeck, Tanya. *Public Rape: Representations of Violation in Fiction and Film*. New York: Routledge, 2004.

Hotel Rwanda. Dir. Terry George. Perf. Don Cheadle, Nick Nolte, Sophie Okenedo. United Artists, 2004.

Human Rights Watch. "Angola Unravels: The Rise and Fall of the Lusaka Peace Process" (1999). Accessed 13 September 2005. <www.hrw.org/reports/1999/angola/>.

———. "Out of Sight, Out of Mind: Thai Policy toward Burmese Refugees and Migrants." (2005). Accessed 30 May 2006. <http://hrw.org/reports/2004/thailand0204/>.

———. "Overview: Chile." (2005). Accessed 14 June 2006. <http://www.hrw.org/english/docs/2006/01/18/chile12205.htm>.

———. "The Road to Abu Ghraib" (2006). Accessed 15 June 2006. <http://hrw.org/reports/2004/usa0604/>.

———. "'They came and destroyed our village again.' The Plight of Internally Displaced Persons in Karen State" (2005). Accessed 25 March 2006. <http://www.hrw.org/doc?t=asia&c=burma>.

Ignatieff, Michael. "Overview: Articles of Faith." *Index on Censorship* 5 (1996): 110–122.

———, ed. *American Exceptionalism and Human Rights*. Princeton: Princeton University Press, 2005.

Integrated Regional Information Networks. "Rwanda: Focus on Genocide Widows Dying of HIV/AIDS." Integrated Regional Information Networks (UN Office for the Coordination of Humanitarian Arrairs) PlusNews. Accessed 14 June 2006. <http://www.plusnews.org/AIDSreport.asp?ReportID=2597&SelectRegion=Great_Lake>.

Jameson, Frederic. *The Geopolitical Aesthetic: Cinema and Space in the World System*. Bloomington: Indiana University Press, 1995.

Jehenson, Myriam-Yvonne. *Latin-American Women Writers: Race, Gender, Class*. Albany: SUNY Press, 1995.

Jehl, Douglas, and David Johnston. "Rule Change Lets CIA Freely Send Suspects Abroad to Jails." *New York Times* 6 March 2005.

Jones, Gayl. *Corregidora*. Boston: Beacon Press, 1975.

Karpinski, Janis. *One Woman's Army: The Commanding General of Abu Ghraib Tells Her Story*. New York: Miramax Books, 2005.

Kendrick, Michelle. "Kicking the Vietnam Syndrome: CNN's and CBS's Video Narratives of the Persian Gulf War." *Seeing through the Media: The Persian Gulf War*. Eds. S. Jeffords and L. Rabinowitz. New Brunswick, N.J.: Rutgers University Press, 1994. 59–75.

The Killing Fields. Dir. Roland Joffe. Perf. Sam Waterston, Haing S. Ngor, John Malkovich. 1984.

Kimmel, Michael S. "Spanning the World: Cross-Cultural Constructions of Gender." *The Gendered Society*. 2nd ed. New York: Oxford University Press, 2004. 47–65.

Kingsolver, Barbara. *Small Wonder*. New York: HarperPerennial, 2003.

Klein, Naomi. "The US Has Used Torture for Decades. All That's New Is the Openness about It." *Guardian* 10 December 2005. Accessed 15 June 2006. <http://www.guardian.co.uk/print/0,3858,5352636-110878,00.html>.

Kobila, James Mouangue. "Comparative Practice on Human Rights: North-South." *The Globalization of Human Rights*. Eds. Jean-Marc Coicaud, Michael W. Doyle, and Anne-Marie Gardner. New York: United Nations, 2003.

Koshy, Susan. "From Cold War to Trade War: Neocolonialism and Human Rights." *Social Text* 58.17 (Spring 1999): 1–32.

Krain, Matthew. "State-Sponsored Mass Murder: The Onset and Severity of Genocides and Politicides." *Journal of Conflict Resolution* 41.3 (June 197): 331(30).

Kreisler, Harry. Interview with Oliver Stone. Institute of International Studies, University of California, Berkeley. 1997. Accessed 18 February 1999. <http://globetrotter.berkeley.edu/Stone/stone-con1.html>.

Kristeva, Julia. *Powers of Horror: An Essay on Abjection*. New York: Columbia University Press, 1982.

Kureishi, Hanif. *Sammy and Rosie Get Laid: The Screenplay and the Screenwriter's Diary*. New York: Penguin, 1988.

LaCapra, Dominic. *History in Transit: Experience, Identity, Critical Theory*. Ithaca, N.Y.: Cornell University Press, 2004.

Lancaster, Roger N. "Rigoberta's Testimonio." *NACLA Report on the Americas* 32.6 (May–June 1999): 4–7.

Land, Joshua. "Tracking Shots: *Shake Hands with the Devil*." *Village Voice* 17 May 2005. Accessed 12 June 2006. <http://www.villagevoice.com/film/0520,tracking1,64015,20.html>.

Laremont, Ricardo Rene. "Political versus Legal Strategies for the African Slavery Reparations Movement." *Africa Studies Quarterly: The Online Journal for African Studies* 8:2 (Spring 2005). Accessed 5 October 2005. <http://web.africa.ufl.edu/asq/v2/v2i4a1.htm>.

Laub, Dori. "Truth and Testimony: The Process and the Struggle." *Trauma: Explorations in Memory*. Ed. Cathy Caruth. Baltimore: Johns Hopkins University Press, 1995. 61–75.

Lindroth, Collette. "The Waste Land Revisited: Sammy and Rosie Get Laid." *Literature Film Quarterly* 17.2 (1989): 95–98.

Locke, John. *Two Treatises of Government*. Ed. Peter Laslett. Cambridge, UK: University of Cambridge Press, 1988.

Loconte, Joseph. "The U.N. Sex Scandal." *Weekly Standard* 10.16 (3 January 2005): 14(2).

Loshitzky, Yosefa, ed. *Spielberg's Holocaust: Critical Perspectives*. Bloomington: Indiana University Press, 1997.

Lutz, Catherine. "Living Room Terrorists: Rates of Domestic Violence Are among Three to Five Times Higher among Military Couples Than among Civilian Ones." *Women's Review of Books* 21.5 (February 2004): 17–19.

MacCannell, Dean. *Empty Meeting Grounds: The Tourist Papers*. New York: Routledge, 1992.

Maechler, Stephan. *The Wilkomirski Affair: A Study in Biographical Truth*. New York: Schocken, 2001.

Magnarelli, Sharon. "Framing Power in Luisa Valenzuela's *Cola de lagartija* and Isabelle Allende's *Casa de los espiritus*." *Splintering Darkness: Latin American Women Writers in Search of Themselves*. Ed. Lucia Guerra Cunningham. Pittsburgh: Latin American Literary Review Press, 1990. 43–62.

Maja-Pierce, Adewale. "Binding the Wounds." *Index on Culture* 5 (1996): 48–53.

Mamdani, Mahmoud. *When Victims Become Killers: Colonialism, Nativism, and the Genocide in Rwanda*. Princeton: Princeton University Press, 2002.

Marquez, Gabriel Garcia. *100 Years of Solitude*. Trans. Gregory Rabassa. New York: HarperPerennial, 1967; 1998.

Maslin, Janet. "Fighting the Battle of Money and Greed." *New York Times* 1 October 1999.

———. " 'Red Corner': Melodrama cum Credibility Snag." *New York Times* 24 November 1987.

———. "*Schindler's List*: Imagining the Holocaust to Remember It." *New York Times* 15 December 1993.

Matthews, Richard. "Society vs. the Individual: What's the Real Issue in the Singapore Caning Case?" *Atlanta Journal-Constitution* 28 April 1994.

McAlister, Melani. *Epic Encounters: Culture, Media, and U.S. Interests in the Middle East, 1945–2000*. Berkeley: University of California Press, 2001.

McClintock, Anne. *Imperial Leather: Race, Gender, and Sexuality in the Colonial Contest*. New York: Routledge, 1995.

McClintock, Cynthia. *Revolutionary Movements in Latin America*. Washington, D.C.: United States Institute of Peace Press, 1998.

McLeod, Andrew. "Victim of Latin American Torture Claims Abu Ghraib Abuse Was Official US Policy." *Sunday Herald* (Scotland) 12 December 2004. Accessed 30 May 2006. <http://www.sundayherald.com/print46535>.

Mealer, Bryan. "UN Peacekeepers' Response Marks Congo Policy Shift." *Boston Globe* 3 March 2005:

Menchú Tum, Rigoberta. *I, Rigoberta Menchú: An Indian in Guatemala*. Trans. Ann Wright. London: Verso, 1987.

Merish, Lori. *Sentimental Materialism: Gender, Commodity Culture, and Nineteenth-Century American Literature*. Durham, N.C.: Duke University Press, 2000.

Metro-Goldwyn-Mayer Studios. *Red Corner* Web site. Accessed 22 March 1996. <http://www.redcorner.com>.

Meyers, Diana Tietjeus. *Gender in the Mirror: Cultural Imagery and Women's Agency.* New York: Oxford University Press, 2002.

Miller, Fred D., Jr. "Rights." *Nature, Justice, and Rights in Aristotle's Politics.* Oxford: Clarendon Press, 2005. 87–142.

Millett, Kate. *The Politics of Cruelty: An Essay on the Literature of Political Imprisonment.* New York: W. W. Norton, 1994.

Mitsis, Phillip. "The Stoic Origin of Natural Rights." *Topics in Stoic Philosophy.* Ed. Katerina Lerodiakonov. Oxford: Clarendon Press, 1999. 153–177.

Mohanram, Radhika. "Postcolonial Spaces and Deterritorialized (Homo)Sexuality: The Films of Hanif Kureishi." *Postcolonial Discourse and Changing Cultural Contexts: Theory and Criticism.* Eds. Gita Rajan and Radhika Mohanram. Westport, Conn.: Greenwood Press, 1995. 117–134.

Moore, Patrick. "Weapons of Mass Homophobia." *Advocate* 8 June 2004: 24–25.

Morgenthau, Henry. *Ambassador Morgenthau's Story.* London: Tuderon Press, 2000.

Morris, David, and Gary Langer. "Terror Suspect Treatment: Most Americans Oppose Torture Techniques." ABC News.com. Accessed 27 May 2004. <http://abcnews.go.com/sections/us/Polls/torture_poll_040527.html>.

Morsink, Johannes. *The Universal Declaration of Human Rights: Origins, Drafting, and Intent.* Philadelphia: University of Pennsylvania Press, 1999.

Mutua, Makau. *Human Rights: A Political and Cultural Critique.* Philadelphia: University of Pennsylvania Press, 2002.

Nash Information Services. The Numbers. Accessed 1 June 2006. <http://www.thenumbers.com/index.php>.

Neuffer, Elizabeth. *The Key to My Neighbor's House.* New York: Picador USA, 2002.

Nichols, Bill. *Representing Reality: Issues and Concepts in Documentary.* Bloomington: Indiana University Press, 1992.

Nussbaum, Martha. *For Love of Country? Debating the Limits of Patriotism.* Ed. Joshua Cohen. Boston: Beacon Press, 1997.

———. *Poetic Justice: The Literary Imagination and Public Life.* Boston: Beacon Press, 1997.

Ondaatje, Michael. *Anil's Ghost.* New York: Vintage International, 2001.

Ortiz, Dianna. *Blindfold's Eyes: My Journey from Torture to Truth.* With Patricia Davis. St. Paul, Minn.: Orbis Books, 2002.

Partnoy, Alicia. *The Little School: Tales of Disappearance and Survival.* 2nd ed. San Francisco: Cleis Press, 1998.

Pateman, Carole. *The Sexual Contract.* Stanford, Calif.: Stanford University Press, 1988.

Pearlstein, Deborah. "Rights in An Insecure World: Why National Security and Civil Liberty Are Complements." *American Prospect* (October 2004). Accessed 28 February 2005. <http://www.prospect.org/web/page.ww?section=root&name=ViewPrint&articleId=8554>.

Peters, Edward. *Torture.* Philadelphia: University of Pennsylvania Press, 1996.

Peters, Julie, and Andrea Wolper, eds. *Women's Rights, Human Rights: International Feminist Perspectives.* New York: Routledge, 1995.

Pieterse, Jan Nederveen. *White on Black: Images of Africa and Blacks in Western Popular Culture.* New Haven: Yale University Press, 1992.

Power, Samantha. *A Problem from Hell: America and the Age of Genocide.* New York: HarperPerennial, 2003.

Prashad, Vijay. *The Karma of Brown Folk.* Minneapolis: University of Minnesota Press, 2000.

Proyect, Louis. "Looking Back at *The Battle of Algiers.*" *Monthly Review* 8 December 2005. Accessed 12 June 2006. <http://mrzine.monthlyreview.org/proyect120805.html>.

Prunier, Gerard. "A Slightly Off-Key Genocide (*A Sunday at the Pool in Kigali*)." *Spectator* 20 September 2003: 55.

Raban, Jonathan. "The Truth about Terrorism." *New York Review of Books* 52.1 (15 January 2005): 4–6.

Red Corner. Dir. Jon Avnet. Perf. Patricia Arquette, Aung Ko. Metro-Goldwyn-Mayer, 1995.

" 'Renditions Save Lives': Condoleeza Rice's Full Statement." *Times Online* 5 December 2005. Accessed 16 June 2006. http://www.timesonline.co.uk/article/0,,11069-1905274,00.html>.

Richburg, Keith B. "Iraqis Say Lynch Raid Faced No Resistance." *Washington Post* 15 April 2003.

Ricoeur, Paul. *Time and Narrative, Volume 3.* Trans. Kathleen Blamey and David Pellauer. Chicago: University of Chicago Press, 1990.

Rieff, David. *A Bed for the Night: Humanitarianism in Crisis.* New York: Simon and Schuster, 2002.

———. "Multiculturalism's Silent Partner: It's the Newly Globalized Economy, Stupid." *Harper's Magazine* 1 August 1993: 17–19.

Rigaud, Milo. *Secrets of Voodoo.* San Francisco: City Lights, 1985.

Robbins, Bruce. *Feeling Global: Internationalism in Distress.* New York: New York University Press, 1999.

Robbins, Bruce, and Pheng Cheah, eds. *Cosmopolitics: Thinking and Feeling beyond the Nation.* Minneapolis: University of Minnesota Press, 1998.

Robinson, Marcus. "Love in a Time of Genocide: Pierre Mignot Lenses *Sunday in Kigali.*" *Playback: Canada's Broadcast and Production Journal* 9 January 2006: 17.

Robinson, Sally. " 'We're all consequences of something': Cultural Mythologies of Gender and Race in the Novels of Gayl Jones." *Engendering the Subject: Gender and Self-Representation in Contemporary Women's Fiction.* Albany: SUNY Press, 1991.

Rohde, David. *Endgame: The Betrayal and Fall of Srebrenica, Europe's Worst Massacre since World War II.* Boulder: Westview Press, 1998.

Rossi, Alice S., ed. *The Feminist Papers: From Adams to Beauvoir.* Boston: Northeastern University Press, 1988.

Rowell, Charles H. "An Interview with Gayl Jones." *Callaloo* 16 (1982): 32–53.

Russell-Brown, Sherrie L. "Rape as an Act of Genocide." *Berkeley Journal of International Law* 350 (2003): 350–374.

Russo, Mary. *The Female Grotesque: Risk, Excess, and Modernity.* New York: Routledge, 1995.

Sadasivam, Bharati. "The Conference That Wasn't: The Fight over Zionism-Equals-Racism Pushed Aside Many Issues." *Village Voice* 18 September 2001. <http://www.villagevoice.com/news/0137,sadasivam,28057,1.html>.

Salvador. Dir. Oliver Stone. Perf. John Belushi, Tony Plana, James Woods. Hemsdale Films, 1987.

Sammy and Rosie Get Laid. Dir. Stephen Frears. Perf. Frances Barber, Ayub Khan Din. Cinecom, 1987.

Sandercock, Josie, et al., eds. *Peace under Fire: Israel, Palestine, and the International Solidarity Movement.* New York: Verso, 2004.

Sanders, Mark, ed. "Ethics." Special issue of *Diacritics* 32:3–4 (Fall-Winter 2002).

Scarry, Elaine. *The Body in Pain: The Making and Unmaking of the World.* New York: Oxford University Press, 1985.

———. "Consent and the Body." *New Literary History* 21 (1996): 867–896.

———. "Five Errors in the Reasoning of Alan Dershowitz." *Torture: A Collection.* Ed. Sanford Levinson. New York: Oxford University Press, 2004. 281–290.

Schindler's List. Dir. Steven Spielberg. Perf. Ralph Fiennes, Ben Kingsley, Liam Neeson. Universal Studios, 1993.

Schulz, William. "Speech Given by William F. Schulz, Amnesty International's Annual Meeting, Brooklyn, N.Y., 16 April 2004." Amnesty International Partners of Conscience mailing.

Seven Years in Tibet. Dir. Jean-Jacques Annaud. Perf. Brad Pitt, David Thewlis. Tristar Pictures, 1997.

Shelley, Becka, "Protest and Globalization: Media, Symbols, and Audience in the Drama of Democratization." *Democratization* 8.4 (2001): 155–174.

Shestack, Jerome. "The Philosophic Foundations of Human Rights." *Human Rights Quarterly* 20 (1998): 201–234.

Silber, Laura, and Adam Little. *Yugoslavia: Death of a Nation.* New York: Penguin Books, 1997.

Simic, Charles. "Archives of Horror: Review, *Regarding the Pain of Others.*" *New York Review of Books* 50:7 (1 May 2003).

Smith, Karen E., and Margot Light, eds. *Ethics and Foreign Policy.* Cambridge, UK: Cambridge University Press, 2001.

Smith, Steven G. *Gender Thinking.* Philadelphia: Temple University Press, 1992.

Sometimes in April. Dir. Raoul Peck. Perf. Idris Elba, Oris Erhuero, Debra Winger. HBO Original Films, 2004.

Sontag, Susan. *Regarding the Pain of Others.* New York: Farrar, Strauss and Giroux, 2002.

———. "Regarding the Torture of Others." *New York Times Magazine* 23 May 2004

Spiegelman, Art. *In the Shadow of No Towers.* New York: Pantheon, 2004.

Spillers, Hortense. "Mama's Baby, Papa's Maybe: An American Grammar Book." *Diacritics* 17:2 (Summer 1987): 65–81.

Spivak, Gayatri. "French Feminism in an International Frame." *In Other Worlds: Essays in Cultural Politics.* New York: Routledge, 1988. 134–153.

Stallybrass, Peter, and Allon White. *The Politics and Poetics of Transgression.* Ithaca, N.Y.: Cornell University Press, 1986.

Steinberg, David I. *Burma: The State of Myanmar.* Washington, D.C.: Georgetown University Press, 2001.

Stewart, Angus. "Two Conceptions of Citizenship" *British Journal of Sociology* 46.1 (March 1995): 63–78.

Stohlman, Nancy, and Lauriann Aladin. *Live from Palestine: International and Palestinian Direct Action against the Occupation.* Boston: South End Press, 2003.

Stoll, David. *Rigoberta Menchu and the Story of All Poor Guatemalans.* New York: Harper-Collins, 2000.

Stone, John F. "Manifestation of Foreign Culture through Paradox: *Salvador.*" *Journal of Popular Film and Television* 19.4 (1992): 180–185.

Tanner, Laura E. *Intimate Violence: Reading Rape and Torture in Twentieth-Century Fiction.* Bloomington: Indiana University Press, 1994.

Tate, Claudia. "Ursa's Blues Medley." *Black American Literature Forum* 13 (1979): 139–141.

Taylor, Diana. *Disappearing Acts: Spectacles of Gender and Nationalism in Argentina's "Dirty War."* Durham, N.C.: Duke University Press, 1997.

Terreblanche, Stampie. *A History of Inequality in South Africa, 1652–2002.* Natal: University of Natal Press, 2003.

Thomas, Dorothy Q., and Michele E. Beasley. "Domestic Violence as a Human Rights Issue." *Human Rights Quarterly* 15.1 (February 1993): 26–62.

Three Kings. Dir. David O. Russell. Perf. George Clooney, Ice Cube, Spike Jonz, Mark Wahlberg. Warner Brothers, 1999.

Timerman, Jacobo. *Prisoner without a Name, Cell Without a Number.* Trans. Toby Talbot. Madison: University of Wisconsin Press, 2002.

A Time to Kill. Dir. Joel Schumacher. Perf. Sandra Bullock, Samuel L. Jackson, Matthew McConaughey. Warner Brothers, 1996.

Tompkins, Jane. *Sensational Designs: The Cultural Work of American Fiction, 1790–1860.* New York: Oxford University Press, 1985.

Toni Morrison Uncensored. Princeton: Films for the Humanities and Sciences, 2004.

Turits, Richard Lee. "A World Destroyed, A Nation Imposed: The 1937 Massacre in the Dominican Republic." *Hispanic American Historical Review* 82.3 (2002): 589–636.

Tutu, Desmond. *No Future without Forgiveness.* New York: Doubleday, 1999.

Twair, Pat, and Samir Twair. "*Three Kings* Gives Positive Image of Iraqis." *Southern California Chronicle* December 1999: 67–69.

UNICEF. *State of the World's Children 2005.* 2005. Accessed 30 May 2006. <http://www.unicef.org/publications/index.html>.

United Nations. *Convention against Torture and Other Cruel, Inhuman and Degrading Treatment.* Office of the High Commissioner for Human Rights, 10 December 1984. Accessed 14 June 2006. <http://www.unhchr.ch/html/menu3/b/h_cat39.htm>.

———. *Convention on the Elimination of Discrimination against Women.* Office of the High Commissioner for Human Rights. Accessed 9 June 2006. <http://www.unhchr.ch/html/menu3/b/e1cedaw.htm>.

———. *Convention on the Prevention and Punishment of the Crime of Genocide.* Office of the High Commissioner for Human Rights. Accessed 12 March 2005. <http://www.unhchr.ch/html/menu3/b/p_genoci.htm>.

———. *Convention on the Rights of the Child.* Office of the High Commissioner for Human Rights, 1990. Accessed 15 April 2006. <http://www.unhchr.ch/html/menu3/b/k2crc.htm>.

———. "Elimination of All Forms of Racial Discrimination." General Assembly Resolution 3379. Accessed 10 November 1975. <http://www.un.org/documents/ga/res/30/ares30.htm>.

———. "Optional Protocol to the Convention on the Rights of the Child on the Involvement of Children in Armed Conflict." A/RES/54/263. Accessed 25 May 2000. <http://www.unhchr.ch/html/menu2/6/protocolchild.htm>.

———. "Optional Protocol to the Convention on the Rights of the Child on the Sale of Children, Child Prostitution, and Child Pornography." A/RES/54/263. Accessed 25 May 2000. <http://www.ohchr.org/english/law/crc-sale.htm>.

U.S. Senate. Military Commissions Act of 2005. S.3930.ENR. 17 October 2006. <http://thomas.loc.gov/cgi-bin/query/z?c109:S.+3930:>.

Uys, Pieter-Dirk. "The Truth, the Whole Truth, and Nothing But." *Index on Censorship* 5 (1996): 46–47.

Villalobos, Joaquin. "A Democratic Revolution for El Salvador." *Foreign Policy* 74 (Spring 1989): 103–122.

Waldron, Jeremy. "Torture and Positive Law: Jurisprudence for the White House." For publication in *Columbia Law Review*. Accessed 30 March 2006. <http://www.columbia.edu/cu/law/fed-soc/otherfiles/waldron.pdf>.

Webster, Donovan. "The Man in the Hood and New Accounts of Prisoner Abuse in Iraq." *Vanity Fair* February 2005.

Weisel, Elie. *Night.* New York: Bantam, 1982.

Weisman, Steven R. "Powell Says Rapes and Killings in Sudan Are Genocide." *New York Times* 9 September 2004.

Welcome to Sarajevo. Dir. Michael Winterbottom. Perf. Stephen Dillane, Woody Harrelson, Marisa Tomei. Miramax Films, 1997.

Wetzel, Janice Wood. "On the Road to Beijing," *Affilea* 11.2 (Summer 1996): 221–233.

White, Hayden. "Historical Employment and the Problem of Truth." *Probing the Limits of Representation: Nazism and the Final Solution.* Ed. Saul Friedlander. Cambridge, Mass.: Harvard University Press, 1992. 37–53.

White, Mimi, "Site Unseen: An Analysis of CNN's War in the Gulf." *Seeing through the Media: The Persian Gulf War.* Eds. S. Jeffords and L. Rabinowitz. New Brunswick, N.J.: Rutgers University Press, 1994. 121–142.

Wicomb, Zoe. "Translations in the Yard of Africa." *Journal of Literary Studies* 18.4 (December 2002): 209–223.

Wilkomirski, Benjamin. *Fragments: Memories of a Wartime Childhood.* New York: Schocken, 1995.

Woods, Donald. *Biko: The True Story of the Young South African Martyr and His Struggle to Raise Black Consciousness.* New York: Henry Holt, 1978; 1991.

Woods, James. "Parables and Prizes: *Disgrace* by J. M. Coetzee." *New Republic* 20 September 1999: 42–46.

World Health Organization. "Violence by Intimate Partners." *The WHO World Report on Violence and Health.* World Health Organization (2002). Accessed 15 February 2006. <http://www.who.int/violence_injury_prevention/en>.

The Year of Living Dangerously. Dir. Peter Wier. Perf. Mel Gibson, Sigourney Weaver. Metro-Goldwyn-Mayer, 1982.

Yee, James. *For God and Country: Faith and Patriotism under Fire.* New York: Public Affairs, 2005.

Yuval-Davis, Nira. *Gender and Nation.* London: Sage Publications, 1997.

Zernicke, Kate. "Cited as Symbol of Abu Ghraib, Man Admits He Is Not in Photo." *New York Times* 19 March 2006.

INDEX

Kincaid, Jamaica, 139
King, Rodney, 49
Klein, Naomi, 200n18
Kline, Kevin, 42
Kozol, Wendy, 123
Kristeva, Julia, 98–99, 113–114, 122
Kristof, Nicholas, 217n11
Kruger, James, 42, 200n20
Kurdish uprising, 47, 51, 56
Kurdistan genocide, 152
Kureishi, Hanif, 21, 95–97, 101–114, 120, 144, 209–210nn24,25

Lacanian symbolic, 60, 74
LaCapra, Dominic, 25, 165, 177, 188
Land Affairs grant (South Africa), 129
land mines, 219n27
land redistribution, 124, 127, 129
Lanzmann, Claude, 197n1
La Pointe, Ali, 159
Laub, Dori, 13
laughter, women's, 178
Law of the Father, 60
legal contexts, 13, 16, 156–157
Legba, 163
Lemkin, Rafael, 215–216n3
lesbians/lesbianism: and CIA, 209n20; and
    Disgrace, 124, 131; and Sammy and Rosie Get
    Laid, 96–97, 100, 102–105, 108–111,
    209–210n24
Levinas, Emmanuel, 46
Levinson, Sanford, 208n14
Levi-Strauss, Claude, 74
Lifeline Expedition, 139
Literature of Cruelty, The (Millett), 122
Little School: Tales of Disappearance and Sur-
    vival (Partnoy), 157, 217n12
loa, 163, 179
Locke, John, 124–126, 129
longue durée, 1, 9, 39
Loren, Sophia, 175
Los Angeles Police Department, 49
LSD, 74
Lusaka Peace Process (1994), 219n27
Lynch, Jessica, 211n31, 220n3
lynching, 214n13

MacCannell, Dean, 31, 197n5
Mace, Nancy, 210n27
MacKinnon, Catharine, 76
Madres, 215n19
magical realism, 53, 108, 141–142
Magnarelli, Sharon, 141
male rape, 121
Mao, 66–67
Marxism, 104, 106, 195n1, 215n17
masculinist desire, 88, 206n6, 209n22
masculinity: and Abu Ghraib, 119; and
    citizenship, 59; and Salvador, 58, 69, 73–74;
    and Sunday at the Pool in Kigali, 77, 80; and
    Three Kings, 47–48, 54, 56
Maslin, Janet, 28, 30, 53, 201n26
masochism, 129
massacres, genocidal, 216n7, 217–218n16,
    218–219n24

maternal function: and Anil's Ghost, 183; and
    Ararat, 179–183; and genocide, 178–184; and
    Lynndie England, 117, 119, 211n32; as nation-
    alist trope, 97; and witnessing, 156
Mayans, 217–218n16
McAlister, Melani, 114–115, 119
McCabe, Colin, 96, 99, 106
McClintock, Anne, 75–76
McGovern, Jim, 196n10
mediated witnesses, 188
Menchú Tum, Rigoberta, 90, 217n13
Mengele, Josef, 169
metanarrative technique, 25, 156, 174–175,
    177, 179–180
metaphor, 53
Metres Dlo, 163, 179
Miles Foundation, 210n28
militarism, nonwestern, 200n18; and Beyond
    Rangoon, 39–40, 198n11; and gender, 97;
    and Salvador, 57, 69–71, 203n10; and Sunday
    at the Pool in Kigali, 205n18
militarism, U.S.: and multiculturalism/diver-
    sity, 114–115, 210–211nn27–29; and Three
    Kings, 47–56; and torture, 10, 196n10,
    200n18
Military Commissions Act (2006),
    208–209n16
Military Readiness Enhancement Act,
    210–211n29
military recruiters, 210–211n29
Miller, Geoffrey, 211n31
Millett, Kate, 122
Million Little Pieces, A (Frey), 217n13
Milosevich, Slobodan, 5
mimicry, colonial, 44, 78
mind/body split, 88
missione civilizatrice, 62
Mladic, Ratko, 218–219n24
modernity, 53, 68, 70, 72, 106, 168
monarchy, 125
moralists, 185–186
Morgenthau, Henry, 219–220n26
Morrison, Toni, 75
Most Favored Nation status (China), 203n9
Mugabe, Robert, 127
multiculturalism, 114–115
Museum of Memory (Naval Mechanics
    School, Argentina), 216n6
music video, 53, 201n26
Muslim Public Affairs Council Foundation,
    47
My Lai massacre, 12

narrative "I," 90, 206nn8,9
narratives of decline: and Corregidora, 133;
    and Disgrace, 21, 123, 142. See also progress
    narratives
nationalisms, 114, 201–202n2; vs. cosmopoli-
    tanism, 218n21; and Oedipal order, 101; and
    safety, 61; and Sammy and Rosie Get Laid,
    109–110; tropes of, 97, 103, 209n17; and
    witnessing, 165
National League for Democracy (Burma), 37,
    198nn8,9
Native Americans, 152

ABOUT THE AUTHOR

Elizabeth Swanson Goldberg is an assistant professor of English at Babson College in Wellesley, Massachusetts. She has published in the areas of postcolonial and multicultural literature and pedagogy, gender studies, and human rights.